I0084587

Chasing the Wind

Chasing the Wind

REGULATING AIR POLLUTION IN THE COMMON LAW STATE

Noga Morag-Levine

PRINCETON UNIVERSITY PRESS

PRINCETON AND OXFORD

Copyright © 2003 by Princeton University Press
Published by Princeton University Press, 41 William Street,
Princeton, New Jersey 08540
In the United Kingdom: Princeton University Press,
3 Market Place, Woodstock, Oxfordshire OX20 1SY

All Rights Reserved.

Library of Congress Cataloging-in-Publication Data

Morag-Levine, Noga.
Chasing the wind : regulating air pollution in the common law state /
Noga Morag-Levine.
p. cm.
Includes bibliographical references and index.
ISBN 0-691-09481-0 (cl. : acid-free paper)
1. Air—Pollution—Law and legislation—United States. I. Title.
KF3812.M67 2003
344.73′046342—dc21   2002035552

British Library Catalog-in-Publication Data is available

This book has been composed in Postscript Sabon Typeface
Printed on acid-free paper. ∞
www.pupress.princeton.edu

Printed in the United States of America

10 9 8 7 6 5 4 3 2 1

To the memory of my father,

Amotz Morag

Contents

Preface

To most readers of this book, localized air pollution concentrations, or "hotspots," are familiar only as momentary waves of caustic fumes encountered while driving past refineries, steel mills, chemical manufacturers, pulp mills, or other heavy industrial sites. But for the millions of Americans who live in close proximity to these pollution sources, such fumes are a constant intrusion and a persistent source of worry. "Noxious vapours" was the Victorian term for these gases and their multiple sensory assaults. Since the beginning of industrialization, some of those exposed to these vapors have attributed to them a long and consistent set of symptoms and concerns—nausea, vomiting, headaches, stinging throats, constricted chests, burning eyes, and a vague but persistent concern about long-term health effects. The seed of this book was such a worry.

Soon after moving into an Albany, California, apartment, my family noticed the intermittent presence of burnt plastic-like fumes that left an irritating, caustic sensation in the eyes and nose, and a bitter taste in the mouth. The fumes would come and go with the wind, and vary in their intensity. The parents of two young children, my husband and I soon became concerned that the air might be harmful, and we began to inquire as to the fumes' source. After a number of false starts, we were referred to the regional air pollution agency, the Bay Area Air Quality Management District (BAAQMD) and contacted its complaint hotline. The agency registered our complaint under "odors" and sent an inspector, who informed us that the fumes came from a steel foundry located less than a mile away. The fumes were created by the rapid heating of synthetic resins during the metal-casting process, and—as we would later learn—included the emission of benzene, phenol, formaldehyde, and other hazardous air pollutants. We were told that for the Air District to take action, it must first establish that the odor amounted to a "public nuisance." Under district rules, this required, as a first step, that complaints from five separate households be confirmed within a twenty-four hour period.

Encouraged by the prospect of pollution abatement, we began to call and register complaints. Although the agency responded diligently to each such complaint, we found that we often were unable to have our complaints confirmed. In the interval between our phone call and the arrival of the inspector, the odor often disappeared as a result of shifts in wind direction or in the foundry's production processes. The inspector would arrive and sniff the air but neither she nor I could detect any trace of the smell. Apologetic and somewhat embarrassed, I would try to explain that the fumes were evident one, two, or three hours earlier when I called. Sometimes inspectors would even indicate that they had perceived the smell on the way over or even in our parking lot, but without detecting it in our presence, they could record no confirmation. Though we failed to confirm most of our complaints, on occasion luck was on our side and the odor lingered until the moment at which the inspector knocked on our door. Even our hard-won successes in confirmation did not usually trigger action, because five separate confirmations during a twenty-four hour period were required before the Air District would issue a citation to the foundry. Irrespective of the number of days in which two, three, or four complaints were confirmed, with each twenty-four hour period the counting started afresh.

The inspectors seemed to be fair-minded and conscientious people who were referees for a game whose rules were unambiguous in their implementation but inexplicable in their logic. Puzzled, and increasingly frustrated, we began to hear about many others who had shared our experience. We also learned that for several years prior, residents in adjacent neighborhoods had actively mobilized against the fumes. Their efforts had led to the installation of partial fume controls on one of the foundry's three local plants, but left fumes on the remaining two plants uncontrolled. Yet the Air District continued to investigate each and every complaint anew, as if it were constantly defaulting to the assumption that no problem had ever existed. Often the process assumed a surreal quality, with inspectors and complaining citizens together chasing elusive winds in search of fumes that they each detected separately only moments before.

Two years later, as the problem continued unabated, I began my graduate studies, and soon what had started as a personal quest for clean air transformed into an academic preoccupation. As I studied contemporary environmental regulation and the nature of the modern American administrative state, it became increasingly difficult to reconcile the policy literature's characterization of U.S. air pollution regulation as overly rigid and ambitious with the BAAQMD's "odor" policies that seemed better geared to investigation than control. The Clean Air Act's expansive promises of protection against harm from pollution, and the massive regulatory infrastructure that it spawned, appeared to have had little if any impact where our pollution problem was concerned. Instead, we witnessed a reactive "night watchman"-like agency that understood its role as a referee between the competing interests of the neighbors and the foundry, rather than a regulator with an independent pollution control mission of its own. Furthermore, as I was soon to learn, in defining localized air pollution as "odors" and leaving it up to local communities to make the case for "odor abatement," the BAAQMD accorded with the behavior of air pollution agencies nationwide. In fact, compared to most such agencies the BAAQMD devoted significantly greater attention and resources to odor problems.

In our foundry case, over a decade of intensive neighborhood mobilization ultimately yielded extensive pollution control. But this outcome is by far the exception rather than the rule. (Patterns of pollution control in the foundry industry are discussed in chapter 8.) In its strictly reactive stance, this system seemed to create significant inequities, extending both to the communities adjoining uncontrolled industrial sources of air pollution, and the exceptional firms that this system targets for pollution abatement. It conditions intervention on years of sustained and politically savvy mobilization of a type that exceedingly few communities are able to support. At the same time, it demands of some firms, such as the Berkeley foundry in question, expensive pollution control investments that the vast majority of their competitors are able to avoid. Furthermore, it is not even clear that this reactive pollution regime necessarily leaves the majority of (uncontrolled) firms better off relative to a regime that would require uniform implementation of feasible pollution reduction measures. This is due to the uncertainty inherent to this process and to the legal and political costs that this regime exacts by pitting firms against surrounding communities in regulatory battles that neither sought, but that neither can afford to avoid. Caught in the middle are the air pollution agencies that respond by squandering the public resources and goodwill on odor investigation rituals. Despite all these evident shortcomings, this manner of reactive air pollution regulation remains entrenched throughout the United States. It is the persistence of this seemingly anachronistic mode of air pollution intervention that prompted me to write this book.

These pollution control frameworks were particularly puzzling in light of the standard view of the 1970 Clean Air Act (CAA), according to which they constituted a revolutionary statutory response to the perceived failures of the earlier common law regime. Guided by this construction of the act, I initially framed my research around the dissonance between the new federal air quality regime's aspirations and rationale on the one hand, and, on the other, the reality of localized air pollution regulation on the ground. In other words, I found in the prevalent practices of "odor nuisance" regulation evidence that the common law regime is alive and well, albeit in administrative garb. But I perceived this as a residual phenomenon that was inconsonant with the core purpose and logic of the CAA. Ultimately deviating from this conventional view, I came to understand the CAA regime itself as imbued with common law regulatory sensibilities. In this book I argue that the abiding influence of these ideas on the contemporary American air pollution regime can help account for systematic differences between this regime and its European counterparts.

Acknowledgments

I AM GRATEFUL for the generous financial assistance provided at various stages in this book's development by the National Science Foundation (Dissertation Improvement Grant); University of California Chancellor's Dissertation-Year Fellowship; Rackham School of Graduate Studies Research Fellowship; and the University of Michigan Career Development Fund. I would also like to thank the Law and Society Association for permission to incorporate material from my article, "Between Choice and Sacrifice: Constructions of Community Consent in Reactive Air Pollution Regulation" *Law & Society Rev.* 28 (1994): pp. 1035–77, into chapters 7 and 8. Many of the ideas presented here benefited from the feedback of engaged colleagues at professional forums, including a number of panels at meetings of the Law and Society Association and the American Political Science Association, the Michigan Law School Faculty Workshop, and the Center for the Study of Law and Society at the University of California, Berkeley. In making final revisions I benefited greatly from the comments of the two anonymous reviewers. Many thanks for excellent help with all steps of the publication process are due to Chuck Myers and Mark Bellis of Princeton University Press. I am also grateful to Linda Truilo for her careful and expert editing, and her helpful manner.

From this project's tentative first steps to the book's penultimate draft, Bob Kagan provided just the right mix of warm encouragement, critique, and advice. One could not ask for a more engaged and kind guide. I first got hooked on doing interdisciplinary work on law as an undergraduate in Malcolm Feeley's "Courts and Social Policy" class. Malcolm's intellectual energy and his steady support and mentorship have enriched my career from those undergraduate days, through graduate school, and beyond. Among my other teachers at Berkeley I owe special thanks to John Dwyer, Judith Gruber, David Lieberman, Robert Post, Harry Scheiber, Martin Shapiro, and Jeremy Waldron. I also want to acknowledge the unique interdisciplinary space provided by the Jurisprudence and Social Policy program at Berkeley and the license it offered for inquiry that does not fit squarely within a single research niche.

I am thankful for the cooperation and assistance provided by the four air pollution agencies under whose jurisdiction the air pollution disputes that I studied occurred. Particular mention must go to Kenneth Manaster, the former chair of the BAAQMD hearing board, whose insights and candor were a window to understanding the contradictory mandates of contemporary air quality enforcement.

I have benefited from opportunities to discuss aspects of the project with Morton Horwitz and Robert Post. Hanoch Dagan, in a lengthy conversation in a crowded airport restaurant, helped me to get past a major writing block. Michael Lipsett agreed good-naturedly to talk air pollution during far too many family gatherings. Don Herzog generously took time to read and comment extensively on an earlier draft. Since the early days of this project, Cary Coglianese could be counted on for a continuous stream of references and, more importantly, expert insights on regulatory politics.

From her neighboring office, Arlene Saxonhouse provided frequent encouragement and all manner of book publishing advice. I have imposed particular burdens on two additional colleagues and friends at Michigan. For the past five years, Ann Lin has been unstintingly generous with her insightful comments, wise counsel, and heartfelt care. Elizabeth Wingrove was an especially resonant sounding board, listening and talking me through crucial junctures in the evolution of the book, and offering line-by-line feedback on important sections. Both have been steady and inspiring guides through the vicissitudes of academic life. To Mark Brandon, on whose intellectual acumen and personal generosity I continue to draw with great frequency, I owe a particular debt.

Erica Young, Kirsten Carlson, and Megan McMillan worked long hours chasing references and expertly assisting with many research tasks. Ryan Hudson's outstanding editing skills, substantive insight, and willingness to shoulder more than she had bargained for were a lifesaver when things got down to the wire. For the errors that no doubt remain despite these many people's utmost efforts, I'm afraid that I alone am to blame.

From across the world and nearby, the good thoughts of Tamar Morag, Shoshana Morag, and Annie Rose cheered me on to the finish line. From the start it was the example imparted by my three academic parents that led me toward this course. As the years go by, my appreciation deepens for the life lessons that my late father, Amotz Morag, taught me as a young child. I am grateful to my stepfather, Shemaryahu Talmon, for his intellectual example and interest in my work despite its distance from his own areas of inquiry. I especially thank my mother, Penina Morag-Talmon, for being a model of balance between family and work, and for her strength of character, wisdom, and unconditional love. Rose and Hillie Levine, my parents-in-law, have consistently conveyed confidence and support throughout the long haul. Finally, and most profoundly, I thank Jonathan Levine, whose imprint is on each of the pages that follow. For his enormous substantive and editorial contributions, infinite reserves of enthusiasm and patience, and his sense of fun, my gratitude exceeds words. Our children, Shira and Adam, were the reason I became involved in air pollution policy in the first place. Toddlers then, now almost grown up, they have been a continuous source of wonder, inspiration, and pride.

Abbreviations

ABA	American Bar Association
APA	Administrative Procedure Act
APCD	Air Pollution Control District
BAAQMD	Bay Area Air Quality Management District
BAT	Best Available Technology
BPM	Best Practicable Means
CAA	Clean Air Act
CIC	Coply International Corporation
CPSC	Consumer Product Safety Commission
DNR	Department of Natural Resources
EDF	Environmental Defense Fund
EPA	Environmental Protection Agency
GACT	Generally Available Control Technology
HAPs	Hazardous Air Pollutants
HEW	Health Education Welfare
IEPA	Illinois Environmental Protection Agency
LAER	Lowest Achievable Emission Rate
MACT	Maximum Achievable Control Technology
MCAPCD	Maricopa County Air Pollution Control District
NAAQS	National Ambient Air Quality Standards
NESHAP	National Emission Standards for Hazardous Pollutants
NOx	Nitrogen Oxides
NRC	National Research Council
NRDC	Natural Resources Defense Council
NSPS	New Source Performance Standards
NSR	New Source Review
OSHA	Occupational Safety and Health Administration
PM	Particulate Matter
RACT	Reasonable Available Control Technology
SCNV	Select Committee on Noxious Vapours
TSPs	Total Suspended Particulates
VOCs	Volatile Organic Compounds

Chasing the Wind

Introduction

THE CLEAN AIR ACT of 1970 (CAA) is broadly understood as a pivotal moment in the history of U.S. environmental policy, entailing a radical shift away from an earlier common law regime that was operated piecemeal by local and state governments. The CAA superceded these decentralized approaches with federal, uniform, and proactive law. But most importantly, it is thought to embody a shift in priorities away from an earlier deference to industrial concerns toward a new and uncompromising commitment to the protection of public health.

The act's absolutist reputation rests primarily on the ambitiousness of the promise it encodes in a central provision mandating the promulgation of primary ambient air-quality standards.[1] In setting these standards, the act requires the EPA to establish maximum permitted levels of regulated pollutants no higher than what the protection of public health against pollution-induced disease demands. These standards exemplify a broader category of regulatory interventions based on scientific assessment of hazards from pollution exposure, frequently termed "risk-based" or "health-based" standards. In addition, the CAA employs a secondary regulatory framework that sets standards based on the feasibility of pollution mitigation, termed "technology standards." Whereas technology standards are inherently based on feasibility and cost, these considerations may not be taken into account in setting risk standards.

Terms for technology standards include "Best Available Technology" (BAT), "Best Practicable Means" (BPM), "Maximum Achievable Control Technology" (MACT), and many others. All of these approaches employ the similar core logic of setting standards with reference to the pollution reduction capabilities of specific technological means. The standards can take the form of a requirement to install particular pollution-control devices or employ other mitigation measures (prescriptive standards). More commonly, however, these standards impose a percentage reduction in emission that is known to be achievable through technological measures of demonstrated feasibility (performance standards).[2] In the latter case, sources are free to employ alternative means, as long as they afford pollution reduction at least equal to the level of effectiveness that can be achieved by the technology serving as the basis for the standard.

I argue that technology and risk standards represent the current incarnation of alternative responses to the regulatory dilemma posed by air pollution since the beginning of industrialization. By the mid-nineteenth century, the forerunners of the two current regulatory approaches had become institutionalized. In Germany, standard-setting was guided by technological feasibility and was implemented through proactive licensing processes conducted by administrative agencies within a civil law framework. Under English common law, the organizing principle of air pollution regulation was the amelioration of proven harms within a reactive system that depended upon judicial resolution of nuisance disputes. By contrast to the German approach, English common law in principle imposed an absolute duty to eliminate injury from pollution ("absolute liability" in legal parlance). As such, technology and risk standards are planted in the different legal traditions of the civil law and the common law respectively.

In place of the predominant risk-based standards within the CAA, technology standards are the European instrument of choice.[3] This book argues that the continuity between risk standards and nuisance law, or conversely, the incompatibility of technology standards with common law principles, is key to the divergent evolution of the European and American regimes. Differences in styles of implementation follow from the two regimes' core standard-setting rationales, as well. American air pollution regulation accords a much greater role to scientific proof of harm, quantitative risk assessment, and frequent judicial oversight than do the corresponding European processes.

The limited inroads made by technology standards into the U.S. air quality regime have drawn sharp political and scholarly criticism on two grounds: their purported economic inefficiency,[4] and a more profound challenge that they pose to the democratic legitimacy of these standards.[5] The resonance of this latter normative charge in American political discourse is perhaps best reflected in the frequent substitution of the term "command and control"—a term with distinct military, and even authoritarian connotations—for the more neutral "technology standards."[6]

The logic that underpins this democratic critique is not self-evident. In this book I argue that current skepticism regarding the democratic legitimacy of technology standards stems from a long tradition in America of resisting civil-law-inspired reforms as potentially despotic. Since the early days of the United States, such reform proposals were encumbered by their association with the absolutist continental state. By the end of the nineteenth century, against increased efforts by progressives to implement continental-modeled social legislation, opponents turned to the claim that common law strictures delimited the scope of the police power in America as a matter of constitutional law. This conflict came to a head at the turn of the twentieth century, in what has come to be known as the *Lochner* era. Under the predominant view, the question was resolved with the New Deal, settling both the constitutionality and the legitimacy of the administrative state. Democratic critiques of technology standards suggest that late-nineteenth-century divisions on the congruence between continental models of administration and American political values remain with us today. Furthermore, I argue that these common law ideas are of crucial import in understanding why American and continental approaches to environmental regulation evolved along separate tracks.

For the purpose of this discussion, the relevant distinction between the common-law and civil-law traditions is their alternative conceptions of the scope of the state's regulatory authority under the police power. The common law tradition limits that power to interventions whose means are closely tailored to legitimate governmental ends, and accords judges a final say on this fit. Under this view, the traditional parameters of nuisance law circumscribe the regulatory authority of the state itself. By contrast, the civil law tradition, working from assumptions of absolute legislative sovereignty, imposes no similar means-ends rationality constraints.

Means-ends tailoring in the context of air pollution implies the crafting of regulations that are both necessary and sufficient to protect against harm. The purported beneficial outcome of this formula is the avoidance of imposition of sacrifice on neighbors through underregulation, or on firms through overregulation. Like their nuisance-based predecessors, risk standards accord with this commitment for close tailoring of regulation by promising complete protection against all scientifically proven risk. By contrast, since technology standards are based on the feasibility of mitigation, they implicitly acknowledge the likelihood that some pollution that is harmful but infeasible to mitigate may well go unabated. At the same time, by hinging intervention on feasibility rather than scientific proof of harm, they similarly allow for the possibility that mitigation costs beyond those strictly required for public health may be imposed on firms.

Risk standards formally eschew explicit balancing of interests in favor of precisely tailored intervention. Nevertheless, in practice both risk and technology-based systems engage in processes of balancing economic versus environmental interests, though they differ in the method and explicitness with which they carry out this unavoidable function. Risk standards resemble nuisance law in their mechanism for balancing interests. Rather than injecting these considerations at the stage of crafting a remedy, they implicitly balance as part of the process of establishing a legal injury or the existence of risk to begin with. This approach differs from technology-based mechanisms in two principal ways. First, by strictly circumscribing legally recognized harms, it tends to hide the sacrifice it imposes in the form of unremedied negative impacts. Second, it shifts the decision-making authority ultimately empowered to exercise discretion away from agencies and toward courts. Risk-based standards, much like nuisance law, make judges final arbiters of the adequacy of the proof of harm on which the agency based its intervention. Technology standards are subject to judicial review as well, but in their review judges look only to the practicability of the prescribed means; the legality of regulation does not hinge on the (judicially assessed) nexus between means and ends.

This book argues that contemporary critiques of the democratic legitimacy of technology standards accord with the longstanding common law tenet that, absent judicial oversight, governments inherently tend to abuse their power. This idea, deeply rooted in the American legal tradition, has exerted a powerful influence over the development of U.S. environmental regulation. The book points to the imprint of this common law ideology in the behavior and rhetoric of agencies, courts, and interest groups on both the business and environmental side. This is not to argue for any manner of deterministic causal connection between common law ideologies and the regulatory patterns I identify, or to suggest that raw political power is not at play. Across the junctures that I analyze, politics, money, and other influences mattered to regulatory outcomes. But since the beginning of industrialization, powerful interests lined up on both sides of the issue. Unlike advocates of technology interventions, however, opponents could appeal to deeply seated notions regarding the unreasonableness of such means-based regulatory approaches. As such, the common-law-inspired ground rules of the contemporary American policy debate encumber advocates of technology-based regulation with greater political burdens, while they lend rhetorical traction to the arguments of opponents of such intervention. The resulting uphill battle may sometimes be won, as the presence of some technology standards within the Clean Air Act (and other environmental statutes) suggests. Notwithstanding these instances, risk-based standards have won the day in U.S. air quality regulation.

It may be argued that the predominance of risk standards in U.S. environmental regulation needs no legal-ideological explanation; many analysts would choose to highlight the purported economic inefficiency of the technology-based alternative. Departing from the prevailing view, this book contends that standards that begin with the question of what is feasible—as opposed to a determination of the exact level of mitigation that is necessary and sufficient to protect health—more forthrightly acknowledge and cope with the realities of both scientific uncertainty and the impossibility of elimination of all risk from pollution exposure. I seek to contribute a historical perspective to this debate, which has largely centered around present-day empirical and (more commonly) theoretical analysis.

The historical evidence presented in this book establishes, over centuries, the repeated failure of harm-tailored air pollution interventions (whether nuisance- or risk-based) to spur deployment of available and feasible mitigation technologies. From this foundation, the book offers two interrelated arguments: the first pertains to reforms needed in domestic pollution policy to further environmental protection goals; and the second identifies distinctive characteristics of American regulatory governance that distinguish the United States as the quintessential "common law state."

In this connection it is important to highlight relevant differences and similarities between the evolution of the common law tradition in the United States and England. As will be subsequently discussed, the impact of the common law ideologies can be discerned in historical and contemporary patterns of air pollution regulation in Britain as well as in the United States. Nevertheless, there likewise exist important differences between the evolution and impact of the common law in the British and the American cases. Most importantly, England lacks a written constitution and the institution of constitutional judicial review. Instead its common law tradition made room for both parliamentary sovereignty and an unwritten constitutional tradition of limitations on the scope of political power. This difference partially accounts for why a technology-based air pollution regime successfully developed in late-nineteenth-century England, under the Alkali Act, but not in the United States. Any proposal for a technology-based statutory regime in the United States akin to the English Alkali Act would have come against *Lochner*-era limitations on the scope of the police power. By contrast, in England there could be no constitutional impediments to this manner of reform and hence fewer footholds for opponents of this manner of legislation.

In the resilience of nuisance law principles within American air pollution regulation, the book finds evidence of the continuing hold of common law ideologies on the contemporary American administrative state. These ideologies are evident in the Supreme Court's takings jurisprudence[7] as well as its recent lines of decisions on legislative record review.[8] But well beyond their embodiment in Supreme Court doctrine, American doubts about the fit between democracy and the administrative state pervade policy-making at all governmental levels.

The following chapters interweave three themes: the continuities between contemporary American air pollution policy and nuisance law, the environmental and distributive consequences of the ostensibly absolutist commitments of nuisance / risk law, and the common law roots of American conceptions of technology standards as undemocratic instruments of "command and control."

Chapter 1 compares the statutory mandates and styles of implementation of contemporary air pollution regimes in the United States and Germany. The chapter contrasts the German regime's pervasive reliance on partial but uniform technology-based standards with the Clean Air Act's far more ambitious, but ultimately fictitious, commitment to the complete elimination of risk from air pollution.

Chapter 2 finds in contemporary critiques of the democracy of technology standards an expression of centuries-old beliefs in the irrationality, and hence illegitimacy, of regulatory processes that begin from assessments of feasibility rather than judgments on proper regulatory goals. The chapter focuses on the role of this assumption in the Supreme Court's reasoning in *Lochner* v. *New York* (1905) and—seventy-five years later—in its decision to invalidate a technology-based benzene rule issued by the Occupational Safety and Health Administration.

The ostensible commitment of the 1970 Clean Air Act to eliminate all harm from pollution recalls the absolute liability doctrines that nuisance law has brought to air pollution since preindustrial times. Chapter 3 follows the evolution of this body of English doctrine, and how and why demands for scientific proof that the pollution caused particular disease (as opposed to "mere" discomfort or aesthetic annoyance) entered the common law. I argue that absolute liability was a rule directed at the separation of incompatible land uses in a preindustrial era during which such separation was feasible and preferable to incremental mitigation. Separation of pollution sources was no longer a feasible solution in the dense cities spawned by industrialization. But the absolute liability rule continued to serve the interests of landowners who sought to protect their estates and farmlands against encroaching industrialization. The result was a common law regime that adhered in principle to an absolute liability rule, but tended, in practice, to exclude urban pollution from the realm of legally cognizable injuries entitled to such complete protection. This feat was accomplished by raising the evidentiary thresholds placed before plaintiffs in industrial areas by requiring proof of a link between air pollution from specific sources and particular diseases. Without such scientific proof, the symptoms and concerns associated with industrial fumes were dismissed as "trifling inconveniences" of the type to which residents of industrial areas implicitly consent by dint of their very presence in these locales. Rather than acknowledging the pollution sacrifices that it imposed, this regime defined them away as a matter of law. A primary outcome of this legal fiction was a systematic failure to implement available, albeit incremental, means of pollution mitigation. By 1863, this failure prompted Parliament to create a supplementary technology-based administrative regime geared at the control of noxious vapors, under the Alkali Act. The United States, however, imported only the common-law-based side of this bifurcated regime.

As chapter 4 argues, tensions evident throughout the nineteenth century between "continental-police" and "common law" visions of the emergent American administrative state came to a head during the constitutional crisis of the *Lochner* era. But the view that a continental-styled focus on available means cut against American understandings of liberty both predated and outlived the *Lochner* court. The chapter recounts the various doctrinal steps leading to *Lochner* in order to trace how and why understandings of the constitutionality of regulatory interference in the market came to depend on judicial assessments of the adequacy of legislatures' proffered proof of the "nexus" between regulatory means and constitutionally legitimate ends.

Returning to air pollution, chapter 5 relies on analysis of nineteenth- and twentieth-century landmark decisions from Pennsylvania to examine whether and when the American nuisance regime spurred deployment of available pollution reduction means. The chapter finds that for the most part, judges looked to the locale's surrounding conditions, rather than the feasibility of mitigation, in deciding on the liability of defendants and the appropriateness of injunctions. An important but apparently rare exception was the emergence around the turn of the nineteenth century of quasi-administrative Best Available Technology (BAT) injunctions that, while adhering to the absolutist shell of nuisance law, were geared at the implementation of partial pollution reductions, even in industrial locales.

By the early twentieth century, a portion of the air pollution problem— the control of industrial smoke—had been delegated to administrative, rather than strictly judicial, control. This move in principle enabled pursuit of incremental implementation of pollution mitigation measures and public goals beyond balancing the interests of plaintiffs and defendants. Chapter 6 explores the history of smoke regulation in the contexts of the United States and England (where it was not covered by the Alkali Act). Both countries avoided a technology-based regime of the type that Germany had applied to smoke since the mid-nineteenth century, and thereby limited their effective capacity for smoke abatement.

Chapters 7 and 8 move from visible smoke to invisible fumes, examining the regime governing contemporary responses to localized air pollution, or "odors." The "odor" terminology conveys subjective connotations of purely aesthetic annoyance to the problem of localized fumes. Chapter 7 examines the assumptions and consequences that follow from this problem definition. As the chapter shows, this problem definition played an important role in the EPA's 1980 decision to leave the regulation of localized pollution of this sort to the common-law-framed public nuisance regime. This decision came notwithstanding the agency's own failure to control the air toxics that are often at the center of "odor" pollution disputes. The consequences of this decision for the regulation of foundry fumes are the subject of chapter 8.

Building on this historical and empirical foundation, chapter 9 argues for reforms that, following the European model, would forgo the tailoring of interventions to proven levels of harm, in favor of a requirement that the extent of pollution reduction be pegged to technological and economic feasibility and be imposed predictably across all firms in an industrial category. Basing interventions on feasibility rather than mitigation of proven harms implicitly acknowledges the possibility of both underregulation and overregulation, relative to pollution's health risks. Yet history teaches the systematic impossibility of the kind of precise tailoring of interventions that air pollution regulation in the common law tradition demands. In the regulation of air pollutants and other dangerous chemicals, the search for perfection has been the enemy of the good.

Regulating Air Pollution: Risk- and Technology-Based Paradigms

A PLETHORA of regulatory programs currently targets synthetic chemicals in our air, drinking water, food products, and workplaces. Although people had worried about the dangers posed by chemicals to health for centuries, a post–World War II surge in the industrial uses of man-made substances sparked new levels of environmental activism in Western Europe and the United States during the 1960s and 1970s. The immediately visible and undeniable advantages of the chemicals to industrial processes, sanitation, and agriculture lost some of their luster as evidence about the risks posed to health and ecosystems mounted. Although a handful of acute and deadly pollution episodes made some dangers obvious, the hidden and latent effects of chronic exposure constituted a more serious and pervasive concern. By the 1960s, environmental movements across advanced industrial democracies were demanding more governmental protection against hazardous chemicals.[1]

The movement met with considerable success in both Europe and the United States, and an array of new or revamped regulatory mandates subjected industrial activity to regulatory standards determined by recently empowered administrative agencies. Yet despite trans-Atlantic similarities in environmental concerns and modes of public mobilization, the chemical regulation regime created in the United States diverged from its European counterparts both in its definition of the pertinent regulatory task and in the style of its implementation.[2] From the start, the American regime stood apart in the ambitiousness of its scope and the absolute protection it sought to offer. "Clean air, clean water, open spaces" ought to be "the birthright for every American," declared President Nixon in his 1970 State of the Union Address.[3] Protecting these rights justified the extension of federal authority deep into regulatory domains previously ruled by state legislators and common law judges. Consistent with the rationale of protecting fundamental citizen rights, the numerous health and safety statutes enacted by Congress around that time promised virtually complete elimination of hazardous exposure to chemicals.[4]

The gap is particularly evident in clean air legislation. Of all the American federal health and safety statutes introduced during that era in rapid succession, none captures the new regime's ambitious orientation better than the 1970 Clean Air Act (CAA). This act all but declared clean air a right by precluding cost considerations from the decision-making processes that governed the setting of its health-based standards. The Clean Air Act, proclaimed Senator Muskie, the law's chief architect, "intends that all Americans in all parts of the country shall have clean air to breathe within the 1970s."[5] Giving teeth to this pronouncement, the act included a timetable by which "(d)irty air would be made healthy."[6] By contrast, air pollution laws enacted in Europe around that time offered no similar promise.

Germany enacted its first federal air pollution law, the Federal Imissions Control Act (*Bundes-Immissionsschutzgesetz-BImSchG*) in 1974. But unlike its American counterpart, this law did not mandate the elimination of risk from air pollution. Instead, it sought across-the-board reduction in emissions through the use of available and feasible means, or *Stand der Technik*. The term is often translated into English as "state of the art," though its meaning in the original German is "by no means confined to the best or latest technology or management practices."[7] Instead, the cost of the relevant technological solutions (considered both in absolute terms and in reference to the economic circumstances of particular firms) is relevant to the definition of *Stand der Technik*.[8] The German and American laws are thus anchored in two divergent regulatory philosophies the first geared toward the implementation of technological means of pollution reduction, and the second focused on the achievment of regulatory ends.[9]

The primary regulatory instrument of the 1974 German law is the permitting of individual sources by regional and local authorities. In this the 1974 Imissions Control Act, built on nineteenth-century statutory precedents, particularly the licensing-based Prussian General Trade ordinance of 1845.[10] These ordinances enabled local authorities to include requirements for pollution reduction measures in manufacturing permits. The approach was adopted into legislation by the North German Confederation in 1869. By 1895, the law enabled pollution control authorities to issue technical instructions and to require operators to conform with *Stand der Technik* in meeting emission limits.[11]

In justification of across-the-board implementation of *Stand der Technik* pollution reduction measures, the 1974 law offered the *Vorsorgeprinzip*, usually translated as the "precautionary principle."[12] The term is one with multiple and contested meanings, and is currently at the center of significant controversy in domestic and international environmental policy debates. In this context, the principle is commonly paraphrased as "better safe than sorry," and reflects the notion that in the face of scientific uncertainty, it is better to err on the side of excessive environmental interventions.[13] Understood in this way, the principle frequently encounters the commonsensical objection that it provides little guidance on the inevitable balance between "the size of the investment and the speculativeness of the harm."[14] However, the implication that precaution demands the elimination of risk irrespective of its likelihood, or of the costs entailed, cuts against the meaning of the *Vorsorgeprinzip* in the context of the 1974 Imissions Control Act, the first piece of legislation to incorporate this German precept.[15] Instead, within this original framework, *Vorsorge* serves to counsel a policy of incremental reduction in emissions, by all sources, even where there is "insufficient evidence to justify the claim that a particular type of emission was an environmental hazard."[16] Put differently, in the context of German air pollution law, the *Vorsorgeprinzip* stands for the premise that the various adverse impacts of industrial air emissions justify regulatory interventions geared at their control, even if the link between exposure to specific pollutants and causation of particular diseases remains uncertain.

This interpretation accords with the literal meaning of *Vorsorge*, a word that combines notions of foresight and taking care with those of good husbandry and best practice.[17] As such, it is not the concern with the prevention of risk, but rather the obligation "to clean after one's self" that seems to underpin the *Vorsorgeprinzip* in its original, air-pollution-directed, incarnation.

A decade later, an influential 1984 governmental report on the protection of German air quality offered the following elaboration regarding the principle's meaning:

> The principle of precaution commands that the damages done to the natural world (which surrounds us all) should be avoided *in advance* and in *accordance with opportunity and possibility* . . . it also means acting when conclusively ascertained understanding by science is not yet available. Precaution means to develop, in all sectors of the economy, technological processes that significantly reduce environmental burdens, especially those brought about by the introduction of harmful substances [emphasis added].[18]

Within this framework, precaution entails a shift from scientific investigation of the exact levels of harm inflicted by current levels of pollution to the implementation of existing means of pollution reduction and the further development of cleaner industrial processes.[19] At the same time, as evident in the previous quote's reference to "opportunity and possibility," precaution—in direct opposite to the risk-based standards of the CAA— does not imply the prevention of all harm at any cost.

In the context of air pollution, two principal arguments have been advanced in favor of a shift toward a regulatory regime based on available means rather than the end of eliminating risk. The first emanates from pervasive, perhaps insurmountable, barriers to full scientific understandings of the exact hazard posed through varying degrees of exposure to countless atmospheric chemicals and chemical combinations. The second derives from the growing scientific consensus that for many such chemicals there may in fact be no safe threshold.

Scientific uncertainty on the scope of the relevant harms stems from incomplete knowledge of the actual concentrations of dangerous chemicals in the environment, the nature of the interactions among them, and, ultimately, their impacts on human health at varying concentrations.[20] Ethically precluded from conducting randomized human experiments to answer this question, scientists instead must rely on extrapolation or inference from occupational, epidemiological, and animal-based toxicological studies. But the results obtained under any of these methods can never fully remove scientific uncertainty regarding the link between exposure to various levels of air contaminants and the generation of disease. Where epidemiological data are concerned, the primary difficulty derives from the need to account for confounding factors such as smoking and sociodemographic status in evaluating the distribution of specific diseases within various population groups. In occupational studies, questions can arise as to whether patterns of disease associated with workplace exposure are good predictors of risk at the much lower pollutant concentrations typical of most ambient air pollution situations. Likewise, animal-based studies require both extrapolation from high- to low-dose responses and, most problematically, from effects observed in other species. Yet another level of uncertainty pertains to the capacity of biological defense mechanisms to counteract and correct for mutagenic and cellular damage associated with exposure to chemicals in minute concentrations.[21] Given these uncertainties, we should not be surprised that good scientific reasons often support choices among experimental designs and decision rules that yield varying estimates of the risk in question.[22]

Disagreements regarding the proper procedures for assigning risk to chemical exposure notwithstanding, the current scientific consensus holds that any level of exposure to certain chemicals poses some risk, although it might be a small one. Put differently, rather than identifying a single point demarcating safe from unsafe exposure, scientific data often portray a continuum along which risk declines but never fully disappears, even at minute levels of concentration. The relevant uncertainty here—sometimes referred to as statistical risk—is not whether health damage will occur, but who and how many will be hurt.[23] The phenomenon of "zero-threshold" chemicals posits a fundamental challenge to the logic of risk-based regulation. Literally setting standards at the level of zero risk would disallow any emission of chemicals lacking a safe threshold. While such a policy may be an appropriate response to a few, extremely dangerous chemicals, it makes for an unworkable general rule. With respect to such "zero-threshold pollutants," a promise of complete protection amounts either to empty political rhetoric or to a prescription for industrial shutdown. In contrast, means-oriented regulation copes better with these chemicals as it sets for itself the attainable goal of feasible reductions.

Congress's decision to make risk elimination the cornerstone of the CAA regime seems puzzling, even given the state of scientific knowledge at the time of the act's adoption. "Scientists and doctors," Senator Muskie would later allow in 1977, "have told us that there is no threshold, that any air pollution is harmful. The Clean Air Act is based on the assumption, although we knew at the time it was inaccurate, that there is a threshold."[24] Paul Rodgers, Muskie's counterpart in the House, was even more blunt during the 1977 debates amending the CAA: "The 'safe threshold' concept is, at best, a necessary myth to permit the setting of some standards."[25] The myth was necessary, however, only for setting risk-based standards. It remains unclear what benefits Congress found in basing major provisions of the act on the "safe threshold fiction" rather than opting for an incremental technology-based regime along the lines that Germany and other European countries opted for around that time.

As noted, the 1974 German law built on a statutory model dating back to the nineteenth century. Because contemporary technology-based approaches to air and other forms of pollution stem from this German model, they remain marked with the imprint of their origins in the civil law tradition that nineteenth-century German law came to epitomize. In similar fashion, I will argue, the CAA's commitment to the elimination of all scientifically proven air pollution harm adheres to long-standing common law principles under nuisance law. As subsequent chapters will explain, this common law regime revolved around the challenge of reconciling a rule of absolute liability for harm from pollution with the infeasibility of implementing such a rule in the context of the industrial city. The following section highlights similar regulatory dilemmas in the structure and implementation of the CAA.

A RIGHTS REVOLUTION? RISK AND BAT
   IN THE CLEAN AIR ACT

Since the early 1950s, two separate types of air pollution problems propelled the gradual creation of a federal regulatory regime. One was acute pollution concentrations around the country—a long-standing problem that captured national attention after a deadly 1948 pollution episode in Donora, Pennsylvania. The other involved the chronic and much more diffuse "smog" that became an object of serious concern, especially in Southern California.[26] Of the two problems, localized pollution represented a far thornier challenge for federal intervention, since it required the direct imposition of controls on particular sources, traditionally a prerogative of the states. Regional pollution problems like smog could, on the other hand, be more easily addressed through a variety of mitigation measures pertaining to a number of sources that were viewed as fungible in the aggregate. Reduction of total regional emissions per se can be accomplished through numerous alternative strategies; no single facility needs absolutely to be cleaned up, and the moment of truth when the regulator imposes a specific solution—or worse, a shutdown—on a given firm can be avoided. In contrast, where the focus is on localized pollution, specific polluting firms are required to demonstrate reductions, regardless of ostensibly counterbalancing improvements elsewhere in the airshed. By implicitly requiring cleanup of all polluting firms, a local definition of the probem would leave a much narrower range of policy options over which states could employ the discretion delegated to them under the Clean Air Act. Because regional pollution problems allowed the states such discretion, they became the focus of the federal regime, evolving through the 1963 Clean Air Act and, especially, the 1967 Air Quality Act.[27] The latter law specified a series of metropolitan regions for which air quality standards were to be set and implemented by states on the basis of federally researched scientific "criteria documents." The standards were supposed to specify maximum allowable concentrations for a short list of prevalent pollutants in the ambient air that were generated by many sources.[28]

This approach was one with significant political logic, and it had the potential to achieve reductions in the aggregate levels of widespread pollutants. At the same time, it had the distinct drawback of ignoring localized problems. As a senior official at the Public Health Service's Division of Air Pollution remarked in 1966, "Those who live immediately downwind from a particular source of pollution are not comforted by the fact that their problem does not bother the rest of the community. Certainly, their claim to relief regardless of the extent to which the problem may affect others in the community cannot, in good conscience or in good politics, be ignored."[29] The 1970 Clean Air Act sought to rectify this oversight.

In promising "clean air" to "all Americans" across "all parts of the country," Muskie's statement suggested that, unlike its predecessors, the new law would also attend to the concerns of those living in direct proximity to pollution sources within industrial locales. Such a focus would indeed have been a revolutionary departure not only from the course of federal air pollution intervention until then, but also, much more fundamentally, from core assumptions of the nuisance regime based in the common law that had up to this point been the primary regulatory recourse for air pollution victims.[30] The following section considers the extent to which the 1970 CAA lived up to Senator Muskie's promise, in terms of both its initial legislative structure and its subsequent implementation. The discussion focuses on the respective role of risk and technology standards in the act's regulation of both regional air pollution problems (through control of "criteria" pollutants) and localized pollution problems (through the control of "hazardous" and "designated" pollutants).

THE 1970 CLEAN AIR ACT: REGULATORY OPTIONS

Criteria Pollutants and National Ambient Air Quality Standards (Sections 108–110)

As the act's legislative history indicates, pollutants "emitted from diverse stationary and moving sources into the ambient air" were to be subject to National Ambient Air Quality Standards (NAAQS) under sections 108–110.[31] Section 108 instructed the EPA to list multi-source pollutants found to pose a danger to health according to scientific "criteria documents." A number of these documents had already been issued under the 1967 act, and Congress included them as primary candidates for NAAQS control. Section 109 of the CAA called for the NAAQS to be set on the basis of scientific evidence at levels "requisite to protect the public health" with "an adequate margin of safety."[32] Science was to determine the concentration, or threshold, at which each pollutant poses a risk to health; no adjustments were to be made in light of feasibility considerations.

The task of implementing these standards fell to the states, not the federal government. Each state had to submit an "implementation plan" outlining the measures by which it intended to attain these standards. While the regime set absolutist standards on regional pollution, its position remained vague with respect to localized impact.

National Emission Standards for Hazardous Air Pollutants (NESHAP) (Section 112)

Deviating from the regionally defined and state-implemented regulation of criteria pollutants, Congress reserved a much more interventionist approach to a small subcategory of especially dangerous substances. Section 112 defined hazardous air pollutants (HAPs) as those "which may reasonably be anticipated to result in an increase in mortality or an increase in serious irreversible, or incapacitating reversible illness."[33] The EPA was directed by this section to list such pollutants and issue National Emission

Standards regulating them. The law set a stricter standard than the one applicable to criteria pollutants ("*adequate* margin of safety"), mandating that HAPs emission standards provide "an *ample* margin of safety" [emphasis added].[34] More importantly in its reliance on source-specific emission levels that would be set federally, the CAA's HAPs policy diverged from its approach to criteria pollutants. Like the criteria pollutant regime, however, the HAPs regime was to be based exclusively on scientific determinations of risk and was to be applied without regard to cost. The legislative history suggests that Congress intended a small number of extremely dangerous chemicals to be regulated in such a way.[35] But with respect to this selected category, the CAA promised absolute control, even against localized risks.

Designated Pollutants: New Source Performance Standards (NSPS) (Section 111 (d))

New Source Performance Standards (NSPS) constitute the third and final category of standards mandated by the 1970 CAA. As defined by section 111, they were primarily intended to control emissions from newly constructed sources of criteria pollutants.[36] The primary regulatory objects of these standards were industrial categories to be listed by the EPA, rather than particular pollutants, and the standards were to be based on levels of reduction achievable through already available means of pollution control, rather than scientific assessments of risk. In contrast to the standard-setting process applicable to existing sources of both criteria pollutants and HAPs, section 111 explicitly required that cost considerations be taken into account in setting standards for new sources of criteria pollutants.

In addition to regulating new sources of criteria pollutants, the EPA was authorized by section 111 (d) to set standards under the NSPS category for existing sources of "designated" pollutants. This residual category excluded pollutants already listed as "criteria" pollutants or HAPs, but was intended by Congress to include pollutants not "widely present . . . in the ambient air," but "generally confined . . . to the area of the emission source."[37] Section 111 (d) required the EPA to issue regulations mandating that each state submit plans for implementing and enforcing emission standards for "designated" pollutants from existing sources. This approach to the implementation of NSPS for "designated" pollutants from existing sources differed from the more direct federal intervention envisioned for "criteria" pollutants from new sources in the rest of section 111. As the legislative record indicates, Congress intended the "EPA to evaluate its possible control authorities and select the section best suited to regulation of a given substance. EPA's unwavering reliance on section 112 for airborne carcinogens has strayed from this plan and incidentally undermined the effectiveness of the Act."[38]

THE 1970 CLEAN AIR ACT: REGULATORY IMPLEMENTATION

National Ambient Air Quality Standards (Sections 108–110)

The EPA directed its prime regulatory efforts to the implementation of NAAQS for six criteria pollutants: ozone, nitrogen oxides, carbon monoxide, sulfur dioxide, lead, and particulate matter (PM-10).[39] Estimates of the costs of all air pollution control activities nationwide exceed $50 billion annually,[40] an investment that has achieved the nearly total elimination of lead emissions and large reductions in sulphur dioxide and particulates, as well as in volatile organic compounds (the primary precursors of ozone).[41] Nevertheless, many regions across the country remain in violation of one or more of the NAAQS,[42] and some areas may never be able to comply without politically unacceptable social and economic dislocations. Notwithstanding, when it became evident that Los Angeles would not be able to attain ozone standards short of a virtual ban on fossil fuel vehicles, the EPA lacked authorization to approve any alternative, more incremental plan. Rather than revising the absolutist mandate, Congress, under the 1990 Clean Air Act Amendments, extended the deadline for compliance with the ozone NAAQS in Los Angeles by twenty years.[43]

Courts have repeatedly interpreted the CAA statutory directive regarding NAAQS as precluding the EPA from taking cost into consideration.[44] Adherence to the goal of attainment of air quality standards, even if unrealistic, accords with the absolutist promise of the act, which leaves no room for compromise. But the reification of the NAAQS and the single-minded focus on achieving them is curious in light of the standards' inherent arbitrariness, since for many air pollutants there does not exist a defined, scientifically defensible threshold beneath which pollution exposures can be said to be safe. The result has been a regulatory process wherein, "[w]hile recognizing that health-effects thresholds may not exist for some pollutants, EPA has nonetheless generally structured its NAAQS rulemakings as if they do."[45] But this does not change the fact that the NAAQS must be based on some consideration of feasibility if they are to be set above zero, and as such even complete attainment would not provide complete protection. The most important legal challenge to this regulatory fiction resulted in a D.C. Circuit court decision that, until it was overturned by the Supreme Court in 2001, cast doubt on the very constitutionality of the Clean Air Act. At issue were EPA revisions to the NAAQS governing ozone and particulate matter (PM-10), both of which the EPA now considers zero-threshold pollutants.[46] A coalition of industrial interests brought suit against the revised rules in 1997 under the argument that since the EPA could not show ozone and PM-10 to be safe at any level above zero, any nonzero standard was by definition arbitrary, unless the agency took costs into account. A majority of the judges on the D.C. Circuit agreed that the EPA standard-setting process did not offer a justification for the particular numeric limit chosen, or the degree of control required. But the biggest surprise was the D.C. Circuit's decision to invalidate the rule on the basis of the long dormant "delegation doctrine," rather than on administrative law grounds. Under the delegation doctrine, article I, section 1 of the Constitution is interpreted to require Congress to provide "an intelligible principle" to guide administrative discretion.[47]

Using this principle, the court concluded that the EPA's interpretation of its rule-making authority under the act lacked an "intelligible principle" and that the relevant provisions were hence an unconstitutional delegation of legislative authority. In the language of the D.C. Circuit, the "EPA's formulation of its policy judgment leaves it free to pick any point between zero and a hair below the concentrations yielding London's Killer Fog."[48] According to the court, this system lacked a regulatory principle justifying the degree of pollution reduction required by the standard. In *Whitman v. American Trucking Association* (2001), the Supreme Court overturned the D.C. Circuit and upheld the constitutionality of the NAAQS rule-making process.[49] At the same time, the court also reaffirmed its earlier findings that the CAA precluded the EPA from taking cost considerations into account in setting the NAAQS, a conclusion that Justice Scalia argued was dictated by the fact that elsewhere in the statute Congress explicitly allowed for economic feasibility considerations.[50]

The limitations of the NAAQS absolutist scheme have been compounded by distributive considerations. The program is designed to achieve regional pollution reductions, not to avoid localized pollution concentrations. Within this framework, emissions trading schemes have proven useful in easing the burden of compliance by allowing for various offsets or trades in pollution reduction within the relevant airshed. Thus, for example, in an effort to comply with the applicable federal standards, the regional air pollution agency in the Los Angeles area employed a rule allowing major stationary industrial facilities to forgo reductions in their nitrogen oxides (NOx) and volatile organic compounds (VOCs) (the primary precursors of ozone), in exchange for the purchase of pollution credits acquired through the elimination of older, highly polluting vehicles. The program was challenged in 1997 by a coalition of citizen and environmental groups who filed an administrative complaint with the EPA. The coalition claimed the scrapped vehicle rule violated Title VI of the Civil Rights Act of 1964 by contributing to concentrations of toxic air pollutants in the largely poor and Latino South Bay area of Los Angeles.[51]

Challenges to offsets involving VOCs expose a tension between the two-fold threat of this pollutant. VOCs are regulated regionally as ozone precursors under the NAAQS, but they are also toxic pollutants with potentially severe localized impact. Ozone, a primary component of smog and a paradigmatically regional pollutant, results from the photochemical interaction among oxygen, NOx, and VOCs in the atmosphere. For the overall creation of ozone, it indeed matters little where within the region reductions take place, but this is only one dimension of the the the risk posed by these pollutants. The distributive dimension of VOC offsets has been recognized and challenged since the early 1980s,[52] and has received more academic and administrative attention in response to increased environmental justice mobilization.[53]

National Emission Standards for Hazardous Air Pollutants (NESHAP) (Section 112)

As noted earlier, the Clean Air Act reserved control of the most dangerous pollutants to section 112. The EPA's interpretation of that section equated HAPs with carcinogens, a general class of pollutants considered zero-threshold by the EPA. The combination of zero-threshold pollutants, a need to account for localized impacts, and an absolutist legislative mandate all but paralyzed HAPs standard setting under the 1970 act. During the two decades when this mandate was in effect, the EPA listed eight HAPs and regulated just seven out of hundreds of particularly dangerous chemicals.[54] Moreover, even the standards for the seven regulated pollutants were applied to only a small subset of the industrial processes emitting them.[55] In 1980, the EPA attributed the HAPs regime's failure during the act's first decade to the agency's own reluctance to issue the absolutist standards that the HAPs mandate seemed to demand.[56]

Prior to admitting failure, the EPA had attempted to reinterpret its risk-based HAPs mandate in a less absolutist fashion. Under guidelines first issued in 1976, the agency proposed that existing sources of hazardous air pollutants be required to use the "best available technology" to control emissions from source categories presenting significant risks to public health.[57] Without formally adopting this policy, the EPA nonetheless relied on it in developing emission standards for several HAPs, including vinyl chloride.[58] The Environmental Defense Fund (EDF) sued, claiming that cost and technology factors had been considered in deciding to require only a 95 percent emission reduction. In settling this lawsuit, the EPA committed both to revising its proposed vinyl chloride standards and to reformulating its technology-based approach to the regulation of HAPs.[59] Following this settlement, the EPA proposed, but never enacted, revised standards. In 1985 the agency withdrew these revised standards and returned to its 1976 BAT-derived rules, a move that prompted another lawsuit, this time by the Natural Resources Defense Council (NRDC).

In a 1987 decision, the D.C. Circuit ruled that, in relying on BAT to set the vinyl chloride emission standards, the EPA administrator had "substituted technological feasibility for health as the primary consideration" for determining levels of permissible HAPs emissions and thus had inappropriately departed from its risk-based statutory mandate.[60] At the same time, the D.C. Circuit concluded that the EPA was not obligated to set the standard at zero whenever it "cannot determine that there is a level below which no harm will occur."[61] The court explained, "[w]e think it unlikely that science will ever yield *absolute* certainty of safety in an area so complicated and rife with problems of measurement, modeling, long latency and the like. . . . Congress chose instead to deal with the pervasive nature of scientific uncertainty and the inherent limitations of scientific knowledge by vesting in the Administrator the discretion to deal with uncertainty in each case."[62] A difficult question that the vinyl chloride case did not address was the scope of the agency's discretion when the uncertainty pertains not to whether harm will be caused, but to whom and how many are likely to be hurt through low concentration exposure (statistical risk).[63]

New Source Performance Standards (NSPS) (Section 111)

Section 112 was not the only regulatory mechanism available for the control of carcinogens and other forms of localized pollution under the CAA. As noted earlier, the legislative history strongly suggests that Congress intended section 111 (d) to help serve this purpose. Nevertheless, and despite the obstacles encountered in implementing the HAPs regime, the EPA opted to control carcinogens exclusively under section 112. It used its authority under section 111 (d) to designate only a handful of pollutants and industrial categories.[64] NSPS for new and modified sources were used to a greater extent, but only with respect to criteria pollutants.[65]

Localized Pollution and the 1977 and 1990 CAA Amendments

In the 1977 CAA amendments, and again in the 1990 act, Congress enacted significant measures intended to impose technological controls directly on pollution sources. The 1977 amendments required nonattainment areas to revise their State Implementation Plans and to include the use of reasonably available control technology (RACT) for all existing sources.[66] With respect to new and modified major sources of criteria pollutants (in both attainment and nonattainment areas), the 1977 act imposed a requirement for preconstruction permits, under the act's New Source Review (NSR) program. As a condition of such permits, sources had to employ pollution-reduction measures that varied in their severity between attainment and nonattainment areas.[67] The impact of this requirement was, however, weakened by EPA regulations, which had the effect of "grandfathering" many older pollution sources by exempting "routine maintenance and repair" from the definition of major modification under both the New Source Performance Standard and the New Source Review program.[68]

Section 112 was overhauled by the 1990 CAA amendments in response to mounting concern regarding carcinogens and other air toxics left essentially uncontrolled by the 1970 regime.[69] Under the revised section 112, Congress listed 189 HAPs that it directed the EPA to control. Further limiting the agency's discretion, the revised statute required the EPA to list industrial categories associated with the emission of these HAPs and to regulate major sources within these categories through Maximum Achievable Control Technology (MACT) standards. Major sources were defined as those with the potential to emit ten tons of an individual HAP or twenty-five tons of a combination of HAPs annually.[70] Any residual risks remaining after the implementation of MACT would trigger a mechanism for investigating localized risk and promulgating additional, health-based standards under section 112 (f). During its first decade, the revised HAPs regime produced forty-five MACT standards affecting eighty-two categories of major industrial sources.[71] Smaller facilities, referred to as "area sources" by the 1990 act, are to be subject to a significantly less stringent requirement of controlling their emissions through "generally available control technologies" (GACT), with no mechanism for addressing residual risk.

The EPA announced in 1999 an Urban Air Toxics Strategy directed at area sources from thirteen industrial categories with a 2012 deadline for complete implementation. Whether the promises of this iteration will be easier to keep than its predecessors has yet to be seen. As of the fourth decade after the passage of the 1970 act, localized pollution has received meager attention under federal clean air law, in a manner that departs little from the previous situation of state-implemented common law.

In contrast to the CAA's primary focus on reducing ambient concentrations of particular pollutants, the German law required reductions in all forms of air pollution and from all sources. Although a number of ambient air quality standards exist, partially in connection with European Union guidelines, their role is secondary to the German emission control standards, which apply irrespective of whether they are required for compliance with the relevant ambient standard.[72] As such the German regime seeks to implement available means of pollution reduction across all categories of communities and locales.

As to why Congress opted to ignore strong suspicions, if not knowledge, of the absence of safe thresholds, two seemingly contradictory explanations have been proposed. The first views the act's absolutist language essentially as a symbolic gesture designed to reap immediate political benefits while delegating the hard policy decisions to the EPA. In David Schoenbrod's words, "The Clean Air Act was incantation."[73] An opposing perspective pins the act's absolutism, especially with respect to HAPs, on a desire to constrain the EPA's discretion, an exercise in "agency-forcing," so to speak.[74]

The rationale for the need for such constraints came from post–New Deal theories on the vulnerability of agencies to capture by the interests they are created to regulate.[75] Reducing the risks of capture required that courts abandon the deferential stance that they ultimately adopted toward New Deal agencies in favor of closer judicial scrutiny of administrative decisions. This goal, in turn, was better served by a risk, rather than a technology-based, regime.

Risk-based statutory mandates implicitly burden the administrative agencies responsible for their implementation with an interlocking pair of legal evidentiary challenges, one pertaining to the degree of existing or threatened harm, and another to the scope of the required remedial or preventative measures. In other words, should risk-based interventions be challenged, the state must be able to offer adequate scientific proof that pertinent regulatory restrictions are both necessary and sufficient to protect public health or environmental values. Where judges deem proof of either condition inadequate, the regulations are legally invalid. Although courts may, and often do, opt to defer to the judgment of expert administrators—as they ultimately did even in the *American Trucking* case—the scope and exercise of such deference is ultimately up to judges to decide.[76]

Technology standards, by contrast, greatly narrow the opportunities for judicial intervention because they render legally irrelevant the closeness of a fit between the targeted harm and the chosen regulatory means. Firms regulated under technology standards can initiate litigation, but on the much narrower basis of the technical or economic feasibility of the proposed means of mitigation. From this perspective, the key aspect distinguishing absolutist risk standards from their technology-based counterparts was the greater role that they accorded to judicial review.

Environmentalists' distrust of agencies explains the act's absolutist risk provisions, but only in part. Notwithstanding the radical scope of their promise, these were not the provisions that drew the fiercest opposition from industry, or the greatest debate in Congress. Attention instead focused on the act's motor vehicle emission-control deadlines and, to a lesser extent, on the act's New Source Performance Standards (NSPS).[77] While lending some support to the symbolic interpretation of the absolutist risk provisions (particularly those regarding HAPs), industry's seeming affinity for risk standards more strongly illuminates a convergence of preferences emanating from both sides of the political map for giving courts, rather than the agencies, the final say. The courts, most notably the D.C. Circuit, where most challenges to federal agency rules are filed, soon rose to the task and began remanding rules to the agency for the purpose of creating a more substantial evidentiary record for review. Among the most important targets of the "hard look" doctrine were some of the EPA's early CAA rules. The courts' decisions were supportive at times of environmental and at other times of business concerns.[78] The interventionist judicial stance was thus welcomed by members of both camps.[79]

Inside the EPA, the impact of the "hard look" doctrine resulted in a drastic transformation in the agency's standard-setting process. Whereas the first NAAQS were promulgated quickly and informally soon after the initial legislative mandate, by the end of the 1970s, standard setting had become more complex and more formally institutionalized. It became a far slower process designed to create a comprehensive rule-making record that would be available in case of judicial review.[80] Nevertheless, without an established threshold of safe exposure, even a scientifically rigorous record could not make the setting of an exposure standard at any particular level less "arbitrary," since the choice of level inevitably derived from a mix of scientific, economic, and technological concerns, and not the exclusively scientific criterion demanded by the law.

Instead of pursuing a legislative amendment to its mandate that would openly acknowledge these impossible constraints, the EPA, by and large, adhered to the fiction that its standards were dictated by science and not political judgments.[81] Moreover, even where the act called for technology-based alternatives, as in section 111 (d), the EPA opted to interpret its mandate narrowly. The preference for risk-based standards (and the judicialized regulatory process that they entail) was thus shared not only by those wanting to influence the direction of EPA enforcement, but also by the agency itself.

R. Shep Melnick attributes the EPA's apparent preference to the public relations benefits conferred by this science-based approach. As he writes, "[p]resenting national standards as absolutely necessary to the protection of public health adds to the moral force behind emission limitations based on these standards" at the same time that "[i]t allows the EPA to escape from the demand that each and every action be justified on the basis of economic analysis."[82] But if the EPA were determined to use science to justify any and all regulations, one would not expect it to adhere to the "safe threshold" basis for standard setting. Instead, the agency would be vociferously proclaiming the position of "no safe threshold," a stance that would ostensibly justify unlimited and cost-independent national standards. Far from advancing the "no safe threshold" position, the EPA continues to behave as if standard-setting for the full protection of public health can be rationally and objectively based on science. The apparent fealty to science nevertheless legitimates the regime, though from a different direction. The fiction of a safe threshold, together with its attendant science-based mandate and regulatory process supports the illusion that a risk-based regulatory regime can avoid imposing any sacrifices.

While the appeal of this response to the "tragic choice dilemma" of zero-threshold pollutants is evident,[83] it is not the only possible response, as the example of the German air pollution regime suggests. Rather than guaranteeing immediate (though fictitious) protection against all harm from chemicals, the German regime's *Vorsorgeprinzip* promises incremental, but continuing, improvement in levels of environmental protection. As discussed, in some of its provisions the CAA regime followed a similar technology-based route, though these circumscribed deviations from risk have generated much controversy in the American context.

RISK VERSUS BAT: THE POLICY DEBATE

The main economic deficiency attributed to technology standards is the propensity of a standard-setting process grounded in feasibility both to "overregulate" and to "underregulate." Since technology standards do not tailor their interventions to particular harms, they are liable to produce either insufficient or excessive protection against the relevant risks. The latter happens when regulations require reductions in pollution well below levels that have been scientifically demonstrated to be harmful, or when the application of uniform abatement measures across industrial categories fails to capitalize upon contextual differences in the costs and benefits of pollution control. Elements likely to influence relevant costs include the nature of the industrial processes in question, as well as the availability and effectiveness of alternative control technologies. The benefits of pollution control vary with climate, geography, population density, and, according to some, the particular environmental tastes or preferences of those living in the area. Uniform technology standards ignore these differences, and, it is argued, thus stand in the way of more finely tuned, less costly, and ultimately more rational solutions to environmental problems. As Stewart and Ackerman write, "uniform BAT requirements waste many billions of dollars annually by ignoring variations among plants and industries in the cost of reducing pollution and by ignoring geographic variations in pollution effects."[84] Furthermore, uniform technology standards are the antithesis of the firm-by-firm solutions that are considered one of the principal attractions of incentive-based means of control, such as pollution pricing and exchange mechanisms like emission trading.[85]

In addition, technology-based standards have also been criticized for impeding pollution control innovations by tying regulatory demands to available technology and failing to offer incentives for investment in new and superior control strategies.[86] By contrast others point to evidence of the capacity of technology standards—when properly designed—to induce technological innovation,[87] and a small but growing number of American legal scholars deviate even further from the prevailing view, arguing that the technology-based approach is preferable overall to risk-based regulation because the former has demonstrated its capacity to deliver better pollution control results.[88]

Among the first exponents of this position within the American debate was Howard Latin, who challenged the very possibility of tailoring pollution reduction requirements to levels scientifically proven to be safe. Without disputing the notion that technology standards are highly imperfect, Latin wrote in 1985 that "[i]n many environmental protection contexts, society's real choice may be to rely either on crude regulation or on no regulation."[89] Imperfect regulation is the only realistic alternative because "the practical consequence of making particularized risk estimates legally relevant—indeed mandatory—is to emasculate the regulation of carcinogens under prevailing conditions of scientific uncertainty."[90]

Similarly to the CAA's risk standards, nuisance law began by offering an absolute guarantee against harm by air pollution, irrespective of technological or economic feasibility of mitigation. But this absolutist orientation virtually compelled nuisance doctrine to evolve in a way that tightly circumscribed the harms against which its complete protection came into force. A primary constraint was to vary the definition of air pollution injury by location, such that much more pollution was tolerated in urban and industrial locales than in more bucolic settings. Within such industrial locales, victory in air pollution lawsuits was made virtually dependent on plaintiffs' capacity to prove that, beyond its discomforts, pollution caused disease. Adhering to this regulatory tradition, the CAA's risk-based standards hinge the scope of the state's regulatory authority upon scientific evidence of harm at the same time that it all but ignores problems of localized pollution in industrial locales.

Throughout the nineteenth century, common-law-based principles regarding the meaning and content of reasonable regulation were invoked against efforts to introduce European-modeled legislation to the United States. As the following chapter argues, the same common law sensibilities account for contemporary challenges to the democratic legitimacy of technology standards.

CHAPTER TWO

"Command and Control": Means, Ends, and Democratic Regulation

ENCODED into the term "command and control," widely used as a synonym for technology standards, is a fundamental challenge to the legitimacy of this regulatory approach.[1] The military and Cold War connotations of the phrase lend it considerable resonance in American political discourse, and its increasingly familiar presence in our regulatory vocabulary has allowed its shorthand critique of technology standards as vaguely authoritarian, and hence undemocratic, to masquerade as a neutral, almost technical, term. This chapter probes the charge that technology-based regulatory standards are democratically deficient. The basis for this critique is not immediately apparent, as it does not stem from simple majority-rule sensibilities; clearly technology standards can be and are enacted by democratically elected regimes. Suspicion that technology-based standards go hand in glove with an undemocratic character must therefore be rooted in principles related to the content of the legislation rather than the process that enacted it.

The most explicit argument offered regarding technology standards' undemocratic character is their supposed centralizing tendency and their putative vulnerability to "factional control."[2] But the fear of factions ties to a deeper equation of technology standards with arbitrary, irrational, government intervention, and the charge of democratic deficiency stems directly from the absence of regulatory tailoring to a proven level of harm.

The requirement for close tailoring of regulatory interventions to legally proven harm marked the divide between opponents and proponents of common law limits on the police power through much of the nineteenth century. Opposing conceptualizations of the police power—whether limited by common law or absolute—divided nineteenth-century legal opinion, with the demand for means-end rationality serving precisely as the line separating the two positions. This nineteenth century controversy ultimately came to a head in 1905 with *Lochner v. New York*.[3]

This chapter argues that the debate on the legitimacy of legislation independent of proof of harm was not laid to rest with the *Lochner* court. Rather, echoes of this controversy continue to reverberate in the charge that in failing to respond to scientifically proven harm, technology standards run afoul of democratic principles. More importantly, this influence remains evident in judicial review of administrative rules governing zero-threshold chemicals. This chapter illuminates this claim by analyzing in parallel the Supreme Court's reasoning in *Lochner* and seventy-five years later, in *Industrial Union v. American Petroleum Institute* (1980), a decision that overturned an occupational benzene exposure rule.[4]

MEANS, ENDS, AND DEMOCRATIC REGULATION

A leading exponent of the "democracy deficit" of technology standards is Richard Stewart, who focuses on the intertwined centralizing tendencies of Best Available Technology (BAT) regimes and their factionalizing results.[5] He depicts the federal environmental protection regime as "a massive effort at Soviet-style central planning of the economy to achieve environmental goals," and concludes that this "centralized command system is simply unacceptable as a long-term environmental protection strategy for a large and diverse nation committed to the market and decentralized ordering."[6] The drawbacks of centralization stem in part from the greater efficiency of more locally responsive regimes. But in addition, Stewart posits a direct link between "the dominant reliance on legalistic 'command and control' strategies to achieve national goals" and the emergence of "a faction-ridden maze of fragmented and often irresponsible micro-politics within the government." Unable to make the thousands of detailed decisions entailed by prescriptive regulation, Congress is forced to delegate the actual setting of standards to subcommittees and agencies, which have themselves become beholden to economic and ideological interest groups. In place of a robust pluralist process, the centralized regulatory state has thus spawned a new form of factional domination within functionally specialized agencies, and Stewart holds reliance on prescriptive technological standards largely to blame.[7]

The argument shares some parallels with Theodore Lowi's thesis in *The End of Liberalism*. Lowi, who analyzed social regulation programs of the 1960s and 1970s, worried, like Stewart, about the tendency of broad statutory delegations of regulatory power to confer an unfair and undemocratic political advantage on those who can turn administrative discretion to their benefit. But in contrast to Stewart, Lowi singled out some of the new regime's risk-oriented formulas, rather than its technology standards, as being particularly likely to yield to interest group-driven bargaining processes.[8] A 1970 report by a Ralph Nader study group likewise located greater barriers to citizen participation in risk- rather than technology-based standards. According to the Nader report, the difficulty of relating particular source emissions to ambient standards (as required under the 1967 Air Quality Act) in particular created "insurmountable barriers to public participation" and contributed to "the already well-established tyranny of the indentured experts of corporations."[9]

Which of the two types of standards in fact gives interest groups a greater capacity to influence the regulatory process is an empirical question that has yet to receive systematic investigation. There currently does not appear to be empirical support for an a priori assumption that this threat attends technology-based standards more closely than their risk-based counterparts. As a practical matter, risk-tailored standards may offer at least as much discretion as those focusing on technology, particularly in light of the problems of scientific uncertainty discussed earlier. Similarly, it is unclear why interest groups might be expected to be any better able to bring their influence to bear when a regulatory decision hinges on the scientifically complex (and often ambiguous) question of risk, rather than on technological feasibility.

The notion that risk standards are more amenable than technology standards to active public participation nonetheless remains influential. In an article advocating regulatory reform to create a less costly and more democratic regulatory state, Richard Pildes and Cass Sunstein rely on Stewart's argument to suggest that there is indeed something distinctive about the impediments to public participation posed by BAT standards, versus those that are more directly health based.[10] A particular locus of their concern is the opening that BAT standards afford to actors with a financial stake in the adoption of particular technological means of pollution control. However, the following statement hints at even deeper fears regarding the democratic appropriateness of such "means-focused" regulatory processes:

> [T]he BAT approach is itself troubling from the standpoint of a well-functioning political process. That approach ensures that citizens and representatives will be focusing their attention not on what levels of reduction are appropriate, but instead on the largely incidental and nearly impenetrable question of what technologies are now available.[11]

Barriers in the form of expertise and access are thus not the only, or even the primary, source of the democratic deficiency inherent in BAT. More fundamentally, technology-based standards are held to be incompatible with well-reasoned legislative and public deliberation. The objective, claim Pildes and Sunstein, is not deliberation per se but a deliberative process that keeps the "key issues" of "risk levels and risk comparisons" front and center.[12] Only after resolving the underlying question about the appropriate level of protection, ought "a well-functioning political process" move to choosing from the array of available means of implementation. Because BAT standards deviate from this ends-to-means sequence, they offer deliberative opportunities inferior to those of risk standards.

Pildes and Sunstein do not elaborate what democratic principle is at stake in adhering to this ends-means sequence. Moreover, there is some tension between an insistence on this adherence and Sunstein's critique elsewhere of what he terms the use of a "common law baseline" in contemporary constitutional doctrines. Along a spectrum of issues ranging from affirmative action to campaign finance reform, the status quo is imbued with an air of neutrality, while deviations from existing distributions are seen as unprincipled and politically partisan intrusions—Sunstein has argued in an article entitled "*Lochner*'s Legacy."[13] As he explains, the link between *Lochner* and present-day constitutional issues lies in the continued hold of *Lochner*-era understandings of the place and meaning of neutrality within the American constitutional order. Regulatory interventions consistent with such neutrality, under *Lochner*, are those that can be shown to derive from a sequential process that appropriately tailors means to permissible governmental ends.[14] This test, according to Sunstein, amounts to a fallacious establishment of a common law baseline as the measure of neutral governmental action.

Building upon Sunstein's reading of the Court's reasoning, the following sections argue that *Lochner* similarly presages contemporary democratic critiques of BAT. This is because the question at the heart of *Lochner*'s means-ends test was ultimately that of the state's authority to regulate without scientific proof of harm.

MEANS, ENDS, AND *LOCHNER*

At issue in *Lochner* had been the validity of an occupational standard, namely section 110 of the New York Labor Law, which stated that "[n]o employee shall be required or permitted to work in a biscuit, bread or cake bakery or confectionery establishment more than sixty hours in any one week, or more than ten hours in any one day."[15] Enacted in 1897 after prolonged lobbying by organized labor, the law, like most labor legislation of the era, was inspired by and patterned upon the workers' protection statutes in continental Europe.[16] Joseph Lochner, the owner of a bakery in upstate New York, was convicted and fined $50 for allowing one of his employees to work more than the permitted sixty hours a week. After losing two rounds of appeal before the New York courts, Lochner saw his conviction overturned by the Supreme Court, which found that the statute's restriction of work-hours violated the constitutional right to freedom of contract embodied in the Fourteenth Amendment. Laws interfering with this constitutionally protected liberty, explained the court, were valid only when they advanced legitimate health and safety goals, a condition not met by the work-hour restriction in question. Valid legislative restrictions on economic liberty, Justice Peckham's majority opinion further elucidated, must serve "as a means to an end" and that end "itself must be appropriate and legitimate."[17]

Beginning from the Supreme Court's own previously quoted construction of the principle at stake, Sunstein describes the interpretive approach adopted by the majority in *Lochner* as a two-step process that began by asking whether the statute had been designed to advance a permissible governmental end (as distinct from redistributive or paternalistic measures, for example) and then continued by scrutinizing the relationship between the permissible end invoked and the means by which the state opted to promote it. Too loose a nexus between means and ends would call into question whether the end formally advanced in support of the statute was the legislature's true motivation. In the absence of sufficient evidence justifying the work-hour restriction as a health measure, the court concluded that the law had been passed from motives other than health and was subsequently invalid. The court does not specify what these other (presumably union-driven) motives were, but, as Sunstein notes, the implication is one of a legislative process tainted by illegitimacy.[18] What makes the law suspect from a constitutional perspective is not direct evidence of its having been enacted out of any improper motive, but rather the a priori absence of a proven health-based rationale.

The similarity between this manner of reasoning and elements of the debate regarding the democratic legitimacy of feasibility-based standards begins to be discernible at this point. But the development of this argument requires a further look at the manner in which the *Lochner* majority reached the decision that the law was not a proper health measure. The risks of prolonged exposure to flour dust and intense heat from baking ovens were the chief health-based rationales that New York offered for the work-hour restriction. The state backed this claim with a number of studies linking such exposure to respiratory inflammation, rheumatism, cramps, and increased morbidity. To counter this evidence, *Lochner* and the larger bakers' organizations that supported his case presented studies blaming unsanitary conditions, not long hours, for the health problems associated with employment in some bakeries. Judges on both courts that initially reviewed the law were divided as to whether the state's evidence sufficiently established a health-based justification, although the majority voted to uphold it in both cases. The tables turned at the Supreme Court when the *Lochner* majority, siding with the New York courts' dissenting position, viewed the state's evidence as lacking a "reasonable foundation for holding this to be necessary or appropriate as a health law to safeguard the public health or the health of the individuals who are following the trade of a baker."[19]

The New York labor law that included the work-hour restriction contained additional provisions allowing for the inspection and detailed regulation of bakeries, down to the location of washrooms, the placement of tiles, and the specification of ceiling heights. Notwithstanding this significant encroachment on bakery owners' autonomy, these regulations were seen by the Supreme Court as unproblematic extensions of the state's police power because there existed a direct connection between the regulatory measures in question and improved sanitary conditions. What distinguished the work-hour limitation from valid legislation was the lack of the means-end rationality required for it to qualify as a reasonable legislative intervention. The relationship between hours of employment in bakeries and damage to the health of bakers or the public who consumed their bread, concluded the court, was simply too speculative to support a reasonable interpretation of the law as a police power measure directed toward health.

It was with respect to this issue, and this issue alone, that justices Harlan, White, and Day dissented from the majority. Agreeing that "there is a liberty of contract which cannot be violated even under direct legislative enactment,"[20] these three dissenters departed from the majority only in their conclusion that the work-hour provision in question was a proper exercise of the police power and consequently did not violate liberty of contract under the constitution. They considered the scientific and other evidence presented in the case sufficient to establish that the work-hour restriction bore a substantial enough relation to the state's legitimate interest in protecting public health. Justice Holmes's dissent diverged from that of Harlan, White, and Day in assuming that the law was constitutionally valid without regard to the state's effort or ability to support a health-based rationale.

As a matter of constitutional law, Justice Holmes's minority position is the one that ultimately prevailed. Yet, as the following section argues, the underlying notion that the legitimacy, if no longer the constitutionality, of regulatory interventions demands a proven nexus between means and ends has remained powerfully influential, not only in contemporary critiques of BAT, but also, most importantly, in judicial review of administrative lawmaking. In this connection, the Supreme Court's 1980 decision in *Industrial Union* stands as a prime manifestation of "*Lochner*'s Legacy."

Between *Lochner* and *Industrial Union* (the Benzene Case)

Industrial Union concerned a benzene workplace exposure standard that the Occupational Safety and Health Administration (OSHA) issued in

1978. Established only five years earlier as an agency within the Department of Labor, OSHA in its early years focused on improving occupational safety by preventing workplace accidents, not on potential long-term threats to workers' health. This focus allowed the agency to take quick and visible action with respect to issues of long-standing concern to unions and others seeking greater workplace regulation, yet to avoid the complex science-policy disputes entailed in setting standards for control of industrial chemicals. OSHA soon met criticism of both its alleged insistence on trivial and expensive workplace adjustments that were likely to yield few, if any, safety benefits, as well as its failure to regulate dozens of occupational carcinogens that the National Institute for Occupational Safety and Health (NIOSH) had identified.[21]

In 1977, following President Carter's election and his appointment of Eula Bingham as OSHA Administrator, the agency made the control of workplace carcinogens its leading regulatory priority.[22] The effort began with the formulation of a generic carcinogen policy that started from the premise that no safe threshold of exposure to carcinogenic chemicals existed. On these grounds, the proposal endorsed a regulatory course that would set exposure standards at the lowest feasible level, rather than in response to a quantitative risk assessment.[23] Like the German policies discussed in chapter 1, OSHA's proposed policy was not intended to provide absolute protection against all carcinogenic risk. In fact, it assumed that such a degree of absolute control would be impossible. Instead, the policy hoped to shift the standard setting process away from what the agency had come to see as a fruitless search for perfectly tailored protection toward a more pragmatic focus on feasible improvements.

The language governing the Occupational Safety and Health Act offered more than a modicum of support for this interpretation. Section 6 (b) (5) of the act directs the agency "in promulgating standards dealing with toxic materials or harmful physical agents" to "set the standard which most adequately assures, to the extent feasible, on the basis of the best available evidence, that no employee will suffer material impairment of health or functional capacity."[24] In the face of significant doubt that any level of exposure to carcinogens could be deemed safe, OSHA contended that its duty under this section was to protect workers to the best extent feasible, and it soon put this theory to the test.

Adopted in February 1978, OSHA's revised benzene standard reduced the permissible level of exposure from ten parts per million (ppm) (measured over eight hours) to one ppm with a ceiling exposure of twenty-five ppm and allowances for brief exposures of up to fifty ppm. Although quantitative risk assessments were available and could have been used to justify the standard chosen by OSHA, the agency expressly avoided relying on these data, in accordance with its generic cancer policy.[25] The prin-

ciples underlying this policy stood front and center in the preamble to
the proposed rule, and OSHA acknowledged the presence of significant
scientific uncertainty as to the exact levels at which exposure to benzene
is likely to affect human health adversely.[26] The agency nevertheless argued that because benzene was a known human carcinogen, and because
no safe levels of exposure to carcinogens had been demonstrated, exposure ought to be reduced to the greatest extent feasible.[27]

The bulk of OSHA's rule-making accordingly focused not on the degree of risk posed by exposure to benzene at levels higher than one ppm,
but on the technological and economic feasibility of reducing exposure
to that level. In making its case, OSHA assessed separately the modes
and costs of compliance for each of the two major industrial categories
subject to the standard: rubber manufacturing, and petroleum production and refining. Of the two, it was the rubber industry that employed
most of the workers likely to benefit from the new standard, and it was
there, contended OSHA, that compliance could be achieved at a relatively low cost by replacing benzene-containing solvents and adhesives
with reduced-benzene or benzene-free materials that were already available and effective.

OSHA conceded that compliance would be significantly more costly
for the petroleum refining industry, which could not simply substitute
lower-benzene inputs, but instead required potentially expensive engineering solutions to capture emissions or dilute their concentration. The
higher cost notwithstanding, the agency concluded that the one part per
million (ppm) standard was feasible because the firms comprising this
industrial sector were generally large and economically stable and would
thus be able to absorb the costs of compliance or pass them on to consumers. It should also be noted that, during this period of standard setting,
OSHA used the same grounds of feasibility to reject union proposals that
would have further reduced permitted exposure and eliminated the allowances for significant short-term and exceptional benzene exposures.[28]

The petroleum industry successfully challenged the benzene rule before
the Fifth Circuit, which vacated the standard in 1978, largely due to
OSHA's failure to conduct any form of cost-benefit analysis in its justification for the standard. In *Industrial Union*, a sharply divided Supreme
Court upheld the Fifth Circuit's finding that the standard was invalid, but
on somewhat different grounds. OSHA's error, Justice Stevens's plurality
opinion argued, lay not in the absence of a cost-benefit analysis, but in its
failure to establish a threshold level above which exposure to benzene
constituted a significant risk.[29] Against OSHA's contention that, in the
absence of established safe thresholds, the previously quoted section 6
(b) (5) made feasibility the regulatory criterion of concern, the court held
that all standards enacted under the act must meet with Section 3 (8)'s

definition of such standards as those "reasonably necessary or appropriate to provide safe or healthful employment and places of employment," and that this in turn meant they served "to remedy a significant risk of material health impairment."[30]

In overturning OSHA's benzene rule in *Industrial Union*, Justice Stevens carefully described the threshold requirement: "that a 'significant' risk be identified is not a mathematical straitjacket; OSHA is not required to support its finding that a significant risk exists with anything approaching scientific certainty." All that was necessary was for OSHA to show "on the basis of substantial evidence, that it is at least more likely than not that long-term exposure to 10 ppm of benzene presents a significant risk of material health impairment," a burden that OSHA had not even attempted to carry, concluded Justice Stevens.[31]

It is noteworthy that the burden of establishing a threshold finding of risk before promulgating any regulatory interventions fell upon OSHA no matter what the cost of compliance with such regulations. Even relatively trivial costs could not be imposed in the absence of some manner of formal risk assessment. As far as the benzene standard was concerned, this principle precluded OSHA not only from ordering expensive engineering controls for petroleum manufacturers, but equally from demanding the far cheaper product substitution solutions that would have sufficed to achieve compliance in the rubber industry, which was where the bulk of workers facing the risk of benzene exposure on the job were employed. The "significant risk" requirement did not leave any room for administrative differentiation of benzene exposure standards across different industrial sectors based on feasibility.

The court's decision that the agency was bound by law to establish a "significant risk" prior to regulating a toxic substance was "a judicial creation" in so far as it had "little direct basis . . . in the text or history of the Act," according to Sunstein.[32] Somewhat surprisingly, he concludes that this does not detract from the soundness of the opinion, since the judges' interpretation of the statute was properly governed by considerations of good public policy.[33] Sunstein argues that the particular policy principle advanced by the decision is that of "*de minimis* exceptions to social and economic regulation." In other words, some problems or risks are simply too small to warrant regulatory interventions. When regulatory authorities ignore this principle, it is the task of the courts to fix that mistake.[34] Elsewhere in the same book, Sunstein hints at a possible root of the problem that generates the need for such a judicial fix. He attributes "[t]he OSHA statute's draconian provision for regulation of toxic substances" in part to the "lobbying efforts of unions," and he treats this as an example of regulatory pathologies resulting from "the problem of interest-group power."[35]

The argument thus echoes the distinction between legitimate and illegitimate motivations for legislation that Sunstein specifically identified with the *Lochner* decision. Importantly, a *de minimis* argument very similar to the one guiding the Benzene decision can likewise be found in Justice Peckham's statement that "the mere fact of the possible existence of some small amount of unhealthiness" through employment in bakeries cannot suffice "to warrant legislative interference with liberty."[36] Justice Stevens similarly wrote in the Benzene case that a safe workplace "is not the equivalent of 'risk free.' There are many activities that we engage in every day—such as driving a car or even breathing city air—that entail some risk of accident or material health impairment; nevertheless, few people would consider these activities 'unsafe.' Similarly, a workplace can hardly be considered 'unsafe' unless it threatens the workers with a significant risk of harm."[37]

The *de minimis* argument does not respond, however, to the regulatory rationale underlying OSHA's generic cancer policy and its benzene-rule test case. The logic behind the rule was one of feasibility and not absolute protection (which is why OSHA rejected demands to set the standard below one ppm). OSHA's goal for its carcinogen policy was to disentangle matters of scientific proof from the scope of its regulatory authority. But the Supreme Court incorrectly equated with absolutist protection the agency's deliberate choice to ground the permitted exposure limit in feasibility rather than scientific proof.

Rather than the *de minimis* principle, it appears that the reasoning behind the court's plurality may be better described as the principle that counsels narrow construction of "statutes in derogation of the common law."[38] Although the act itself makes no mention of proof of "significant risk" as a precondition for regulatory intervention, the court in *Industrial Union* read this requirement into the statute's definition under section 3 (8) of a health and safety standard as "reasonably necessary and appropriate to provide safe or healthful employment."[39] Rejecting OSHA's claim that, with respect to known toxic substances, "reasonably necessary and appropriate" at most required that the standard "not be totally irrational," the court insisted that without a threshold finding that current legal levels of exposure created a significant risk, a regulatory standard could not be deemed reasonable under the act. The reason for this, Justice Stevens's opinion explained, was that "[i]n the absence of a clear mandate in the Act, it is unreasonable to assume that Congress intended to give the Secretary the unprecedented power over American industry that would result from the Government's view of Section 3 (8) and 6 (b) (5)."[40] Unlike the *Lochner* majority, Justice Stevens does not question Congress's constitutional authority, if it so chooses, to put "unreasonable" legislation into law. Nevertheless, short of explicit language to this effect, common law-based and harm-tailored notions of reasonable regulation are to apply.

The similarity between *Lochner* and the plurality opinion in *Industrial Union* was first noted in the dissenting opinion to the latter, written by Justice Marshall and signed by three more justices. Charging the plurality with having distorted the plain meaning of the act's relevant provisions to make them conform with its "own views of proper regulatory authority,"[41] Justice Marshall explicitly likened their opinion to that of the *Lochner* majority, and he predicted that "the approach taken by the plurality today, like that in *Lochner* itself, will eventually be abandoned, and that the representative branches of government will once again be allowed to determine the level of safety and health protection to be accorded to the American worker."[42] As this language suggests, the dissent's critique echoes the conventional view of the issue raised by the *Lochner* case as one of insufficient deference to the legislature. However, the parallels cut much more deeply. In both cases what is at stake is the legitimacy of regulatory interventions that are not tailored to a particular harm. And it is in this sense that *Industrial Union* properly belongs to the list of common-law-based public law decisions that constitutes "*Lochner*'s Legacy."

Unlike the Supreme Court's constitutional review in *Lochner*, judicial review of the type of administrative rules practiced in *Industrial Union* leaves the door open for a legislative "end run." Since such judicial action is based on interpretation of the governing legislation, new laws that eliminate ambiguity regarding the intent of the legislature can be enacted. Yet, as Martin Shapiro has argued, the difference between *Lochner*-era constitutional doctrines requiring substantive due process and later judicial scrutiny of agency rules is greater in theory than in practice. Citing *Industrial Union*, he contends that "justices are certainly prepared to substitute their own interpretation of the statute for that of the agency. And their idea of what Congress wants quite often appears to bear a striking resemblance to what the justices themselves seem to want."[43] Although Congress may in theory respond to any such interpretations with legislative amendments, political reality makes such corrections difficult to undertake. This leads Shapiro to conclude that in the final analysis, "we are not so far from the turn of the century after all."[44] If the constitutionality of means-focused legislation has largely been resolved since the New Deal, the compatibility of this type of legislative mandate with broader American notions of the rule of law has not been put to rest. Instead, the continuing purchase of the view that democratic governance implies substantive limits on the proper ends of regulation accounts for distinctive features of American administrative rule, among them the penchant for risk-based, rather than technology-based, mandates.

Critiques of the democratic legitimacy of BAT have centered on both the discretion that this type of regulatory mandate confers on agencies and the factionalized, interest-group-dominated regulatory processes such discretion is presumed to yield. Yet in circumscribing the authority of agencies, risk standards ultimately give judges a greater say. In ruling on the validity of these standards, judges cannot avoid the imposition of sacrifices inherent to the regulation of zero-threshold chemicals. But in allocating sacrifice of this type, judges are able to rely on scientific uncertainty and *de minimis* definitions of the relevant (statistical) harm to render any such sacrifice legally invisible. As the following chapters discuss, this method is one with deep roots in nineteenth-century common law air-pollution adjudication.

CHAPTER THREE

Regulating "Noxious Vapours": From *Aldred's Case* to the Alkali Act

"NOXIOUS VAPOURS" was the Victorian era's term for the combination of fumes, gases and smells that surrounded a range of economic activities. Facilities in which animals were raised or animal products processed (such as slaughterhouses and tanneries) had long been a source of such pollution. But over the course of the nineteenth century, smells and gases from metal smelting and chemical manufacturing became the primary vapors of concern. Especially notable among the air-polluting industries of the era were the copper smelters and alkali works of Great Britain. Two classes of harm provoked concern regarding their emissions: injury to land as manifested by denuded forests, wilted vegetation, and failed crops; and injury to human health, including both immediate physical discomforts and worry about long-term disease. The severity, urgency, and multidimensionality of this problem can be seen in an 1862 account depicting the blighted environs of St. Helen's:

> The sturdy hawthorne makes an attempt to look gay every spring; but its leaves . . . dry up like tea leaves and soon drop off. The farmer may sow if he pleases, but he will only reap a crop of straw. Cattle will not fatten . . . and sheep throw their lambs. Cows cast their calves; and the human animals suffer from smarting eyes, disagreeable sensations in the throat, and irritating cough, and difficulty of breathing.[1]

Located in the industrial midlands of England, not far from Liverpool, the town of St. Helen's is closely associated with local landowners' mid-nineteenth-century antipollution campaigns. These efforts, directed both at securing compensation for loss to property and the implementation of pollution mitigation measures, ultimately resulted in a bifurcated regime: compensation continued to fall under the auspices of the common law, but mitigation became the product of a technology-based statutory regime under the 1863 Alkali Act. That regime was geared at incremental reductions in both classes of harm (injuries to land and health) through implementation of available technology—even in the face of imperfect scientific knowledge regarding harm to health. In contrast, the common law regime denied compensation for "unproven" health effects of noxious vapors, but sought full protection against harm to property.

The chapter begins with an account of the common-law nuisance regime's emergence in the early seventeenth century. That regime defined the defilement of air as a substantial injury deserving of protection whether or not there existed feasible technical means, short of relocation, of mitigating the problem. Against the predominant view, the chapter argues for the need to read the absolutist protection created in the initial regulatory regime less as an expression of natural-rights conceptions of property, than as a function of available solutions (through land-use separation) that made absolute protection of property *and health* feasible and economically rational. The viability of separation as a solution to such conflicts, rather than an a priori refusal to balance the relevant interests, underpinned this regime.

Once entrenched, however, the common law's absolutist approach endured even as industrialization reduced the feasibility of separation as a solution for protecting residential land uses. The logic of the industrial city was based on proximity and mixed land use (residences, markets, transportation, and industry).[2] These circumstances seem to call for a regime capable of incremental implementation of mitigation measures as these become available, rather than relying solely on better land-use separation. This kind of approach would require a regulatory regime to distinguish pollution that can feasibly be mitigated from that which cannot, but such balancing judgments were incongruous with the nominally absolutist protections of the common law. This chapter argues that the common law approach to this problem was to circumscribe the zone of protection, limiting compensation to injury to land, not to the "trifling inconveniences" of noxious vapors' injury to health. This development in Great Britain did not stand alone, however; at the same time that the common law regime was trivializing the problem, a statutory regime was being assigned the task of implementing available controls for noxious vapors. This was not the case, however, in the United States, where the common law's trivializing problem-definitions soon became entrenched, but without a supplementary, technology-based administrative regime for the control of industrial gases.

Sic Utere: Absolute Liability as a Separation Regime

The course of the common law's response to noxious vapors was set in motion by an early 1600s dispute over the stench of a pigsty between one William Aldred and his hog-farming neighbor, Thomas Benton. Benton moved into the property adjoining Aldred's house in September 1608 and proceeded to keep hogs and sows in a pigsty within his garden. Complaining that the pigs' "fetid and unwholesome stink" seeped and flowed into his house so that he and his servants "could not stay there without danger of infection," Aldred brought suit before the Norfolk Assize. Ten months later the jury found for him and awarded damages.[3] Benton appealed for arrest of judgment, arguing that "it is lawful for anyone to make a hog-sty, even in a market town, for one cannot be so tender-nosed."[4] The judges upheld the jury's award despite this claim. Next, Benton took his appeal before the King's Bench, but this time, instead of defending the legality of the location, he emphasized the economic benefits of the activity: "(T)he building of the house of hogs was necessary for the sustenance of man and one ought not to have so delicate a nose, that he cannot bear the smell of hogs."[5] Rejecting Benton's plea, the King's Bench upheld Aldred's damage award in a decision that Sir Edward Coke's report would subsequently entitle *Aldred's Case* (1611). According to that report, the principle behind the King's Bench rejection of Benton's "necessity" claim traces to an ancient maxim: *sic utere tuo, ut alienum non laedas,* or "use your own (property) so as not to harm another."[6] For centuries henceforth, common law judges would wrestle with the meaning of this rule as they sought to adapt its core logic to rapidly changing economic conditions.

Like many of his ex post facto legal summaries, Lord Coke's reading of an otherwise unremarkable case became a definitive statement regarding an aspect of legal doctrine that had previously been in flux or otherwise uncertain. He presumably selected *Aldred's Case* for attention because it typified a larger category of nettlesome actions that had begun to come before the royal courts with growing frequency during the 1500s—land-use conflicts entailing sensory intrusions from agricultural, commercial, or manufacturing facilities upon their residential neighbors. Exposure to fumes or odors (as in *Aldred's Case*) was a common basis for action, but pertinent sensory intrusions also included noise, vibrations, or interference with light, an eclectic array of encumbrances that common law tort doctrine came to lump under the vague heading of "nuisance."

The increased salience of what might be termed "sensory nuisance" disputes of this type stemmed from intertwined processes of legal and social change. The sixteenth century was an era of political and economic transformation from a fast-declining feudal order to a nascent industrial capitalism. Growth in trade and manufacturing triggered population mobility, and increased density in English cities began creating more opportunities for friction between residents and neighboring economic activities. Acting in concert, the royal courts expanded their jurisdiction by lowering doctrinal barriers that had previously excluded all but freeholders of land from their docket.[7] Against this backdrop, Lord Coke set out in his report on *Aldred's Case* to articulate the principles by which the competing interests at stake in this category of land-use disputes were to be governed.

The plaintiff Benton cogently outlined the parameters of these disputes when he raised his "sustenance of man" defense. Conflicts of this type pit against each other the right to well-being and enjoyment of life on the one hand, and the right to make a living and the need of the community for goods and services on the other. Lord Coke implicitly accepted this framing of the problem by adducing two further examples of likely sources of conflict analogous to Benton's hogs: smoke from lime-kilns and water contaminated by the processing of animal skins. Common to all these cases is a conflict between economic activities and the rights of adjoining neighbors to clean water and air. What manner of response, if any, did *Aldred's Case* offer to Benton's "sustenance" claim? The meaning of *sic utere* depends on the answer to this question, but two possible inter-pretations present themselves. The first, a more absolutist interpretation, would view the "sustenance of man" argument as irrelevant to its goal of protecting the plaintiff's rights, without regard to any economic conse-quences. An alternative interpretation, however, would start from the as-sumption that where there exist more suitable locations for raising pigs the "sustenance argument" need not trump competing interests in land, saying nothing of whether such sacrifice ought to be required where there exist no feasible means of accommodating all the relevant public and pri-vate interests.

The predominant interpretation in contemporary legal historical schol-arship has viewed Coke's opinion and, more broadly, the early nuisance regime it put in place, as embodying a single-minded commitment to cor-rective justice and a rejection of any attempt to balance competing inter-ests. This interpretation of the starting point of the nuisance regime is part of a larger thesis regarding its later trajectory; if the early nuisance regime is seen as one that resolutely abstained from any balancing of inter-ests, then the evident balancing compromises that it made in the nine-teenth century are perceived as indicating a fundamental shift in the re-gime's underlying principles.[8] This perspective is captured by the claim that earlier era "courts had considered only the rights of the individual parties in nuisance actions," but by the later nineteenth century, "the focus in nuisance law was no longer *solely* on the plaintiff's injury [em-phasis added]." Instead, out of concern for the interests "of the defendant entrepreneur . . . nuisance law was transformed."[9] Important historical disagreements exist concerning the magnitude and timing of this shift, the extent to which it typifies a broader transformation in nineteenth-century tort law,[10] and—perhaps most importantly—the relative roles of eco-nomic motivations and ideological commitments on the part of judges in shaping subsequent common law reasoning.[11] Such disagreements not-withstanding, these entire debates share the underlying assumption that the starting point of *sic utere* unambiguously shunned any balancing in favor of an exclusive focus on injury.

A transformation of nuisance law from its deepest agrarian roots can hardly be denied. Air pollution with impacts far exceeding those of Benton's pigs would, by the mid-nineteenth century, be exempted from regulation by common law judges. But our understanding of the meaning of this transformation would be altered if the starting point of *sic utere* embodied a value set that differed in important ways from that which is commonly assumed. This chapter argues that *sic utere*, from its inception, was grounded in (or at least compatible with) pragmatic policy considerations that were concerned not only with protecting property rights against injury, but also with balancing countervailing private and public interests. Far from being a process of linear reasoning from harm to remedy that eschewed any balancing, the *Aldred's Case* rule embodied two distinct balancing processes. First, judges had discretion to decide whether or not to define the pigs' odors as a legally cognizable injury, and in this could, and did, weigh competing interests. Second, the common law's decision to employ an absolute liability in air pollution nuisance disputes of this type ought not be equated with judicial obliviousness to economic concerns; instead the logic behind the rule appeared to have been that of encouraging better separation of incompatible land uses during a preindustrial era in which separation was both a feasible and a complete solution.

In his eighteenth-century summation of the principles of nuisance law, William Blackstone paraphrased the *sic utere* rule of *Aldred's Case*, defining as a nuisance "any thing that worketh hurt, inconvenience, or damage."[12] This authoritative restatement worked to entrench an absolutist interpretation of the *sic utere* rule as a common law promise of compensation for all injury. Yet the "anything" to which Blackstone refers would more appropriately be defined as "any *legally actionable*" injury. Here and elsewhere in the common law, judges engage in balancing and impose sacrifices, but they do so through the distinction between abstract notions of injury (*damnum*) versus legally actionable injury (*injuria*).[13] Judges had to decide when the *damnum* constituted *injuria* and when it did not, a question of law rather than fact. The common law thus recognizes the existence of "*damnum absque injuria*" or "loss, hurt, or harm without injury in the legal sense"; this circumstance does not trigger any legal remedy.[14] The acknowledgment that not all manner of injury is (or ought to be) remediable by law is thus a core principle of common law reasoning. Some plaintiffs will have to go uncompensated, neither because they suffered no injury nor because they failed to prove it, but because the party that harmed them did not breach a legal duty. The relevant question clearly is what constitutes such legal harm—that is, how did judges distinguish actionable from inactionable harms?

This question lies at the heart of *Aldred's Case* and the common law nuisance regime that it established. *Sic utere*, the case was careful to explain, was not a categorical prohibition against all manner of harm brought by interfering land uses. Aldred prevailed because his complaint concerned "matters of necessity, such as wholesome air,"[15] but he would have lost, as the opinion makes clear, had the issue been one of "matters of delight," such as "prospect" (a pleasant view), even though the value of the latter is acknowledged: "it is a great commendation of a house if it has a long and large prospect."[16] *Aldred's Case* does not explain the rationale for exempting "matters of delight," but implicitly harks back to another ancient maxim: *de minimis non curat lex*, "the law does not bother with trifles." A narrow interpretation of this maxim would imply that the only inactionable losses are those of trivial magnitude. Yet in its explicit recognition of the importance of some such "matters of delight" (such as "a long and large prospect"), *Aldred's Case* openly acknowledged that some substantial losses may go uncompensated. It therefore follows that what qualified as "legal injury" and what as a "trifle" depended on a policy judgment allowing for balance of competing interests, rather than a strict or abstract measurement of the scope of the relevant harm.

Nuisance, the doctrinal heading governing this area, is a term coming from the Latin word for "harm." Nevertheless, it is not synonymous with harm as conventionally understood; rather it is a legal "term of art" distinguishing those "annoyances which are singled out as unlawful."[17] This distinction affords judges significant flexibility in legal interventions; where the legal relevance of the injury itself is a pliable matter for judicial determination, judges are able to interject a range of policy considerations into their decisions. In other words, by incorporating this distinction, *sic utere* was a doctrine that, somewhat tautologically, promised legal protection against all injuries deemed worthy of such protection. The setting aside of balancing considerations is triggered only once a harm has been defined as a legal injury. Any injury that does not pass this test is, by implication, a "legal trifle"; thus a regime based on this reasoning has an option to define away sacrifice rather than eliminating it.

The illusion of a legal protection that does not rely on a balancing of interests is further strengthened by application of the liability rule in *Aldred's Case*, which made irrelevant to Benton's liability the question of whether there existed any measures that could have reduced the odor of his pigs, had Benton not neglected to take them. The liability rule appears to impose a prohibition against inflicting any legal injury, to offer a guarantee of complete relief from all such injury, and to do so irrespective of an offender's capacity to achieve any feasible mitigation. In modern tort doctrine this sort of standard is known as an absolute liability rule. In contrast, a negligence standard makes liability contingent upon the quality of the defendant's behavior, rather than the nature or scope of the harm suffered by the plaintiff.[18] Under the latter standard, parties that had taken reasonable precautions are not liable, even if they have caused harm. Intrusions that an offending party has taken all reasonable measures to avoid, therefore, become sacrifices that, at least implicitly, may be legally imposed. The negligence standard thus appears to be the antithesis of an absolute liability rule that is nominally committed to corrective justice at any cost. Whereas absolute liability with respect to land-use conflicts is seen as the product of a refusal to balance competing interests, a negligence standard in the same context implicitly accepts the inevitability of some injuries by pollution, noise and other such interferences as a form of utilitarian sacrifice. But, as I will argue next, absolute liability itself can also be seen to ensue from a balancing process when the choice of whether or not to impose that standard is guided by the availability of geographic separation as a viable and appropriate solution.

The economic and geographical circumstances of the times provided the escape route that made an absolute liability regime feasible; I argue that this line of reasoning was the rationale behind the choice of an absolute liability standard in *Aldred's Case*. This is evident both in the language of Lord Coke's report and its subsequent and classic common law interpretation by Blackstone. William Blackstone's justification for the absolute protection that nuisance law offers against "anything that worketh hurt, inconvenience, or damage" is explicitly predicated upon the evident availability of the solution of spatial separation. Embedded in his proximity-based definition of the problem is the solution that could offer the complete protection that the *Aldred's Case* rule demands. The conflict that he perceived was not between economic activity and nonactivity, but rather the relative location of incompatible land uses:

> [I]f one erects a smelting house for lead *so near* the land of another, that the vapor and smoke kills his corn and grass, and damages his cattle therein, this is held to be a nuisance. . . . [I]f one does any other act, in itself lawful, which yet *being done in that place* necessarily tends to the damage of another's property, it is a nuisance: for it is incumbent on him to find some other place to do that act where it will be less offensive [emphasis added].[19]

Though his example reflected industrial advancements that had occurred in the intervening century and a half, Blackstone followed the language of *Aldred's Case* closely:

> [T]he building of a lime-kiln is good and profitable; but if it be built so *near* a house, that when it burns the smoke thereof enters into the house, so that none can dwell there, an action lies for it. So if a man has a watercourse running in

a ditch from the river to his house, for his necessary use; if a glover sets up a lime-pit for calve skins and sheep skins so *near* the said water course that the corruption of the lime-pit has corrupted it, for which cause his tenants leave the said house, an action on the case lies for it [emphasis added].[20]

The proximity-based problem definition—together with its a priori determination of separation as the appropriate solution—calls the traditional interpretation of *Aldred's Case* into question. Interpretations of the case as supporting absolute protection and rejecting any balancing of economic interests must presume, by implication, that the defendant's claim regarding the necessity of raising pigs to the "sustenance of man," went unanswered. The proximity-based problem definition shows that this is not the case, and that the *Aldred's Case* judges saw the flourishing of economic activity as "good and profitable"—the only question being the spatial arrangement of such activity.

Far from standing as a refusal to acknowledge the imperative of balancing interests, the case instead reflects a judgment that an appropriate—and readily available—solution to problems of incompatible land uses lay in their separation. Put differently, the availability of a viable and complete solution to the air quality problem at hand (through the hog house's relocation) was relevant to the court's selection of an absolute liability rule rather than the equally available negligence rule. The finding of a legally cognizable injury thus derived not from an abstract inquiry into the impact of the relevant air quality problem, as the traditional interpretation would have it, but rather from an intertwined assessment of not only the severity of the harm, but also—and perhaps more importantly—the availability of a feasible preventative solution through the separation of incompatible land-uses. Benton was liable for nuisance not because he raised inevitably malodorous pigs, but because he did so in the wrong place—in close proximity to other neighbors, rather than in a more isolated locale.

Importantly, the salient principle of *Aldred's Case*—absolute liability protection by means of land-use separation—may well have been an innovation introduced by Lord Coke. A reading of the decision in the lower court (which was upheld by the King's Bench) shows that the three presiding judges make a point of emphasizing that "a man may make his hogsty adjacent to his neighbour's house if he keeps it clean."[21] Since even a frequently cleaned pigsty is likely to produce some unpleasant odors, the original decision actually falls somewhere between a negligence and an absolute liability standard. This is a different kind of response to Benton's claim regarding the necessity of pigs for the "sustenance of man"; merely clean up, the court seems to be telling him, and you will be able to maintain your enterprise at its current location. Coke's later report makes no mention of this type of incremental solution, opting instead for the *sic utere* absolute liability rule.[22]

The damage award ostensibly left the decision whether to move or incur future damage payments in Benton's hands. But in imposing an absolute liability rule, *Aldred's Case* offered a strong incentive for losing nuisance defendants to relocate. Under absolute liability, a decision to remain in place would entail unknown future costs, since litigation from new parties (even those newly moving into the area) would expose Benton to the threat of new liability suits; as long as his animal husbandry techniques failed to eliminate all odors, he would be subject to evaluations by future neighbors and judges about the level of odor. Only through relocation could he achieve reasonable certainty regarding his future costs. Moreover, absolute liability in this context may tend to discourage the option of mitigation at the original location—the reason being that even Herculean cleanup efforts would not provide assurances against future liability should it prove impossible to eradicate odors completely.

Although separating land uses had been an eminently feasible solution to sensory interferences in an agrarian environment, its sufficiency plummeted as the industrial revolution got underway, and rapid growth in the scale and number of enterprises accelerated the discharge of industrial pollutants. The separation of industrial from residential areas remained a sensible planning ideal, but it was extremely difficult to implement because of the size of the areas subject to pollution, the need for proximity between industry and its workers, and urban growth dynamics that spurred the encroachment by one land use upon another. The absolute air quality protection that had previously been afforded by adequate separation of conflicting uses was no longer a feasible goal. At best, incremental air quality improvements could be achieved by introducing pollution prevention and control technologies as they became available. As the following section demonstrates, nuisance adjudication proved an inadequate regulatory tool for this purpose.

CONTROLLING NOXIOUS VAPORS FROM COPPER AND ALKALI WORKS IN NINETEENTH-CENTURY BRITAIN: TECHNOLOGICAL AND EVIDENTIARY BARRIERS

The two primary sources of noxious vapors during the Victorian era—copper smelters and alkali works—resembled each other insofar as they both posed serious and similar environmental threats. However, the two industries differed considerably with respect to the ease with which these threats could be addressed with existing technological know-how. A common law regime based on absolute liability did not, however, consider this difference relevant, since the decisive factor was legally actionable injury to a plaintiff (rather than a defendant's conduct or ability to control the offending source). British law and policy of the era was thus torn between a technological imperative to dissimilate treatment of the two industries on the one hand, and a common law refusal to assess liability relative to any capacity for mitigation on the other. In light of this tension, the pragmatic need to apply different rules to industries with differing technological characteristics encouraged either the abandonment of absolute liability in favor of a negligence standard within the common law or the creation of a statutory regime to supplant or augment it.

Due to its heavy reliance on coal, the older industry of copper smelting took place near coal mines in the Swansea district in South Wales and around Lancashire.[23] Lancashire was also the birthplace of the alkali industry in the early nineteenth century, producing soda (sodium carbonate) for the manufacture of soap, glass, and textiles.[24] By 1862 the industry employed 19,000 men, produced finished goods valued at £2,500,000, and was the pillar of Britain's chemical manufacturing industry.[25]

The primary air pollutants emitted by each industry differed with their respective production processes. Copper ores contained sulfur (often at high concentrations) and fluorspar. Roasting and melting these ores produced sulfur dioxide and hydrogen fluoride, which reacted with moisture in the air to form sulfurous, sulfuric, and hydrofluoric acids, as well as large quantities of smoke mixed with sulfur, arsenic, lead, antimony, silver, and metal particles. Alkali works emitted hydrogen chloride, which became hydrochloric acid upon contact with airborne water. While the chemical content of the two industries' emissions varied, exposure to their fumes caused similar injuries to vegetation and discomfort to animals and people.

Motivated by a combination of political pressure from local governments, fear of legal actions, good citizenship, and the economic incentive of recovering raw materials, individuals within both industries energetically sought ways to reduce emissions during the first third of the nineteenth century.[26] In the alkali industry these efforts met with relatively quick success when effective, scrubber-like devices known as "Gossage towers" (after their inventor) were developed in the 1830s. These devices took advantage of long-standing knowledge about the water solubility of hydrochloric acid, which explains the quick development of this important, albeit imperfect, solution.[27] However, the different chemical properties of the sulfuric acid (namely its insolubility in water) impeded the search for technological mitigation of copper smelting pollution.

The smelter Vivian and Sons of South Wales led the industry in its search for technological solutions during the early nineteenth-century. In 1822, John Henry Vivian invested £6000 to develop a device similar to the Gossage towers that would treat copper smelter smoke with water.[28] The device received considerable attention when it "was strongly commended by the judges" at a Swansea competition held the same year through a fund "for obviating the inconvenience arising from the smoke produced by smelting copper ores."[29] But water ultimately could do little to abate the copper smoke's insoluble sulfuric acid, and Vivian's company abandoned its water-based attempts at mitigation. As would become evident over time, reducing sulfuric copper smoke required a more technically sophisticated approach that oxidized sulfur through improved furnace design.[30]

If the primary obstacle to pollution mitigation had simply been technological feasibility, one might have expected differences in the ease of pollution control to lead to large differences in the level of mitigation. However, the alkali industry did not show better results than the copper industry. According to a parliamentary committee appointed at the behest of St. Helen's landowners, the readily available Gossage towers went largely unutilized. The committee blamed nuisance law's failure to spur deployment of the new technology on this regime's strict evidentiary burden, which required that injury suffered by a plaintiff be linked to a specific source of emissions.[31] Pinpointing sources had been a simple matter in the era of *Aldred's Case*, when most agrarian land use conflicts arose between a single source and its neighbor(s), but the concentrated industrial cities of the nineteenth-century engendered an intermingling of emissions from numerous sources that often made specific identification impossible. Moreover, with the advent of the tall smokestack, the remote airborne transport of emissions similarly impeded the legal establishment of a linkage between a plaintiff's damage and a specific factory. In order to establish legal liability under existing nuisance doctrines, a landowner had to trace emissions to their source, using visual or olfactory cues. Indeed, physically able individuals could even find employment as runners who would painstakingly, and often unsuccessfully, attempt to follow emissions to their source. The inherent difficulty of identifying specific sources ultimately led major landowners to abandon their quest for judicial relief.[32]

Behind the burden of source identification loomed the even more daunting challenge of establishing a causal linkage between pollution and harm suffered. Whereas the *Aldred's Case* regime unquestioningly presumed the injuriousness of "unwholesome" air, nineteenth-century common law burdened plaintiffs with proving that particular emissions had caused a particular injury, be it to vegetation or to health. Of the two harms, the former was somewhat easier to prove. An 1812 visitor to Swansea captured the blighting effects of the fumes on flora: "About a mile or two towards the entrance of Swansea, the appearance is frightful, the smoke of the copper furnaces having entirely destroyed the herbage; and the vast banks of scoriae surrounding the works, together with the volumes of smoke arising from the numerous fires, gives the country a volcanic appearance."[33]

The visible devastation notwithstanding, two separate 1830s lawsuits by the South Wales farmer Thomas David failed to convince juries of a necessary causal link between the copper smoke and his crop damage. In the first case, David led a group of eleven farmers who sought a public nuisance indictment against Vivian and Sons. The plaintiffs contended that smoke and fumes from the smelter had destroyed their crops, killed or sickened their cattle, and diminished their own health and well-being. They spoke of losing cattle and sheep to what they termed "Effryddod" (Welsh for crippling disease), a bizarre ailment whose symptoms included large lumps on the animals' legs, loose teeth, and inability to eat. Represented by Sir James Scarlett, one of England's most successful advocates, the defendant countered that the plaintiffs provided nothing more than circumstantial evidence insufficient to establish a causal link between copper smoke and any of the alleged injuries. Scarlett blamed bad farming and herding methods for the losses of crops and animals, not the smoke. Crops wilted because they were deprived of sufficient manure, and animals sickened because of dampness and exposure to wet winds.[34] David and his coplaintiffs lost the case. The following year David brought another action, this time for damages against another major copper manufacturer in the area, winning one shilling. The jury found that while the smoke had indeed damaged David's land, his own farming practices were partly to blame. It fell to David to establish the portion of damage attributable to the emissions, and he could not complete this task to the jury's satisfaction.[35]

Difficult as it was to establish a causal linkage for crop failure, efforts to prove impacts on human health encountered virtually insurmountable obstacles. Some physicians expressed concern about health effects of copper fumes as early as the beginning of the nineteenth century, but this minority view received little attention. The consensus view, embodied in a report on copper works presented to the 1842 Royal Commission on Children's Employment conceded that copper smoke seriously affected "vegetable and animal life," but nevertheless concluded that "the inhalation of it does not appear to operate prejudicially upon human health."[36]

In fact, an influential theory of the time argued quite the reverse—that industrial fumes were actually beneficial because of a supposed disinfectant effect. Doctors who testified before the Commission on Large Towns in 1845 attributed prophylactic qualities to copper smoke, with one even going so far as to claim it "insured [Swansea] from the terrible destructive disease the Asiatic Cholera."[37] Cholera truly was the major health worry of the day; epidemics struck first in 1831–32 and three more times in the subsequent thirty-five years, and tens of thousands of deaths accompanied each outbreak.[38] Among the remedies proffered against a frightening disease that struck suddenly and killed its victims quickly,[39] chemical fumigation was one of the least far-fetched. Its plausibility as a potential public health measure provided a convenient defense in litigation against polluters that weighed against the serious health concerns associated with the emissions.

Such concerns were particularly evident in Liverpool, where James Musparatt had opened the first English factory for soda produced by the Leblanc process.[40] A letter that appeared in the *Liverpool Mercury* in October 1827 captured these fears: "For my part I don't mind if they [the walls of St. Martin's] are as black as Warren's blacking, provided the church is white inside. But I am more concerned for my lungs, and likewise for the minister and congregation; if there should be a north-wester when they meet, I am sure they will feel more for their lungs than they will for the colour of the church walls, because Mr. Musparatt's smoke will enter the sacred pile as well as my humble cottage."[41] Yet four years later the disinfectant theory helped acquit Musparatt of public nuisance charges, albeit in the midst of the first cholera epidemic.[42]

Against a similar use of the disinfectant claim by defendants in the *David v. Vivian* case, plaintiffs complained of adverse physiological and psychological responses to the fumes, including "a dry sensation in the throat, a bitter, metallic taste in the mouth, loss of appetite, shortness of breath, tightness across the chest, smarting eyes and frayed tempers."[43] These immediate symptoms were both an object of concern in themselves and a trigger for vague worry about more ominous, if as yet unsubstantiated, threats to health. Nonetheless, the jury returned a verdict of not guilty after the judge had instructed them that "the distress of a handful of farmers did not constitute the public nuisance required for an indictment against the company."[44]

These instructions to the jury indicate both a transformation in the common law definition of a legal nuisance and the instrument of that change: while the *sic utere* doctrine nominally remained in force, its meaning was changing, in part, through the mechanism of jury instructions whereby the judge defined what did or did not constitute a public nuisance and essentially told the jury to exclude the plaintiffs' complaints (regarding vegetation, domestic animals, or health symptoms) under that definition. In this way the substantive doctrine could be maintained at face value, while the change in evidentiary burdens all but gutted the protections afforded by the original regime. By the late 1850s, the appropriateness of jury instructions that explicitly abandoned the *sic utere* model in favor of a negligence regime lay at the center of a major legal controversy. Ultimately, as the following section discusses, the House of Lords would insist upon upholding only a façade of the *sic utere* rule in an 1862 decision involving copper smoke.

ABSOLUTE LIABILITY AND "TRIFLING INCONVENIENCE": THE ROAD TO THE *ST. HELEN'S* REGIME

Three landmark decisions between 1858 and 1862 hinged on the content of jury instructions in noxious vapors litigation. At issue during this period, as during the *Aldred's Case* era, was the choice between absolute liability and negligence rules for the adjudication of air pollution disputes. The choice between these competing rules amounted to whether or not to protect industry against suits from landowners in cases where mitigation was infeasible. By this time, the solution of moving an offending source had largely become untenable as industrial activities increasingly needed to be located within urban concentrations. Since negligence focuses on conduct, and not on injury alone, a shift to a negligence rule would exempt industries found not to be negligent from paying compensation for injury to property and vegetation, or for the discomforts or health effects of noxious vapors.

Such a shift had the potential to introduce a more transparent balancing of competing interests: when it exempts from liability those harms arising from nonnegligent actions, the negligence rule visibly imposes sacrifice on those who have suffered such harms. By the same token, a negligence rule could facilitate increased deployment of available pollution-control technology. For example, alkali manufacturers who did not use or adequately maintain Gossage towers might be held liable for having failed to take reasonable precautions. In contrast, the alternative of absolute liability under a nuisance rule implied that plaintiffs' interests would not be sacrificed but protected by the possibility of compensation for landowners harmed by neighboring industrial activities. However, a consistent application of strict liability in the industrializing cities of nineteenth-century Britain would have threatened economic development by rendering entire urban populations deserving of compensation for discomfort. Thus, standing by the strict liability rule virtually compelled the construction of a rationale for exempting these discomforts from compensation. The scaffolding was already in place, thanks to the precedent of early nineteenth-century demands for proof of a specific causal link between pollution and disease.

The contest between the negligence and absolute liability regimes appeared for a short moment to tilt in favor of the former. In *Hole v. Barlow*, an 1858 nuisance case that centered around noxious vapors from brick burning, the judge instructed the jury "that no action lies for the use, the reasonable use, of a lawful trade in a convenient and proper place, even though some one may suffer annoyance from its being carried on."[45] Under this formulation, manufacturers whose behavior is "reasonable" and who conduct their business in a "proper place" for trade are not liable for damage. The emphasis on "proper place" might seem, at first, to hark back to Blackstone's emphasis on the role of location in determining the propriety of an economic activity, but, in fact, the geographical assumptions of the two judges differ crucially. For Blackstone, the proper place for a polluting economic activity was by definition one that ensured sufficient separation to prevent harm. However, for the *Hole v. Barlow* judge, the "proper place" now fell within the densely populated manufacturing town. As long as the firm's conduct was "reasonable," the certainty that harm would be caused was of no legal import. Without this provision, wrote the judge, "the neighbourhood of Birmingham and Wolverhampton and the other great manufacturing towns of England would be full of persons bringing actions for nuisance arising from the carrying on of noxious and offensive trades in their vicinity to the great injury of the manufacturing and social interests of the community." But the judge did not leave urban plaintiffs without any resort; offsetting the above limitation on their capacity to bring action was a corresponding lifting of the demand for strict proof of harm to human health, as his instructions clearly conveyed: "(T)o entitle the plaintiff to maintain an action for an injury of this nature, it is not necessary that the thing complained of should be injurious to health: it is enough if it renders the enjoyment of life and property uncomfortable."[46]

The Court of Common Pleas upheld his direction to the jury, with an explicitly utilitarian rationale: "private convenience must yield to public necessity."[47] This language represents an explicit attempt to break with the "tradition" established by *Aldred's Case* (recall that the failure of Benton's claim regarding the necessity of pigs to the "sustenance of man" had been interpreted as a rejection of utilitarian balancing). Unsurprisingly, landowners denied compensation by the *Hole* rule were quick to seek a return to the legal status quo ante.

Four years later their efforts met with success when the Exchequer Chamber in *Bamford v. Turnley* rejected *Hole's* negligence rule. Like *Hole*, the case concerned fumes from brick burning. The plaintiff relied on the strict liability rule of *Aldred's Case* to argue that *Hole* had been wrongly decided, and the court ruled in his favor.[48] In his concurring opinion, Judge Bramwell articulated most forcefully the rationale for reverting to the earlier *sic utere* rule—in an explicit rejection of utilitarianism, he wrote that the "law to my mind is a bad one which, for the public benefit, inflicts loss on an individual without compensation."[49] Offering an economic rationale, he added that "(i)t is for the public benefit there should be railways, but it would not be unless the gain of having the railway was sufficient to compensate the loss occasioned by the use of the land required for its site; and accordingly no one thinks it would be right to take an individual's land without compensation to make a railway."[50] The lack of unanimity behind this decision nonetheless evidenced an ongoing constituency for the earlier, pro-utilitarian view of the *Hole* court. Against the majority's view, one dissenting judge wrote, "The compromises that belong to social life, and upon which the peace and comfort of it mainly depend, furnish an indefinite number of examples where some apparent natural right is invaded, or some enjoyment abridged, to provide for the more general convenience or necessities of the whole community."[51] Against this backdrop of conflicting precedents and divisions on the bench, an appeal from a St. Helen's Smelting Company put before the House of Lords the choice between a negligence and an absolute liability rule in the adjudication of noxious vapors from copper smelting.[52] The legal dispute was designed as a test case of this issue. It differed from the *Hole* and *Bamford* decisions in one important aspect: whereas the earlier brick-burning cases had concerned only human discomforts and health concerns from noxious vapors, in *St. Helen's* the copper smelting pollution harmed vegetation as well ("the hedges, trees, shrubs, fruit, and herbage, were greatly injured; the cattle were rendered unhealthy").[53] Tipping, the plaintiff in the case and the owner of a 1,300-acre estate outside St. Helen's, testified to the "damage done to his plantations, and to the very unpleasant nature of the vapour, which. . .affected persons as well as plants in his grounds."[54]

Under the *Hole* jury instructions, Tipping most likely would not have received damages for either injury, as St. Helen's was an industrial area and thus matched the "proper" location criterion of *Hole*. Furthermore, negligence was not at issue, since the plaintiff did not challenge defense testimony that no means existed by which the process could be conducted in a less polluting fashion.[55] But the different instructions given to the jury explicitly altered the *Hole* decision rule. Unlike the *Hole* instructions that had emphasized both the centrality of location to assessment of legal liability on the one hand, and relaxed the standard of proof of damage to health on the other; instructions to the *St. Helen's* jury amounted to a complete reversal. Location was to be irrelevant to liability, and injury to health an implicit requirement for clearing the *de minimis* threshold. The *St. Helen's* judge, Mellor, began by restating the *sic utere* absolute liability rule of *Aldred's Case*: "every man. . .was bound to use his own property in such a manner as not to injure the property of his neighbours."[56] As the judge made clear, however, not every injury justifies remedy. He qualified the above statement by adding, "that the law did not regard trifling inconveniences." This, too, seems to be a mere restatement of the *Aldred's Case* distinction between "matters of delight" and "matters of necessity." But in contrast to the *Aldred's* era, when "wholesome air" fell squarely into the latter category, Mellor trivialized the human discomforts brought about by odors and fumes as "trifling inconveniences."[57] To qualify as an injury beyond trifling "in an action for nuisance to property, arising from noxious vapours," the judge explained, the injury must "visibly" diminish "the value of the property and the comfort and enjoyment of it."[58] Whether "visibly" here means "obviously" or "so as to be visible by the eye or sight"[59] remains unclear. Either way, the emphasis on the strength of evidence of harm exempts, by implication, difficult-to-prove health impacts from liability, although more evident damage such as wilted crops met the threshold of legal injury.

Without specifying the nature of the harm being compensated—whether comfort, harm to property, or both—the jury awarded damages. The defendant appealed, ultimately bringing the issue before the House of Lords, and arguing that the judge's directions should have followed the *Hole* location / negligence rule. The Lords upheld the instructions, and in so doing unequivocally rejected *Hole's* negligence rule.

In reaffirming *sic utere*, the Lords appeared to be further developing a nuisance regime that would be highly responsive to pollution's affronts. However, language in the Lords' opinion suggests that the distinction between remediable and nonremediable injury from noxious vapors—i.e., the "trifling inconveniences" exemption—was central to their decision, even if not strictly part of the holding of the case.[60] Lord Wesbury, the Lord Chancellor, put the distinction between "material injury" and what he termed "sensible personal discomfort" front and center:

> With regard to the latter, namely, the personal inconvenience and interference with one's enjoyment, one's quiet, one's personal freedom, anything that discomposes or injuriously affects the senses or the nerves, whether that may or may not be denominated a nuisance, must undoubtedly depend greatly on the circumstances of the place where the thing complained of actually occurs. If a man lives in a town, it is necessary that he should subject himself to the consequences of those operations of trade which may be carried on in his immediate locality, which are actually necessary for trade and commerce. . .and of the public at large.

However, added the Lord Chancellor, a similar expectation for the submission of personal interests to the greater good would *not* apply "to circumstances the immediate result of which is sensible injury to the value of property."[61]

In practical terms, an important outcome of the *sic utere* regime was its allowance of compensation for landowners (based on visible damage) and its simultaneous denial of compensation for residents of large industrial cities (whose injuries were less apparent, though no less real).[62]

Moreover, this outcome was achieved not by explicitly balancing interests or acknowledging sacrifices, but was instead accomplished by marginalizing the pollution concerns of the residents of industrial cities: "Where great works had been erected, and carried on, persons must not stand on their extreme rights, and bring actions in respect of every matter of annoyance."[63]

In its earliest agrarian manifestation, *de minimis* (or "matters of delight") spoke to conventional understandings about the kinds of reciprocal injuries that neighbors tended to tolerate. The *St. Helen's* regime transformed it, however, into a prescriptive standard tinged with communitarian admonitions regarding the sacrifices that (some) individuals ought to make for the common good. At the same time, it diminished the significance of such sacrifices with definitions that trivialized the relevant injury and interpreted residence in polluted locales as proof of consent to an interference already deemed inconsequential.

Although the language of absolute liability appeared to promise maximum protection, it should not be surprising that, in practice, a regime that categorized most effects of air pollution on humans as "trifling inconveniences" would fail to spur investment in incremental pollution control technologies in urban industrial areas where visible damage to land and crops was limited. The regulatory logic behind the *St. Helen's* decision, however, cannot be understood in isolation. The "trifling inconvenience" doctrine of *St. Helen's* was put in place two years after the passage of the 1863 Alkali Act and was therefore only one element in an interlocking common law / statutory regime. The institution of the Alkali Act and the civil service cadre it spawned made it possible to deploy available technological solutions without regard to either the evidentiary burdens or the trivializing problem definitions of the common law.

THE ALKALI ACT REGIME

William Tipping's 1862 suit against the St. Helen's Smelting Company was contemporaneous with the appointment of a Parliamentary Select Committee to explore legislative alternatives for the control of noxious vapors. The Earl of Derby, a former Tory prime minister and leader of the opposition, pushed for this committee at the behest of landowners in the St. Helen's area, most notably the Gerard family. The landowners' long-standing complaints about alkali pollution had been accompanied by numerous suits against Musparatt and other manufacturers during the 1840s. The next decade, however, saw the suspension of litigation due to frustration; it remained extremely difficult to prove causation, and lawsuits had to be brought repeatedly, even when they succeeded. Their difficulties in court notwithstanding, the Gerards' connections with the Earl of Derby appeared to bear fruit; the Parliamentary Select Committee came into being within a week of the earl's initial action in the matter. He himself was appointed chairman of the committee of fourteen, which also included two scientists and four estate holders from the area.[64]

The committee heard evidence from nearly fifty witnesses, including eminent scientists, representatives of local authorities, and spokespeople for manufacturing and farming interests. The proceedings focused on the dual industrial pollution threats of the day: alkali-manufacturing fumes and copper-smelting emissions. The committee took testimony both about the extent of the damage caused by these pollution sources and the technologies available for mitigation.

The discussions of pollution's harms centered on injury to property, rather than health effects, an agenda that was likely influenced by the concerns of the landowning interests pushing for this legislation. The focus on property may also indicate skepticism about the health impacts of the emissions, or at least about the prospect of tying health-related problems conclusively to pollution sources. In any case, the committee concluded that the emissions had indeed been causing broad injury to property and so demanded a legislative remedy.

No longer would the locally crafted judicial solutions of the common law do. Overcoming the inherent limitations of nuisance law could be achieved only through legislative intervention, a significant change of institutional locus. The Select Committee identified multiple flaws of the traditional common law approach that justified this shift:

> "Partly in consequence of the expense such actions occasion, partly from the fact that while several works are in immediate juxtaposition, the difficulty of tracing the damage to anyone, or of apportioning it among several, is so great as to be all but insuperable; and, that, even when verdicts have been obtained, and compensation, however inadequate, awarded, a discontinuance of the nuisance has not in most cases been the result."[65]

Thus it was finally acknowledged at the national level that solutions to industrial pollution based on nuisance law faced severe impediments: unrealistic evidentiary demands regarding proof of harm; expensive litigation that placed these solutions out of the reach of all but the wealthy; and a potentially endless stream of lawsuits against the same industrial polluters, since damage awards usually did not compel abatement of the offending emissions.

The committee justified its recommendations in terms not only of the inadequacy of nuisance law for treating the industrial pollution problem, but also of the extensive testimony regarding the availability and economic feasibility of technological means of controlling the emissions. Divergent conclusions regarding the potential for pollution abatement by the two industries within its mandate emerged from the committee. It found Gossage towers effective and economically feasible for the alkali industry, but failed to uncover any economically feasible solutions for copper-smelting emissions.

Despite their effectiveness, few firms used Gossage towers in the absence of sufficient regulatory incentive. The committee accordingly recommended that new legislation be passed in order to prompt manufacturers to use the available technology. Since their rationale rested heavily upon the availability of control technology, rather than upon remediation of injury, the committee also advised against including copper manufacturers in the new regime "as, unhappily, no means have yet been devised of neutralizing those effects (though they may be mitigated) consistent with the carrying on of this important branch of industry."[66]

The legislative outcome of the committee's work was the Alkali Act, formally entitled "An Act for the More Effectual Condensation of Muriatic Acid Gas in Alkali Works." This law, as its name suggests, was a narrow piece of legislation.[67] It passed with the consent of the alkali industry and received the Royal assent in July 1863 for a temporary trial run of five years. The committee resolved "not to prescribe the specific process by which the nuisance should be prevented." Instead, the law mandated 95 percent condensation, a level known to be achievable given the state of technology at the time.[68]

Enforcement of the act fell to a specially created "Alkali Inspectorate." The inspectorate's mission was to achieve centralized and uniform enforcement of emissions law for the alkali industry by removing that function entirely from the realm of local control. A prominent sanitary chemist by the name of Robert Angus Smith headed the inspectorate. The five-year trial period proved effective, with all sixty-four factories throughout Britain condensing at least 95 percent of their emissions within three years of the act's passage. In 1868 the act was extended without limit.[69]

Notwithstanding the act's success in significantly reducing emissions of hydrochloric acid from specific sources, the overall air quality of the industrial cities of Great Britain saw little improvement, due to both growth of industry and the fact that the act applied only to hydrochloric acid from alkali works.[70] This failure helped stimulate the passage of an 1874 amendment to the Alkali Act that entailed three major changes: (1) the 95 percent condensation requirement became a volumetric standard for the allowable emission of hydrochloric acid from alkali works, making inspection and enforcement easier than under the former standard; (2) a mandate for the inspection of copper works using a salt-based process that released hydrochloric acid (not regular smelting) importantly expanded the scope of the act beyond the alkali manufacturing realm and took the first step toward control of pollution from copper smelting; and (3) alkali manufacturers were required to employ "best practicable means" in the control of all other noxious vapors, thereby extending the domain of the act beyond hydrochloric acid to other gases. Even more significantly, the amendment introduced a novel and flexible legislative formula—best practicable means (BPM)—which, in Smith's words, would allow for future air-quality improvements without need for further legislation by "enforcing the acquisition of ascertained improvements."[71] Despite the innovative nature of the legislation, interventions could not keep pace with the overall air quality problem of nineteenth-century industrial Britain, and the air remained foul. In February 1876 the Duke of Cumberland asked for a Royal Commission to "inquire into the working and management of works and manufactories from which sulphurous acid, sulphuretted hydrogen, and ammoniacal and other vapours and gases are given off, to ascertain the effect produced thereby on animals and vegetable life, and to report on the means to be adopted for the prevention of injury thereto."[72]

The commission's mandate thus bound together questions of both harm and technological means for its abatement, and the decision whether or not to extend the act to additional industries and gases would hinge on this two-pronged assessment. The 1862 Select Committee that drafted the first Alkali Act had paid little attention to the gases' impact on health, finding sufficient justification for intervention in evident injury to property. Although the Royal Commission ultimately drew a similar conclusion, it did, unlike the earlier committee, hear extensive and conflicting testimony regarding noxious vapors and health. The Royal Commission heard from doctors, who reported an elevated incidence of chest diseases around St. Helen's and testified that "patients who suffer from heart disease, asthma, tubercular diseases of the chest, and all chest affections are aggravated very greatly by the effect of these cases [primarily chemical wastes] upon the lungs."[73] Another witness, a vicar, spoke of seeing people vomit in the streets and of himself becoming ill in church because of chlorine in the air. Their testimony was countered by those who denied that the fumes caused any such ill effects, attributed bad health among industrial workers to drink rather than fumes, and invoked the earlier mentioned theory regarding the gases' beneficial disinfectant quality.[74]

John Simon, the preeminent public health reformer of the Victorian era, sought to redefine the problem, calling for a move away from the endless debate over scientific proof of a causal link between the vapors and disease:

[T]he expression "injurious to health," in many of these discussions had been used in a sense to impose upon the person who is charged with the duty of protecting health, an obligation to prove that typhoid fever, or small pox, or dysentery, or ringworm, or something of that kind, some definite disease that we name in our catalogue of diseases, is produced by those vapours. I do not think we are bound when it is a question of sanitary injury, to show injury of that kind. To be free from bodily discomfort is a condition of health. If a man gets up with a headache, *pro tanto* he is not in good health, if a man gets up unable to eat his breakfast, *pro tanto* he is not in good health. When a man is living in an atmosphere which leaves him constantly below par. . .all that is an injury to health, though not a production of what at present could be called a definite disease.[75]

This was not a novel move. As discussed earlier, the immediate discomforts associated with exposure to industrial fumes had long been the object of complaints and litigation. The question had become whether they ought to be categorized as legal injury deserving of compensation or as "trifling inconveniences" willingly assumed by residents of industrial locales. In the context of the Royal Commission's debates, the question of injury to health became less a matter of legal liability than a political debate about the justifiability of legislative intervention.

Unable to reach a justification based on injury to health, the Royal Commission nonetheless found ample justification for intervention in injury to property. Regardless of the specific worry that spawned it, the ensuing regime's scope—that is, where and how much it was to intervene—was not dictated by injury or even especially tailored to it. Instead, it rested upon the growing feasibility of technological solutions. The commission accordingly recommended a significant expansion in the number of industrial gases to be regulated under the act, as well as an increase in the size and resources of the Alkali Inspectorate.

The technology-driven nature of this regime can clearly be seen in its decision not to include copper smelters among the regulated industries, despite the commission's evident enthusiasm for a broad pollution-control mandate. After listening to considerable testimony regarding the costs of improving furnaces, along with estimates of their potential effectiveness at controlling pollution, the market for recovered by-products, and the copper industry's financial situation, the commission overrode the opinion of Smith, the Alkali Inspectorate's chief, and accepted the copper manufacturers' view that an across-the-board requirement for the installation of new furnaces would be prohibitively expensive. The Royal Commission therefore recommended that the Alkali Inspectorate monitor copper works with an eye only toward developing technological solutions.[76]

The Alkali, etc., Works Regulation Act of 1881 enacted most of the commission's recommendations into law. Under this legislation, the BPM formula was applied to sectors beyond the alkali industry and to gases other than hydrochloric acid, including producers of chemical manure, gas liquor, nitric acid, chlorine, sulfate, and chloride of ammonia.[77] The number of chemical works covered quadrupled from 240 to close to 1000, and the staff of the inspectorate was doubled.[78] Thus, from an initially narrow focus on a single industry and pollutant, this regime expanded quite rapidly through a series of legislative amendments. Another amendment in 1905 authorized the inspectorate to regulate thirteen separate gases. Subsequent legislation empowered the ministers overseeing the Alkali Inspectorate to add gases and processes to the list, thereby allowing the regime to continue expanding gradually as new technologies became available, without needing to return to Parliament every time. This regulatory framework governed industrial gases in Britain until the passage of the Control of Pollution Act in 1974.[79]

Pressure from St. Helen's landowners with political connections to Lord Derby was the proximate trigger for the creation of the Alkali Act regime. But more importantly, this regime was the product of larger transformations in the climate of British regulatory politics during the 1860s and 1870s. As David Vogel discusses, the era was marked by a shift in public attitudes toward governmental regulation of business. This change was in part precipitated by the publication of various government inspectors' reports that documented the lot of the working classes and urged the implementation of governmental remedies. The result was a string of legislative reforms, including the expansion of the factory acts and culminating with the passage of the Public Health Act of 1875. The introduction of a centralized air-pollution control regime occurred within the larger context of these developments.[80]

Nevertheless, the Alkali Act also differed from many of these larger reforms in that it lacked a clear public health rationale due to the existence of significant uncertainty regarding the health impacts of the regulated gases. Instead, it was the pollution's obvious damage to vegetation and property that formally justified the act. As the Royal Commission on Noxious Vapours wrote in its 1878 report, the Alkali Acts "were the first and only Acts which sanction the expenditure of public money on inspection in cases where the object of such inspection is simply or at any rate mainly the protection of private property."[81]

The noteworthiness of this lack of an explicit health rationale makes sense only as a byproduct of a new, nineteenth-century attempt to define harm arising from noxious vapors in terms of provable links to particular diseases. In a significant move away from the confident assertion of a relationship between impure air and ill health of the earlier *Aldred's* regime, the nineteenth-century common law approach held that in the absence of a specific disease, no injury existed, and a need for scientific proof therefore became a new prerequisite to the establishment of harm. The need for scientific proof played a central role in the absolute liability regime; the guarantee of compensation upon establishment of the occurrence of an injury provided incentive to treat scientific uncertainty as a loophole that would enable a nominal commitment to the maintenance of absolute liability without halting economic progress. Air pollution falling below the threshold of proof of injury to health hence came to be defined as noninjury under the "trifling inconveniences" doctrine.

Fortunately for Britain, this definition of the problem of injury to health was complemented by a statutory regime that called for the implementation of technology as it became available. The United States, however, imported only the common law half of this regime without enacting an American version of the Alkali Act. Chapter 5 will consider how the common law in its U.S. incarnation subsequently dealt with demands for the implementation of available pollution-control technologies, following an examination in chapter 4 of the legal-ideological impediments that the U.S. context posed to the implementation of an Alkali Act–styled regulatory regime to require abatement independent of provable injury to health.

CHAPTER FOUR

On the "Police State" and the "Common Law State"

THE 1863 HOUSE OF LORDS arbitration of the St. Helen's copper smoke dispute had a U.S. parallel four decades later, when the State of Georgia brought suit before the Supreme Court against air pollution from two Tennessee smelters.[1] In a 1907 opinion written by Justice Holmes, the court unanimously issued an injunction requiring abatement of the smelters' smoke.[2] In a short concurring opinion, Justice Harlan offered the following rationale: "Georgia is entitled to the relief sought, not because it is a State, but because it is a party which has established its right to such relief by proof."[3] In this, Harlan departed from Justice Holmes's interpretation of the nature of Georgia's claim and the source of its authority to intervene. "The case has been argued largely as if it were one between two private parties; but it is not," Justice Holmes wrote, explaining that "[t]his is a suit by a State for an injury to it in its capacity of quasi-sovereign. In that capacity the State has an interest independent of and behind the titles of its citizens, in all the earth and air within its domain. It has the last word as to whether its mountains shall be stripped of their forests and its inhabitants shall breathe pure air."[4] For Holmes, unlike Harlan, the state has an independent and legitimate interest in seeking clean air, and as such its ability to act does not depend upon proof of injury to citizens' property or other rights.

Yet in the end, it was not the state's sovereign power as such, but rather proof of injury that served as the rationale for the court's decree. Most likely in order to avert a dissent by Harlan, and perhaps by others on the court, Holmes's opinion explicitly concluded: "we are satisfied by a preponderance of evidence that the sulphurous fumes cause and threaten damage on so considerable a scale to the forests and vegetable life, if not to health."[5] Why did the two justices go to the trouble of highlighting a seemingly theoretical disagreement with so little relevance to the case at hand? Their purposes are difficult to divine within the confines of this case alone. Instead, the exchange is better read as the continuation of an ongoing debate between justices Harlan and Holmes regarding the origin and scope of the state's authority to regulate. This division had been most clearly expressed two years earlier in *Lochner v. New York* (1905).[6]

Justices Holmes and Harlan had written separate dissents in *Lochner*, splitting on the necessity of proof of harm to the validity of the state's exercise of regulatory police power. In contrast to Holmes, Harlan reasoned that the work-hour restriction in question was valid because it was reasonably related to harm, not because its enactment was the state's sovereign prerogative. The point of difference between the *Lochner* majority on the one hand, and Harlan and the two other justices who joined his dissent on the other, pertained to the sufficiency of the scientific and other evidence presented by the state; the latter three believed the state had provided enough proof to render the work-hour restriction a valid exercise of the police power, while the majority found the evidence insufficient. Yet despite their conflicting reading of the evidence, the dissenting trio and the majority did agree on the relevant decision rule: substantive limits on the scope of the police power require the state to offer proof of the existence of an injury requiring remedial intervention. While the three dissenters were willing to extend a significant degree of deference to the state's finding regarding the dangers of long hours of employment in bakeries, they would most probably have refused to uphold the law had the state failed to offer any health justification. In this they and the court's majority departed importantly from Holmes, who found no such proof necessary to the constitutionality of the statute.

Chapter 2 argued that both *Lochner* and the much later benzene case shared a common law–derived assumption that legal interventions insufficiently grounded in proof of harm are unreasonable. This chapter returns to *Lochner*, this time in order to trace how and why concerns about the constitutionality of regulatory interference in the market came to hinge upon judicial assessments of the adequacy of legislatures' proffered proof of the "nexus" between regulatory means and constitutionally legitimate ends. The immediate impetus for this judicial scrutiny, the chapter argues, was a perceived threat posed by German-inspired "social legislation." Taking a longer view, the case represents the culmination of tensions evident throughout the nineteenth century between "police" and "common law" visions of the emergent American administrative state. These tensions far predated the *Lochner* era, and, this chapter concludes, were not resolved by its demise.

"*LOCHNER* REVISIONISM" AND AMERICAN EXCEPTIONALISM

In his dissent from the previously discussed 1980 *Industrial Union* (benzene) decision, Justice Marshall tarred the majority position as tantamount to that of the *Lochner* court, casting both decisions as illegitimate and unprincipled acts of judicial usurpation of the lawmaking power of other branches. Justice Marshall failed to offer any explanation why *Lochner* was not just wrong but also unprincipled, but no explanation was really needed since his reference matched the nearly universal inter-pretation of the case. This consensus broke down, however, in the two decades following *Industrial Union* as a diverse body of scholarship—collectively lumped under the rubric of "*Lochner* revisionism"—chal-lenged earlier understandings of the decision as politically partisan, and rethought the view that its reasoning was idiosyncratic to the laissez-faire judges of that particular age.[7]

The motivation for some "*Lochner* revisionists" reaches well beyond the actual case in an attempt to redeem the idea of liberty of contract as a substantive constitutional constraint on the regulation of property. Others are primarily concerned with what *Lochner* has to teach about the relation-ship between law and politics in judicial decision-making, or about the legitimacy of judicial activism in other contemporary constitutional de-bates.[8] Most of these observers share the belief that *Lochner* represented neither a judicial usurpation of legislative prerogative per se, nor an un-grounded, early-twentieth-century swing to an extreme free market ideol-ogy. Rather, this scholarship views *Lochner* as the fruition of a long-stand-ing distinction in nineteenth-century jurisprudence between valid and invalid regulatory interventions, a distinction which implied that the state's regulatory authority under police power was limited rather than absolute.

Scholars differ in their understanding of the criteria distinguishing valid from invalid regulation. For some, such as Howard Gillman, the primary division is between "class neutral policies" that advanced "a public pur-pose" and invalid laws that "merely promoted the interests of some classes at the expense of others."[9] For Robert Post, the societal domain into which particular regulatory instruments seek to intrude forms the relevant crite-rion: The Court used the doctrine of substantive due process to separate the domains of social life in which persons could routinely be objectified according to the dictates of administrative expertise, from the domains of social life in which these dictates could be subject to constitutional chal-lenge.[10] As Post makes clear, where our sensibilities differ from those of the *Lochner*-era judges is not in the belief that there exist domains into which the state's managerial power ought not intrude, but in the proper place-ment of market relations within that constitutionally protected sphere. In-sulating the market from "managerial control" in no way meant an immu-nity from regulatory intervention by the state. Rather, the common insight cutting across this body of scholarship pertains to the readiness of judges to uphold legislation deemed necessary to protect the "health, safety, mor-als, or public welfare" of the community.[11] But the same judges balked where the nexus between the regulation and these common-law compati-ble ends was seen as insufficient, as in the *Lochner* case.[12]

Lochner-revisionist scholarship connects here to a larger debate, some-times referred to as "American exceptionalism," on the uniqueness of the

American state during the nineteenth century, and the extent to which it diverged from its European counterparts, whose police power was clearly less constrained. The stronger version of the exceptionalist thesis envisions a nineteenth-century U.S. government enfeebled to the point of nonexistence. The weaker version of the thesis begins from the premise that, far from being powerless, the American state acted in myriad ways: it regulated, developed infrastructure, and promoted economic growth. But under this view, courts and other U.S. institutions shaped and restrained the exercise of state authority in a fashion that did not occur in Europe.[13] Moreover, this uniqueness did not occur by chance, but stemmed from a deliberate rejection upon the republic's founding of "the organizational qualities of the state as they had been evolving in Europe over the eighteenth century."[14]

William Novak's extensive study of the long reach and multifaceted character of common-law-based regulatory authority in the United States during the nineteenth century thoroughly refutes the extreme version of the American exceptionalism hypothesis. The state was alive and active, and its regulatory impact could be felt in arenas ranging from the protection of public safety to the construction of a public economy, and from the policing of public space to the imposition of restraints on public morals.[15] The result, concludes Novak, was a vigorous regulatory regime that bore little resemblance to the passive, laissez-faire state it has sometimes been construed to have been. Neglecting this has contributed to a "cult of American exceptionalism," Novak argues, under which "the degree to which older European ideas and institutions remained vital parts of the American polity" is discounted.[16]

Novak supports his conclusion with a detailed and rich account of the various legal instruments that ordered American life during the nineteenth century. This legal regime served as "the cornerstone of the well-regulated society" that was the United States during the 1800s.[17] Within this society, "civil liberty" was "liberty restrained by *law*," but, as Novak notes, the law that could legitimately restrain liberty was "not just any law"; only the common law could serve as "the legal foundation of the well-regulated society."[18] For influential American elites, the force of the distinction between common law and non-common-law-based means of regulation lay in the view that, in contrast to the coercive underpinnings of other legal theories of the time, the common law's authority was based in the consent of those it governed.[19] The conceptualization of a "common law state" that this notion spawned, is key to distinguishing the U.S. regime from contemporaneous European regimes.

Novak's demonstration of the multiple ways in which common-law-based regulation shaped many areas of economic policy in nineteenth-century America clearly contradicts the strong version of the American exceptionalist thesis. Yet in its highlighting of the common law's distinctive incarnation in the American regulatory regime, his argument may in fact reinforce the weaker version of the thesis. That is, the very fact that the state's regulatory authority was conceived of and exercised within this common law framework constituted a qualitative and significant difference between the American regime and its continental counterparts framed by civil law.

THE "POLICE STATE" AND THE "COMMON LAW STATE"

"It must, of course, be conceded," wrote Justice Peckham in *Lochner*, "that there is a limit to the valid exercise of the police power by the State. There is no dispute concerning this general proposition. Otherwise . . . [t]he claim of the police power would be a mere pretext—become another and delusive name for the supreme sovereignty of the State."[20] Yet, as is often the case when matters are declared to lie beyond contention, there was in fact sharp disagreement surrounding these propositions; it was the growing influence of the idea that there existed no a priori substantive limits on the realm of "police power" legislation, rather than its self-evident falsehood, that served as *Lochner's* true subtext.

The work-hour restriction at issue in *Lochner* was hardly the only instance of such legislation. Mandating a shorter workday had been a central objective of the American labor movement during the 1880s and 1890s, and similar laws were passed in many states and with respect to multiple industrial sectors.[21] The inspiration came from Europe, where parliaments during the 1880s began to pass "social legislation" aimed at improving the life of the working class. The leader in this movement was Bismarck's Germany, where these laws emerged as one element of a two-pronged strategy to defend against the perceived threat of the rising socialist workers' movement. Legal suppression of all Social Democratic, socialist, and communist associations, assemblies, and pamphlets constituted the first prong of this campaign. But in addition to these restrictive measures, Germany enacted far-reaching legislative reforms of labor conditions, most famously, a series of compulsory insurance laws in the 1880s that increased economic security for workers in the face of disease, industrial accidents, and old age.[22]

The last quarter of the nineteenth century saw unprecedented trans-Atlantic exchange spurred by easier and more frequent modes of travel and communication. Since the 1870s, Germany in particular had become a fashionable destination for postgraduate study by American students, who would return home with "an acute sense of a missing 'social' strand in American politics and a new sense, as unnerving as it was attractive, of the social possibilities of the state."[23] More concretely, they carried with them the statutory blueprints that would later be grafted to progressive reform agendas. As Charles McCurdy writes, "American progressives talked incessantly about the enactment of 'social legislation' to protect the weak and poor from exploitation, to provide some security for those unable to obtain it themselves, and to effect a modest redistribution of wealth and opportunity."[24]

The 1905 *Lochner* decision makes no mention of social legislation, and, for the most part, courts of the era avoided the term.[25] Instead, the *Lochner* court relied on the language of "police power" and the "supreme sovereignty of the state"—language that, at the time, evoked the social legislation program and the German state from which it came. The key to this connection and to the place of the police power in the *Lochner*-era constitutional crisis lies in the pivotal role of the concept "police," or "*Polizei*," in the evolution of the modern contintental state.

Polizei initially meant the condition, or the ideology, of a good communal existence. The term bore communitarian overtones, connoting a state of affairs of collective rather than individual well-being, or the public good rather than the personal happiness of its individual constituents. Sometime during the fifteenth or sixteenth century, the meaning of the term broadened to include not only the goal of communal well-being, but the institutional methods needed to bring it about. The "police power" (or *Polizeigesetze*, meaning police regulation) thus became the institutional means needed to realize the goal of police.[26]

This shift corresponds with Germany's fifteenth-century "reception" of Roman law and the early beginnings of the state that this adoption facilitated.[27] As Kenneth Dyson writes, "[T]he continental European legal theories of the state were the product of the renewed study of Roman law." In this respect the "decisive contribution of Roman law was the idea that somewhere in the community, whether in the people or in the prince (or in both combined), there existed a supreme will that could alter laws to suit the changing requirements of society."[28] In this fashion, Roman law offered both a structure and an ideology conducive to the displacement of feudal ideas and the rise of centralized, sovereign states. Originally equated with the monarch, state sovereignty in time became institutionally embodied in the legislature whose own lawmaking power, like that of the monarch, was seen as absolute and superior to any competing norms or customs.

This transformation is most famously associated with the French Revolution's replacement of the old regime's "*gouvernement des juges*"[29] by a legislated legal order that, following Rousseau, identified legislation with the general will, legislators with popular sovereignty, and such sovereignty with democracy.[30] At the center of this legal order ultimately stood the *Code Napoléon* a comprehensive set of civil, criminal, commercial, and procedural statutes aimed at displacing French customary law and its attendant aristocratic privileges. The spread of the revolution brought similar codes to other countries in Europe, most notably Germany, whose code ultimately surpassed that of France in its level of detail.[31]

The codes' precursors in the German context were evident as early as the fifteenth century, when municipal "public order" measures targeted realms ranging from religious observance to construction and hygiene standards.[32] Continuing this tradition, the nineteenth-century Prussian state enacted a series of public health regulations under the rubric of "medical policing," including the certification of physicians and midwives, the control of epidemics, the inspection of food supplies, and the regulation of prostitution.[33] This era also saw the foundation of social insurance programs upon which Bismarck would later build.[34] German social legislation of the late nineteenth century may have been most immediately prompted by a sense of a working-class threat, but it was nevertheless very much the product of a centuries-long German political ideal of "*Polizeistaat*" (police state).

In the Anglo-American tradition, the term "police state" carries distinctly repressive and even tyrannical connotations, in contrast to its traditional continental meaning. As Bismarck's banning of socialist political expression illustrates, this state was clearly capable of repression, but it entailed a more complex mix of attributes, including the state's obligation toward citizens, and collective responsibility for public welfare. At the deepest level, the term "police state" contains within it the notion that state action on behalf of a public interest—which the state is entitled to define—is necessary and appropriate.[35] That the connotations of "police state" in Anglo-American usage are exclusively authoritarian attests to the victory of a common law ideology that rejected both the repressive and the communitarian aspects of the *polizei* tradition as one.

Like its continental counterparts, the British Parliament came to possess unlimited sovereign legislative authority. However, in contrast to Europe, where political revolutions sought to uproot the old legal order and replace it with new and explicitly reformist positive law, England's more evolutionary political transformation allowed for a greater coexistence of customary and parliamentary law. Unlike continental countries where both Roman law and the state it bolstered aimed to displace preexisting local legal traditions and the feudal allegiances in which they were grounded, English "feudalism had bequeathed a conception of law that was not only flexible and adaptable to the practical exigencies of a changing society but also defended by a well-established and independent judicial profession." The result was a British state in which law derived legitimacy from the consent of the governed, rather than the will of the king.[36]

In contrast to continental rulers, the English sovereign was expected to abide by long-standing norms and traditions of the common law, even though he was technically empowered to repeal them.[37] The seventeenth century made evident conflicts over competing claims to sovereignty by Parliament and the monarchy, but neither side sought to uproot a common law tradition that had by then assumed the status of an "ancient custom" existing "time out of mind of man," or the restraints that this tradition imposed on the exercise of political power.[38] If the result was a sometimes inconsistent legal system in which parliamentary sovereignty somehow coexisted with doctrines allowing judges to void statutes as "contrary to reason," this inconsistency was one that the English were prepared to accept.[39]

The United States inherited and built upon this common law tradition but did so without assimilating British theories of parliamentary sovereignty. Absolute sovereignty in its continental, or even its British, form was what America's founding fathers strove to avoid when they purposefully obstructed any branch of government from acting effectively alone. Furthermore, in a direct inversion of the continental codes' antijudicial bias, those who designed America's constitutional structures considered legislative majorities a potentially far greater threat to liberty than the judges who staffed the "least dangerous branch."[40]

The question of whether judges or legislators ought to have the final say regarding the reasonableness of legislation was at the forefront of a nineteenth-century clash between the idea of "police" and an emerging ideology of "rule of law," which held law both separate from, and superior to, the authority of the state. In Prussia the concept of the *Rechtsstaat* (state of law) emerged to modify absolutist ideas of police administration by building on "seventeenth-century constitutional theory, natural right theory, and the philosophy of rationalism to construct a domain of public law (*ius publicum*) whose task, among others, was to determine the boundaries of the state's power to rule."[41] But it was in the common law countries of England and the United States first and foremost that "police" was subsumed into a "rule of law" paradigm. In this process, as Chris Tomlins writes, "the administrative capacity of the state—'the police power'—was reinvented within this law paradigm and made an object of judicial contemplation, its legitimate use an issue for juridical, not political, determination."[42] It was also within this context that "policing" became the task of providing for security, rather than social welfare as such, and the term "police state" assumed its contemporary authoritarian connotation.[43]

NUISANCE LAW AND PUBLIC HEALTH ADMINISTRATION

Like Germany, both England and the United States saw extensive administrative interventions into public health, safety, and morality during the nineteenth century. As Novak notes, there was "a plethora of bylaws, ordinances, statutes, and common law restrictions regulating nearly every aspect of early American economy and society, from Sunday observance to the carting of offal."[44] Yet despite a similar breadth of regulation, significant differences remained in the manner in which this regulatory authority was justified. Actions that in Germany constituted "medical policing" were constituted in England and the United States as public nuisance abatement. The difference goes deeper than simple terminology, extending both to the legal demand for proof of harm and to the locus— judicial or legislative—of the authority to determine the legitimacy of the interventions.

The incompatibility of the "medical policing" regulatory model with principles of English law was noted by Edwin Chadwick, the Bentham-inspired leader of the British sanitary movement in the early nineteenth century. Although he aspired to a centralized approach to public health regulation modeled on that of France, he also recognized the political need to implement the model in terms compatible with the common law. Toward the end of his famous 1842 *Report on the Sanitary Condition of the Labouring Poor* he thus turns to the question of legislation and the sort of instruments that could put his agenda into practice.[45] In this regard, he noted that the German medical policing model could not be transplanted to the English context; despite the "striking" success of German regulations and policies created "with a view to the health and pleasure of the population," he acknowledged that Germany's "medical police" concept is "scarcely applicable to the substantive English law." His common-law-compatible alternative was regulation via nuisance, which provided remedies for anything "by which the health or the personal safety, or the conveniences of the subject might be endangered or affected injuriously."[46] Largely in response to Chadwick's report, the British Parliament passed the Public Health Act of 1848, thereby creating administrative Boards of Health with extensive authority to abate nuisances. The "concept of nuisance was retained as the substantive core of the law, but its administration shifted from the courts to the Boards of Health and their medical officers."[47]

The term "nuisance" here refers to a public law concept, in contrast to the private nuisance doctrine discussed in the previous chapter. Under both categories of nuisance, interventions depend upon proof of legal injury, but in the case of public nuisance the injury must be to a significant number of people or to the public at large. The plaintiffs in private nuisance cases are those individuals whose property rights have been injured, whereas in public nuisance cases, a public regulatory body traditionally initiates the suit. This difference may be traced to two distinct doctrinal origins for public and private nuisance. The doctrine of private nuisance stemmed from limitations on interference with the enjoyment of individual property, while that of public nuisance had its beginnings in criminal action brought against infringements of the public right and the king's peace.[48]

The boundaries between the two types of nuisance started to blur when, during the sixteenth century, courts began to allow private plaintiffs to sue under public nuisance for particular damages that they, as distinct from the public at large, had incurred.[49] Henceforth public nuisance was actionable both by means of a criminal indictment for interference with public rights and via private action for the particular damages that a private plaintiff might suffer. This made for a hybrid legal concept that straddled private and public law categorizations.[50] This ambiguity, and the attendant legal requirement for proof of harm, distinguished public nuisance regulation from German "medical policing." Whereas the latter was rooted directly in the state's sovereignty, the former derived its regulatory rationale from injury suffered by citizens with the state acting on their behalf. Yet, as Chadwick noted in his report, nuisance law was a ready and effective instrument where there existed evident threat to public health.

Originally, public nuisance injunctions required specific proof that, in the particular time and place under consideration, the action in question imposed an unreasonable interference. Over time, judges began to distinguish between "nuisance in fact," where liability depended upon context-specific proof of harm, and "nuisance per se" where the relevant "act, occupation, or structure" is considered "a nuisance at all times and under all circumstances."[51] The long and eclectic list of behaviors that courts found to constitute per se nuisances includes the keeping of hogs and diseased animals, storage of explosives, shooting fireworks in the streets, practicing medicine without qualifications, prostitution, illegal liquor establishments, gaming houses, indecent exhibitions, and public profanity.[52] In all such cases, evidence that the defendant had engaged in any prohibited category of behavior was sufficient grounds for injunction. Although defendants could defeat prosecution under some of these categories by showing that they had not, in fact, caused or threatened injury, under others, most notably those concerning matters of public morals and decency, findings of nuisance per se imposed absolute liability.[53]

In both England and the United States, nineteenth-century legislators appropriated the "nuisance per se" terminology as a means of reconciling an array of preventative statutory measures with the common law's reactive logic. This strategy allowed land uses considered hazardous or undesirable to be declared nuisances per se and consequently prohibited. The relevant hazard could be physical, economic, or moral, and targeted business activities ran the gamut from saloons to slaughterhouses.[54] In addition to outright exclusions, the nuisance per se formula also provided a way to regulate potentially dangerous land uses instead of completely prohibiting them. In these cases, the statutes defined failure to take specified health or safety measures in the course of particular economic and other activities as a nuisance per se. For instance, by the start of the nineteenth century, a number of American cities had passed ordinances restricting the use of wood and other flammable materials in newly constructed buildings and had declared noncomplying structures to be abatable nuisances. As Novak explains, unlike traditional public nuisances such as slaughterhouses, wooden buildings were not inherently noxious or hazardous, but "became a nuisance solely because the legislature or municipality drew an arbitrary line . . . known as a 'fire limit' around a community declaring otherwise innocent conduct within that boundary 'offensive' as a matter of law."[55] Statutory nuisance per se formulas thus functioned as a legislative fiction capable of conferring the common law's imprimatur on what were in fact proof-independent precautionary measures. Despite this resemblance to continental regulation, two key differences remained: the interventions were presumed to be closely tailored to proven harms; and the courts retained the prerogative of invalidating them should they stray too far from this nexus.

Under the common law, the abatement of nuisances depended upon judicial orders for injunctive relief. Nuisance statutes in many nineteenth-century American states delegated this authority to administrative bodies and authorized them to serve in a quasi-judicial capacity. One example is an 1867 New York statute under which boards of health could enact individual orders "concerning the suppression and removal of nuisances and concerning all other matters in their judgment detrimental to the public health."[56] Though they varied in the size, mission, and scope of their authority, many such boards of health possessed extensive inspection, enforcement, and, eventually, legislative powers. But this authority was framed as an extension of the state's long-standing power to abate nuisances, and it thus ultimately remained subject to judicial findings that a nuisance existed. In tying intervention to the establishment of nuisance, rather than to continental-style police power, the common law state ultimately conferred upon judges the power to determine what counts as regulatory reasonableness.

BETWEEN NUISANCE AND SUBSTANTIVE DUE PROCESS

Of the police power, Justice Shaw wrote "[i]t is much easier to perceive and realize the existence and sources of this power, than to mark its boundaries, or prescribe limits to its exercise" in *Commonwealth v. Alger* (1851).[57] The case is one of the most extensive and influential judicial expositions during the nineteenth century on the scope of the police power. Yet in the end, as the above statement suggests, the case did not resolve, but rather highlighted the ambiguities that surrounded the grafting of the continental concept of *polizei* onto a common law base. Two decades later in the *Slaughter-House Cases*, Justice Miller quoted Shaw and added that "this power is, and must be from its very nature, incapable of any very exact definition or limitation."[58] Neither justice explained why the police power's scope is inherently vague. To the contrary, instead of probing the contradictions at the heart of this conceptual ambiguity, both opted to embrace it. What this solution lacked in logical consistency, it made up for in its capacity to avert, at least in the short term, the political crisis that was bound to result from a more clear-cut definition of the scope of legislative authority in America.[59]

At the crux of *Alger* stood a law that, deviating from the prevailing nuisance framework, limited the length of private wharves protruding into Boston Harbor. The deviation lay in the absence of a state claim to the abatement of a specific nuisance, or even the definition of an overly long wharf as a nuisance per se (presumably because of the impossibility of setting a nonarbitrary threshold). Instead, the wharf regulation set a quantitative standard in the style of continental codes. Alger fought an indictment brought against him for building a wharf that exceeded the length specified by the law, arguing that his wharf did not obstruct navigation or otherwise interfere with the public's rights. In other words, since it did not create a common law wrong (or legal injury), it ought not to be punished. This argument implied that the state could only regulate in response to a proven harm and that legislation not tailored to harm in this fashion would be invalid. Without disputing Alger's claim that his wharf inflicted no harm, the state insisted it was justified in setting and enforcing the length restriction, thereby putting the question of a priori limitations on the police power squarely at the center of the case.

Justice Shaw's opinion upheld the law irrespective of the state's failure to link it to a proven harm. As he noted in the opinion, "[t]hings done may or may not be wrong in themselves, or necessarily injurious and punishable as such at common law; but laws are passed declaring them offenses, and making them punishable, because they tend to injurious consequences; but more especially for the sake of having a definite, known and authoritative rule which all can understand and obey."[60] Whether this statement, and the larger opinion of which it is part, ought properly to be read as allowing for the existence of legislative authority not constrained by common law's demand for proof of harm would provide grist for constitutional and legal historical debate for at least another century.[61]

Shaw's endorsement of the "definite, known and authoritative rule" may bring to mind the language and logic standing behind the codification of civil law, but the very fact that his statement was expressed in a judicial opinion reviewing the validity of a statute places his conception of the police power within the common law. Only by drawing on long-standing judicial authority to determine the reasonableness of statutes under the common law could Justice Shaw take for granted, without any discussion, his own authority to review the legislation in question. Shaw is clearly willing to defer to legislative judgments on such matters, and even to divorce notions of legislative reasonableness from traditional tests of harm (substituting the need for authoritative and clear rules as a viable alternative). Yet nowhere does he entertain the idea that the validity of the law is established in legislative sovereignty as such, and, in that, adheres to the common law's basic paradigm.

It is important to note that *Commonwealth v. Alger* was not a constitutional case. The court's authority to review the reasonableness of the legislation was grounded strictly in common law, not constitutional interpretation. Only later during the Reconstruction era did this authority begin to be associated with a constitutional form of review. Triggering this development was the recognition by leading members of the American bar that the Fourteenth Amendment opened a broad range of state regulation to constitutional scrutiny. Although it sought to protect the rights of recently emancipated blacks against legislative encroachment by states, the Fourteenth Amendment further facilitated judicial review of the substance of state laws that had little to do with the amendment's original intent, including commercial regulations. Over the next four decades, what had begun as a daring, if not outlandish, idea gradually made its way from legal briefs to Supreme Court dissents until, at last, a majority of the court in *Lochner* voted to invalidate a statutory provision on the grounds that it violated liberty of contract as protected under the Fourteenth Amendment's due process clause.[62]

This process began with the 1872 *Slaughter-House Cases*, which challenged an 1869 Louisiana statute that restricted all slaughtering to one centralized facility, in accordance with a model that had already been implemented successfully in Paris. The law had a clear public health rationale: the disposal of offal in the Mississippi River had prompted over a thousand citizens to sign a petition against a situation described as both "revolting" and "prejudicial to health."[63] But granting the right to run the central facility to one company meant the law benefited particular butchers at the expense of others, and credible accounts indicated that the choice partially resulted from financial favors provided by the chosen company to Louisiana legislators. A group of Louisiana butchers and stockholders characterized the law as a spoils scheme masquerading as a public health law and, as such, an invalid exercise of the police power. The challengers' brief made the novel claim that, in lacking a real public health rationale, the law imposed an unconstitutional interference with property under various provisions of the Fourteenth Amendment.

A majority of the court upheld the law as a legitimate health measure, accepting Louisiana's claims that good public health reasons supported the centralization and control of butchering activities, and that the created enterprise was not a monopoly because the company was obliged to allow other butchers to use its facilities at a reasonable charge. In no uncertain terms, Justice Miller rejected in his majority opinion any idea that the law violated the Fourteenth Amendment due process clause, writing that the Louisiana law did not violate any "construction of that provision that we have ever seen, or any that we deem admissible."[64]

Four justices dissented, among them Justice Field, who carefully noted the broad scope of regulations to which the police power properly extends: "That power undoubtedly extends to all regulations affecting the health, good order, morals, peace, and safety of society, and is exercised on a great variety of subjects, and in almost numberless ways."[65] But the statute under consideration, he concluded, ought not to stand because it had been passed "under the pretence of prescribing a police regulation" rather than as an authentic health measure. Justice Field's dissent did not, however, invoke a Fourteenth Amendment due process claim in drawing this conclusion (although Justice Bradley, in another dissenting opinion, did).[66]

It was not until his dissent four years later in *Munn v. Illinois* (1876), which concerned the regulation of Chicago grain elevators, that Justice Field explicitly tied the due process clause to a duty incumbent upon the Supreme Court to ensure that legislators not misuse their police power authority "under pretence of providing for the public good."[67] This time he argued that the pretext for statutory regulation had been the public nature of grain elevators as, in the language of the majority opinion, property "affected with a public interest." Field held grain elevators to be private, not public enterprises. His dissent constructs the relevant constitutional question as one pertaining to legislative authority to control not the price of privately provided services, but the use of property; he answers that such economic controls are clearly inadmissible.[68] But, Justice Field emphasized, there remain large realms of property use over which regulation is clearly constitutional, and he offered as illustration an extensive array of fire safety, sanitary, and other extant police power measures for public health. The relevant distinction lies between regulatory restrictions on property "having for their object the peace, good order, safety, and health of the community," and those seeking other, presumably illegitimate, ends.[69]

By 1887 this position was no longer the sole purview of dissenters within the Supreme Court. In *Mugler v. Kansas*, the court upheld a state law prohibiting the manufacture and sale of liquor, but it did so on the basis of its own assessment of the reasonableness of the legislation rather than out of simple deference to the law's formal purpose. "There are, of necessity, limits beyond which legislation cannot rightfully go" wrote Justice Harlan. He continued,

> The courts are not bound by mere forms, nor are they to be misled by mere pretences. They are at liberty—indeed, are under a solemn duty—to look at the substance of things, whenever they enter upon the inquiry whether the legislature has transcended the limits of its authority. If, therefore, a statute purporting to have been enacted to protect the public health, the public morals, or the public safety, has no real or substantial relation to those objects, or is a palpable invasion of rights secured by the fundamental law, it is the duty of the courts to so adjudge, and thereby give effect to the Constitution.[70]

Such adjudication, the court later explained in *Lawton v. Steele* (1893), subjects statutes to the following judicially administered, two-step test: "first, that the interests of the public generally, as distinguished from those of a particular class, require such interference; and, second, that the means are reasonably necessary for the accomplishment of the purpose, and not unduly oppressive upon individuals."[71] The *Lawton* case arose from a suit brought by fishermen whose nets had been expropriated under a New York statute protecting game and fish against extinction. This expropriation, the court concluded, did serve the state's legitimate police power interest in protecting fish and game and was consequently a valid regulatory measure. However, the court made sure to emphasize that the legislature's "determination as to what is a proper exercise of its police powers is not final or conclusive, but is subject to the supervision of the courts."[72] In other words, the court's endorsement of this particular regulation notwithstanding, it ought not be assumed that other legislative acts would necessarily pass judicial muster.

Over a decade later, the process that had begun with the *Slaughter-House Cases* culminated in *Lochner v. New York*. Concluding that the bakery work-hour restriction lacked sufficient connection to any legitimate public health rationale, the Supreme Court voiced the suspicion that "many of the laws of this character, while passed under what is claimed to be the police power for the purpose of protecting the public health or welfare, are, in reality, passed from other motives."[73] Rejecting New York's argument and evidence about the dangers posed by long hours of bakery employment both to the bakers and the public that consumed their bread, the *Lochner* court declared the work-hour limitation to be "wholly beside the matter of a proper, reasonable and fair provision, as to run counter to that liberty of person and of free contract provided for in the Federal Constitution."[74]

The belief that American democracy was inextricably bound up with its common law roots prompted Justice Peckham to imply in *Lochner* that, in America, an unlimited police power was a contradiction in terms. In his eyes (and those of the influential elites for whom he spoke), civil-law-inspired threats to the supremacy of the common law amounted to nothing less than an attack on American democracy. Under the seemingly arcane rubric of police power jurisprudence, the ensuing constitutional crisis pitted two fundamentally divergent visions of the emerging American administrative state against one another.

The vision defended by the *Lochner* judges was hardly that of an economic free-for-all, but rather one in which a police power bound to common law would ensure that judges, rather than legislators, would have the final say on the validity of regulatory restrictions on the use of property. By the end of the nineteenth century, the scope of this common-law-bound police power was beginning to expand well beyond the traditional nuisance categories. Thus Judge Cooley, the era's leading constitutional scholar, wrote in 1890 of the compatibility of common law frameworks with far-reaching regulation of the employment of women and children, and even with controls on prices charged by monopolies. Nevertheless—and this is of the essence—he insisted that there existed substantive constitutional limits on the scope of police power interventions in the market and that the task of enforcing these limits belonged to the courts.[75]

Lochner hinged the constitutionality of statutes on legislators' ability to prove to the satisfaction of reviewing courts that restrictions imposed by a new law reasonably advanced a legitimate collective end. It would be well into the New Deal before the Supreme Court, in a nearly complete turnaround, conferred a presumption of constitutional validity upon all economic legislation and required challengers of the legislation's constitutionality to show that it failed to rest "upon some rational basis within the knowledge and experience of the legislators."[76] The "rational basis" test marked the seeming victory of those who had long sought to divorce police power authority from its restriction to traditional common law ends. If the court did not go so far as to concede legislative sovereignty (because it left the door open for future forms of substantive judicial review), it gave legislators almost total freedom to intervene in market relations for whatever purposes and by whichever means they saw fit.

But the retreat of substantive constitutional review of economic legislation in no way signaled the common law's capitulation before an administrative state modeled on civil law. Under the New Deal, detailed legislation like the bakery regulations in *Lochner* was increasingly becoming a thing of the past. The growing centrality of administrative bodies in the implementation of regulatory policy shifted the spotlight from judicial review of legislation to review of regulatory action as the primary terrain over which those who admired, and those who feared, the continental administrative state now turned to do battle.

ADMINISTRATION, DELEGATION, AND THE RULE OF LAW

Continental administrative theory arrived in the United States largely through the writings of German-educated, progressive reformers such as Woodrow Wilson and Frank Goodenough.[77] This theory espoused an apolitical administrative autonomy characterized by the technical application of specialized knowledge. Putting this expertise to optimal use required that agencies not be subject to ephemeral political whims, but instead be given extensive discretion to make and implement policy, since autonomy was seen as a prerequisite to the exercise of professionalism. In turn, this meant that pertinent statutory mandates had to be framed broadly in order to give agencies the leeway to fill in missing details, and that agencies' decisions had to be insulated from legislative or judicial interference and thus subject only to administrative, that is, expert, modes of review.

Because continental parliamentary systems already blur the boundaries between the legislative and executive branches (by making the leader of the majority party in Parliament the head of the executive branch), statutory delegations to agencies within these systems present relatively little difficulty from the perspective of democratic theory. In the United States, however, both delegation and the administrative state created thereby were fundamentally contested moves. "That Congress cannot delegate legislative power is a principle universally recognized as vital to the integrity and maintenance of the system of government ordained by the Constitution," the Supreme Court declared in an 1892 decision, while upholding the congressional law in question.[78] During the next half-century, those who hoped to halt, or at least slow, the advance of the administrative state were to challenge the constitutionality of broad legislative delegations. The strategy succeeded briefly during the early New Deal era, but the court's capitulation on this and related areas of conflict with the Roosevelt administration sent the nondelegation doctrine into retreat.[79] Nevertheless, the underlying constitutional tensions that had first given rise to this doctrine had by no means disappeared.[80]

Delegation could confer significant administrative autonomy only to the extent that agency decisions were to be insulated from judicial interference. In postrevolutionary France this understanding led to the creation early in the nineteenth century of a new hierarchy of specialized adjudicative bodies that to this day oversee relations within and among government agencies, as well as between bureaucracies and private citizens. At the head of this hierarchy sits the *Conseil d'état*, comprised not of judges but of the very elite of the French civil service. This model was emulated by most European countries, where the task of protecting against illegal governmental action was taken out of the courts and given to administrative tribunals staffed by bureaucrats rather than legally trained judges.[81]

This practice, wrote Alfred Dicey in 1885 in *Introduction to the Study of Law of the Constitution*, is fundamentally incompatible with British understandings of the rule of law. What we mean "when we speak of the 'rule of law' as a characteristic of our country," Dicey wrote, is "not only that with us no man is above the law, but (what is a different thing) that here every man, whatever be his rank or condition, is subject to the ordinary law of the realm and amenable to the jurisdiction of the ordinary tribunals."[82] In fact, he declared, "In England, and in countries which, like the United States, derive their civilization from English sources, the system of administrative law and the very principles upon which it rests are in truth unknown."[83]

In contending that administrative adjudication violated core notions of common law legality, Dicey's assertion paralleled the constitutional line of argument used to deflect continental-inspired legislation in the United States of the same time. Lacking a constitutional judicial review option, Dicey and the larger English liberal school he represented looked to judicial review of administration as the central line of defense against the encroachment of an unfettered police power. As Martin Shapiro writes, what "condemned continental administrative law in the eyes of English liberals" (and those Americans who followed their lead) was the special status accorded to the state as the guardian of the public interest under this model of administrative law.[84] On the opposite side stood progressive reformers for whom European-styled administrative justice was indispensable to the capacity of agencies to advance public policy and protect the interests of the public at large.[85] Well ensconced within most state and federal agencies, these reformers were able to create de facto administrative rule-making and adjudication procedures. These soon came to be criticized as undemocratic, in a mode familiar from common law encounters with continental legal models.

Roscoe Pound labeled extant regulatory procedures "administrative absolutism" in a 1938 report prepared on behalf of the American Bar Association (ABA),[86] which was part of a larger campaign spearheaded by the ABA to pass congressional legislation that would increase judicial oversight over administrative rule-making (quasi-legislative) and enforcement (quasi-adjudicative) actions. Rule-making procedures in most of the New Deal agencies were informal in nature and produced little by way of written record. Without such a record, there was little basis for meaningful judicial review since nothing documented the evidence or reasoning behind a rule. The ABA thus sought to eliminate informal rule-making in order to allow greater judicial oversight of administration. Eliminating agencies' informal rule-making powers was a primary goal of an ABA-sponsored bill that passed both houses of Congress in 1940. Known as the Walter-Logan Bill, the law was vetoed by President Roosevelt, who referred to it as a "high water mark of judicialization" and the work of lawyers "who desire to have all processes of government conducted through lawsuits."[87] World War II put the issue on the back burner, but Congress returned to it soon after the war ended and in 1946 enacted the Administrative Procedure Act (APA). This compromise act recognized the legitimacy of administrative rule-making but gave regular courts a final say on matters of administrative legality. The ABA's most visible and immediate success under the APA had to do with the requirements governing agency quasi-judicial decisions, in other words, those regulatory enforcement actions having at stake the economic and legal interests of particular parties. Here the ABA successfully pushed for the separation of administrative adjudication from other agency functions, the imposition of court-like procedures upon these quasi-adjudicative proceedings, and, most importantly, judicial review of any such administrative decisions under the potentially scrutinizing standard of "substantial evidence."[88] By contrast, where agency quasi-legislative functions were concerned, the ABA failed in its efforts to eliminate informal rule-making in favor of exclusive reliance on the formal rule-making process. Instead, the APA generally allowed agencies to choose between formal and informal rule-making processes, each subject to different levels of potential judicial scrutiny. Formal rule-making was court-like in producing a written record that agencies could use to justify their adopted policies or standards. The standard of judicial review in these cases was "substantial evidence" on the record. Usually, however, a formal rule-making process was not necessary, and agencies could rely on a streamlined, informal process requiring only that they give notice of their intention to promulgate a rule, receive comments from interested parties, and print the final rule together with a "concise general statement of basis and purpose."

As to the standard for judicial review of informally enacted rules, the APA vaguely prescribed that they be set aside only when found to be "arbitrary, capricious, an abuse of discretion, or otherwise not in accordance with law."[89] In conventional parlance, "arbitrary and capricious" behavior is that which appears extremely irrational, pointless, or even absurd. Taken literally, this standard would seem to require judges to uphold agency rules in all cases but those where no rational explanation for the chosen course of action exists—"a lunacy test," so to speak.[90] This interpretation, however, does not accord with the long-standing meaning of arbitrariness under the common law, where the term has generally served as a synonym for unreasonableness or the absence of adequate proportionality between regulatory means and ends. In opting for the latter, seemingly narrower "arbitrary and capricious" standard, those who drafted the APA may well have intended to signal to courts an expectation of greater judicial deference than that historically associated with "reasonableness" review under the common law. The message was one that a new generation of New Deal–appointed judges, schooled in the failings of the discredited *Lochner* court, was already politically inclined and professionally socialized to accept. However, even then there were those who understood that the tables could well turn again. By giving judges the ultimate power to decide the limits of deference to administrators, the APA gave the upper hand to common-law-derived notions of administrative legality.[91]

This was made clear when, shortly after the enactment of the federal health and safety risk-control mandates of the 1960s and 1970s, courts abandoned their earlier deference in favor of rigorous review of administrative rules. Making regulatory interventions legally contingent upon proof of risk, these statutory mandates paralleled long-standing nuisance doctrines and gave judges a similar veto power to that which they had always possessed under common law. As such, the "hard look" doctrines of the 1970s are better seen not as a novel mode of judicial scrutiny suggestive of a radically new regulatory regime, but as an extension of courts' traditional role under nuisance law. As the following section argues, democratic critiques of administrative mandates that diverge from the common-law risk model likewise need to be understood as rooted in this debate, which portrays police power as being incompatible with the rule of law.

On the "Absolutism of a Democratic Majority"

This debate ultimately pertains to the relationship between legislation and democracy, asking whether democracy requires limits on the content of legislation enacted by elected majorities. Christopher G. Tiedeman, one of the leading constitutional jurists of the *Lochner* era, gave voice to the sense of crisis some American elites felt in response to "the radical experimentation of social reformers."[92] Introducing his 1886 *Treatise on the Limitations of the Police Power*, he wrote without irony, "The conservative classes stand in constant fear of the advent of an absolutism more tyrannical and more unreasoning than any before experienced by man, the absolutism of a democratic majority."[93]

In labeling continentally inspired social legislation "tyrannical," Tiedeman placed himself squarely in a long tradition of American suspicion of such legal instruments. Since the Revolutionary era, those who sought to infuse the American legal system with the institutions and methods of continental civil law had been vigorously opposed by others who resisted such importation.[94] For example, Charles Pinckney, an influential delegate to the Constitutional Convention, countered such efforts with the claim that "[f]rom the European world are no precedents to be drawn for a people who think they are capable of governing themselves."[95] This view remained highly visible throughout the nineteenth century in rhetoric invoked to fight various codification initiatives, which had emerged for different reasons, including concerns pertaining to the legal profession, suspicions of federalist judges, and, later in the century, dissatisfaction with common law responses to industrial hazards. Almost invariably, opponents of these initiatives cast any move toward continental-style codification as a potentially despotic measure at odds with fundamental American values.[96]

Preserving this rhetoric, James Coolidge Carter, who successfully led the New York Bar Association's anticodification campaign of the 1880s, described codes as "a characteristic feature in those (countries) which have a despotic origin, or in which despotic power, absolute or qualified is, or has been, predominant."[97] The link between codes and despotism, Carter explained, derived not from coincidental association but as a necessary consequence of "the fundamental difference in the political character of the two classes of States." He went on to say, "In free, popular States, the law springs from, and is made by, the people," whereas in despotic countries "the sovereign must be permitted at every step to say what shall be *the law*. . . . He can say it only by a positive command, and this is statutory law; and when such positive command embraces the whole system of jurisprudence it becomes a *Code*."[98]

Carter does not name any specific despotic country, and not by chance. The argument linking codification with despotism derived its resonance from a long-standing American dichotomization of American liberty and continental tyranny. But as European absolute monarchies gave way, first to constitutional monarchies and then to republics, the credibility of equating civil law institutions like codes with despotism came under significant strain. True enough, the parliament of Imperial Germany did rely on traditional elites, and it ruthlessly suppressed dissident movements, but it was nonetheless elected by universal suffrage.[99] This made the earlier contrast between continental law and the law of "free states" whence the law "springs from the people" (to quote Carter) increasingly difficult to sustain. Ironically enough, the continental police power became even more threatening during the later nineteenth century to adherents of common law limitations on the state, precisely because of the democratic legitimacy that majoritarian institutions conferred upon it. In 1925, Charles Evans Hughes (later Chief Justice of the Supreme Court) gave voice to this concern when he contrasted the common law, which he regarded as "springing from custom" and as embodying "the experience of free men," with "those insidious encroachments upon liberty which take the form of an uncontrolled administrative authority—the modern guise of an ancient tyranny, not the more welcome to intelligent free men because it may bear the label of democracy."[100]

While contemporary writers shun much of the hyperbole of earlier eras, echoes of this sentiment continue to reverberate. Feasibility-derived "command and control" pollution standards remain democratically suspect according to reasoning strikingly similar to that which pervaded the debate during the late nineteenth and early twentieth centuries. Like observers of these periods, contemporary scholars worry about the dangers of agency factionalization and undue interest group influence thought to attend interventions of this type. Particularly striking in their continuity are concerns that, under the pretext of protecting the public, technology standards are most likely to be enacted by *dirigiste* regimes to confer windfalls on favored groups.

The modern antithesis of an administrative, technology-based regulatory regime, like its traditional common law counterpart, is not an environmental version of laissez-faire economics. Indeed, it sees pollution control as both legitimate and important. Nor is the modern critique a call for a reversion to a common-law-based nuisance regime for health and safety regulation. Rather, the dispute now centers on the type of administrative state that ought to arise to deal with these issues. Modern critics of technology standards seek a regime that underpins regulatory interventions with specific proof of harm; in this they reveal the sensibilities of a centuries-old common law tradition that sees interventions that lack such tailoring as democratically deficient.

While one may readily construct democratic theory arguments for either side of this issue, the problem from an environmental standpoint is that the level of linkage between harm and remedy sought by a regulatory regime rooted in the common law has remained an insurmountable obstacle to effective pollution abatement in many instances. The following chapters return to the history of air-pollution regulation in the United States to explore the workings of the harm-tailored regime and to demonstrate its systematic tendency to fail to implement feasible controls.

From *Richards's Appeal* to *Boomer*: Judicial Responses to Air Pollution, 1869–1970

UNDER England's bifurcated regulatory regime, it fell to a statutory component—the Alkali Act—to provide incentives for the implementation of available pollution controls for noxious vapors. Meanwhile a judicial component (nuisance law under the *St. Helen's* doctrine) adhered to an absolute liability rule that left some room for compensation for visible injury to property (most often damage to vegetation) but denied relief for "discomforts" stemming from fumes. In the absence of a similar statutory framework in the United States, it was left to common law judges to negotiate between the competing solutions for addressing air pollution disputes: land use separation and/or property loss compensation on the one hand, and pollution mitigation on the other. This chapter traces the trajectory of these judges' decisions, through analysis of landmark air-pollution cases, all but two from Pennsylvania, which span the century following the Civil War. Four categories of judicial responses to such disputes may be discerned, and the structure of the chapter corresponds to this categorization:

1. no remedy (neither injunction nor damages) should plaintiffs fail to prove a causal relationship between emissions and injury to property or health;
2. finding of liability for nuisance, but with damages awarded in lieu of injunction when abatement is deemed economically or technologically infeasible;
3. injunction aimed at shutting down or relocating the polluting facility (total injunctions);
4. Best Available Technology (BAT) injunctions intended, contrary to traditional understandings of injunctions as absolute "cease or desist orders," not to eliminate the pollution problem totally, but to encourage the implementation of feasible means of control.[1]

In Pennsylvania, courts issued total injunctions only when the offending company was located in a residential area. In these rather exceptional cases, the Pennsylvania Supreme Court imposed evidentiary thresholds regarding proof of injury much lower than those demanded of residents of industrial locales, whose suits usually led to responses from the first or, at best, the second categories above. BAT injunctions, which placed quasi-administrative air pollution control functions in the hands of courts, emerged at the end of the nineteenth century as an intermediate solution geared at producing incremental relief, even for those residing in industrial locales.

The efficacy, legitimacy, and continued need for this quasi-administrative judicial function was the issue dividing the majority and the dissent in the well-known case of *Boomer v. Atlantic Cement* (1970).[2] Like all of the cases discussed in this chapter, *Boomer* resulted from a dispute between an industrial facility and its neighbors. In this particular case, neighboring landowners brought an action for injunction and damages against a large cement plant in upstate New York because of injury to property from dirt, smoke, and vibrations. Refusing to issue an injunction due to the large disparity in economic consequences for the economic interests at stake, the New York Court of Appeals awarded damages instead.[3] Writing in dissent, Judge Jasen found damages an inappropriate response to the health hazard and broad environmental injury brought by the cement dust. Instead, he argued for the superiority of an injunction that would give the defendant eighteen months in which to develop a technological solution.[4]

The attention subsequently lavished upon the case by the legal academy is difficult to explain in terms of the novelty or creativity of its reasoning, as others have suggested.[5] The alternative remedies espoused by the majority and the dissent had both already been well established in the judicial repertoire by the end of the nineteenth century in Pennsylvania, New York, and elsewhere. Instead of any particular doctrinal innovation, timing appears to be the key to *Boomer*'s renown. Decided on the eve of Earth Day and Congress's subsequent passage that year of the Clean Air Act, *Boomer* came to symbolize the adaptability and efficiency of a judicially managed, common law regime. However, the association is highly ironic. Far from offering a paean to the common law's air-pollution regime, the *Boomer* opinion highlighted the inherent limits of judicial remedies in this domain and the need for proactive statutory and administrative air-pollution regulation. Writing for the majority, Judge Bergan offered the following explanation of his refusal to issue a postponed injunction along the lines suggested by the dissent:

> A court should not try to do this on its own as a by-product of private litigation and it seems manifest that the judicial establishment is neither equipped in the limited nature of any judgment it can pronounce nor prepared to lay down and implement an effective policy for the elimination of air pollution. This is an area beyond the circumference of one private lawsuit. It is a direct responsibility for government and should not thus be undertaken as an incident to solving a dispute between property owners and a single cement plant—one of many—in the Hudson Valley.[6]

The New York Court of Appeals' refusal to grant an injunction to the *Boomer* landowners in 1970 resembles a decision made a century earlier, when the Pennsylvania Supreme Court, in *Richards's Appeal* (1869), refused to issue an injunction requiring the use of specified smoke reduction measures, and instead pointed to damages as the proper remedy. Although it opted for a similar solution, the message sent by the *Boomer* court spoke not about the sufficiency of damages as a solution, but rather to the need for statutory and administrative interventions under the "direct responsibility of government." As this chapter shows, BAT injunctions emerged as a quasi-administrative judicial function in the absence of a statutory regime comparable to England's Alkali Act. With the arrival of a far-reaching statutory regime in the form of the Clean Air Act imminent, *Boomer* thus seems to suggest that it was time for U.S. courts to relinquish such quasi-administrative tasks.

Pennsylvania is particularly prominent in air pollution adjudication in the century following the Civil War. The wealth of cases derives from the combination of a large population—Pennsylvania was the second most populous state during this period—and the concentration of steel and iron industries within the Commonwealth. The body of jurisprudence thus created represents a more-or-less self-contained system with greater internal consistency across the decades than may appear at first glance.

RICHARDS'S APPEAL (1868): INJUNCTION OR DAMAGES?

The first air-pollution case to be decided by the Pennsylvania Supreme Court, *Richards's Appeal*,[7] reflects that state's economic transformation over the course of the mid-nineteenth century. The plaintiff, L. Harry Richards, was a cotton cloth manufacturer who had built a factory and an adjoining residence for his family in 1830. Seven years later, the Phoenix Iron Company opened and began smelting iron just below the bluff where Richards's property lay. The company continued to expand over the next two decades, adding two more mills in the same area. By the time of Richards's lawsuit in 1864, seventy furnaces' worth of smoke was reaching his business and home, and Phoenix Iron had become one of Pennsylvania's largest smelting companies with 800 to 1000 employees and a capital investment of approximately $0.5 million.

After three decades of coexistence between the cotton cloth manufacturer and the iron smelter, the lawsuit was triggered by a change in the fuels used in the smelter's furnaces. Until 1864 Phoenix Iron had relied primarily upon anthracite coal, but it began switching to the more polluting bituminous variety in the early 1860s. Richards responded in 1864 with a lawsuit complaining of both the "sulphurous, unwholesome and noxious" impact of the smoke on the health of his family and workers and the property damage inflicted by soot on his business. Although Richards asked the court for an injunction, his intent was neither to shut down nor force the relocation of the company. Instead he sought the implementation of available and (by his argument) feasible measures of pollution reduction. He focused on two such potential technological solutions: a reversion from semi-bituminous coal to the less-polluting anthracite variety, or alternatively, construction of chimneys high enough to remove the smoke from his property (as he contended was already common practice). After the trial court refused to impose either of these options, Richards suggested a third potential means of abatement, the deployment of smoke consumption devices.

After losing at the trial level, *Richards's Appeal* came before the state Supreme Court. Significantly, whereas the lower court had followed an absolute liability standard, the state Supreme Court employed a negligence rule. The lower court's specially appointed agent, or "master," had built his report around Richards's failure to establish the existence of a nuisance as such (rather than the question of negligence by the smelter), and it was this report that had justified the court's denial of an injunction. The company, said the master, was not guilty of creating a "nuisance of any sort whatever" since "there was no evidence of any injury to the goods manufactured, or to the health of the family or operatives,"[8] though he conceded that the smoke and soot may have caused annoyance and slight injury to buildings. Under this construction, Richards's failure derived from his inability to prove that the smoke and fumes caused more than a *de minimis* injury.

The state Supreme Court, however, located his failure elsewhere. The language of its conclusion is reminiscent of that adopted in *Hole v. Barlow*[9] and rejected in the *St. Helen's* case, only a few years earlier: "there was neither a negligent nor willful infliction of injury upon the plaintiff or his property in the defendants' mode of operating their works."[10] Conceding that "there may be injury to the plaintiff," the court explained that "this of itself may not entitle him to the remedy he seeks."[11] An injunction, the remedy requested by Richards, requires a plaintiff to demonstrate not only injury but also the existence of feasible means of abatement—and it is this burden that Richards failed to meet.

Going sequentially through the control options proposed by Richards, the court explained its grounds for rejecting each. With regard to the option of raising the furnace stacks, the Court agreed with the master's conclusion that they were already "as high as such stacks are ordinarily built—a material increase of their height would involve enormous expenditure, would destroy their usefulness, and 'is therefore wholly impracticable.' "[12] The court likewise deemed infeasible the option of switching from bituminous coal, since it is "of great value" to the manufacture of iron and "to prohibit the use of it to the defendants would be equivalent to a total suspension of their business."[13] Finally, regarding the possibility of applying smoke consumption devices of the sort recommended in an 1866 *London Quarterly* article for the type of problem at hand, Justice Thompson wrote, "I would require very clear proof of the practicability of the application of the principle." Notwithstanding the technology's success in reducing similar pollution problems, the court concluded that the success of the method remained too uncertain to justify an injunction requiring its use, as "we are not able to say from anything shown, that the evil complained of can be remedied by the application of smoke consumers."[14] Short of such "very clear proof," notwithstanding the existence of what it conceded to be a potentially promising opportunity for pollution reduction, the court refused to enjoin.

Yet, as the court explained, its refusal to issue an injunction said nothing about Richards's right to damages under the common law. In fact, the court went so far as to say, "We have no doubt that an action at law will lie for an injury to property for causes similar to those mentioned in this bill, and if so, why will not the remedy be adequate in such case, and thus the injury be repaired in damages?"[15] As the court emphasized, different considerations govern judicial decisions about remedies in suits for common law damages versus equity suits for injunctions. In suits seeking injunctions, judges must weigh the competing interests of the parties, and they may exercise discretion as to the nature of the relief demanded by the circumstances. As the court emphasized when it effectively encouraged Richards to seek damages in a common law suit, denial of injunction is not tantamount to denial of relief. Instead, the court seemed to be moving here toward the creation of a bifurcated common law / equity judicial regime, with the former geared toward compensation for injury and the latter toward abatement.

The Pennsylvania bifurcated regime differed, however, from England's common law / Alkali Act combination in three interrelated ways: the existence of a feasible technological solution was determined by a judge, rather than an administrative body such as the Alkali Inspectorate; the burden of proof of feasible means of control fell to the plaintiff, not an agency like the inspectorate; and finally, in balancing the equities (and thus the feasibility of abatement) the court weighed only the interests of the plaintiff, rather than the public at large, against those of the company. Thus, to explain why an injunction would make little economic sense, the opinion highlighted the Phoenix Iron Company's claim "that to purchase plaintiff's whole property would be less injury to them than stopping the use of such coal."[16]

It is impossible to tell from the case alone whether or not there were others in that location who suffered from the smoke like Richards. That bit of missing information is important to an understanding of the logic behind the case. Had the area gone completely over to heavy industry, with Richards's home and factory standing as isolated relics from an earlier era, the court's damage remedy could be seen as consistent with the traditional goal of nuisance law to separate conflicting land uses, the distinctive feature of this case being that this time it was the residential land user who was effectively invited to move away, with the help of financial compensation from the company. This would mean that Richards's success or failure in proving the feasibility of the various control alternatives had little to do with the outcome, since the case might have in effect been predetermined by the court's view of relocation as the preferred solution to the dispute.

While separation may well have been the most appropriate solution within the confines of this specific case, it was a solution with two serious drawbacks. First, by failing to demand the implementation of available but generally untested pollution-control technology, it all but ensured that future litigants elsewhere would face similar evidentiary impediments when trying to establish the practicability of particular technological approaches. Second, the economic viability of substituting damages for injunctions depends on the existence of a relatively small number of potential plaintiffs. The large number of potential plaintiffs in most industrial areas meant that, in practice, damage awards presented polluters with an economic threat comparable to, if not greater than, that of injunctions, should such penalties entail ongoing payments to large numbers of affected neighbors. This concern, it appears, soon prompted the Pennsylvania Supreme Court to shift course.

Huckenstine's Appeal (1872): Neither Injunction nor Damages

Huckenstine's Appeal,[17] a similar complaint against injury inflicted by smoke and gas generated by a brick manufacturer, came before the Pennsylvania Supreme Court only four years after *Richards's Appeal*. This plaintiff blamed the brickyard's fumes for extensive injury to his vineyards and orchards, and he offered evidence that smoke from the kilns rendered the "land and the houses on it very inconvenient and uncomfortable as a residence."[18] The defendant countered that damage to the vines arose from the "wet, spouty and swampy" character of the plaintiff's land rather than the fumes. The lower court rejected the latter claim and issued an injunction forbidding smoke, gas, or vapor from the brick-kilns either to injure the plaintiff's vineyards or to render his premises unsuitable for a home. The

Pennsylvania Supreme Court, however, overturned not only the injunction itself, but also the lower court's finding of nuisance liability as such.

Disputing the lower court's conclusion that the smoke had caused the vineyards' decline, the Pennsylvania Supreme Court accepted the "testimony of the defense that the true cause of the blight in the vines is the nature, and cold and wet condition of the soil."[19] As to the alleged ill effects inflicted on those living in the plaintiff's house, the court argued that they did not amount to remediable legal injury, relying somewhat paradoxically on *Richards's Appeal* for support. As the court noted, comfort is the very type of interference for which it had refused to issue an injunction in the earlier case. While this interpretation of the holding in *Richards's* was perhaps consistent with the holding of the trial court, the Supreme Court had emphasized Richards's likelihood of winning damages for the alleged injury under common law. Ignoring its own earlier distinction between the reasoning applicable to liability decisions in common law and the granting of injunctive relief in equity, the court in *Huckenstine's Appeal* imposed what amounted to an insurmountable evidentiary barrier regarding the causal link between pollution and alleged injury to vegetation or health.[20]

To justify its decision, the court looked to Lord Wesbury's argument in *St. Helen's*: "The people who live in such a city or within its sphere of influence do so of choice, and they voluntarily subject themselves to its peculiarities and its discomforts, for the greater benefit they think they derive from their residence or their business there."[21] Thus residence in a polluted locale implied consent to exposure to fumes. But unlike *St. Helen's*, which maintained a distinction between injury to vegetation (for which Tipping won compensation) and the "trifling inconvenience" or discomfort associated with exposure to fumes, *Huckenstine's Appeal* found no legal injury either to property or to health. Vineyards, the court appears to have concluded, were no longer an appropriate land use in that location—a hillside overlooking the city of Allegheny, "whose everyday cloud of smoke from thousands of chimney and stacks hangs like a pall over it, obscuring it from sight."[22] The plaintiff thus faced the choice of putting his land to a (presumably profitable) industrial use or relocating (without compensation) to a different place.

PENNSYLVANIA LEAD COMPANY (1881) AND EVANS V. READING CHEMICAL FERTILIZING CO. (1894): INJUNCTIVE RELIEF AND OUT-OF-PLACE INDUSTRIAL FACILITIES

The ensuing decade brought yet another air-pollution suit against an industrial facility before the Pennsylvania Supreme Court, but this time with the opposite result.[23] In the *Appeal of the Pennsylvania Lead Company*, a farming plaintiff successfully petitioned for an injunction against a neighboring lead-smelter's "offensive, noxious and poisonous gases, fumes and vapors." In justifying the injunction, the Pennsylvania Supreme Court offered that "[a]ll intelligent persons are aware that lead vapors are poisonous, and this the more so as they are often, as in the case in hand, accompanied with arsenic. In this matter we need not chemists and experts to teach us, for common experience is sufficient."[24] Although the Pennsylvania Lead Company denied that its fumes presented any such threat, unlike the previous defendants, it was unable to bring scientific doubt to work in its favor.

While this difference may be partially explained by growing scientific consensus on the toxicity of the emissions in question, the key to the decision appears to lie in the nature of the surrounding locale. As the court explained,

> Again, we cannot but regard this company as unfortunate in the selection of a place for the erection of its works. To undertake the business of lead smelting in the midst of a rich suburban valley, occupied by farms and country residences, was, to say the least of it, not very prudent.[25]

Lead smelting and its attendant environmental consequences would have to go on, the court acknowledged with this statement, but in a less bucolic locale.

A similar logic led the court to uphold an injunction against a fertilizing company in *Evans v. Reading Chemical Fertilizing Co.* (1894).[26] In this instance, unlike that of the lead-smelting situation, there was little evidence to suggest long-term injury to health. The pollution problem instead was that of "an offensive and disagreeable odor" produced in the process of manufacturing fertilizer from animal carcasses.[27] "[W]hile it probably does not cause any serious disease, or injuriously affect the workmen in the factory who are accustomed to it," the court decided that the odor was "offensive and disagreeable to people generally who inhale it, and causes nausea, vomiting and loss of appetite."[28] Despite the company's use of "[t]he most improved machinery and appliances and the best processes known to the business,"[29] the Pennsylvania Supreme Court upheld the lower court's injunction. The court offered the following answer in explanation of its refusal to balance the odors' injury to the plaintiff against the company's greater economic loss: none of the cited precedents "can be authority for the proposition that equity, a case for its cognizance being otherwise made out, will refuse to protect a man in the possession and enjoyment of his property because that right is less valuable to him than the power to destroy it may be to his neighbor or the public."[30]

The absolutist emphasis on protecting property rights, together with the rejection of competing interests, strongly recalls *Aldred's Case* and the general tenor of preindustrial nuisance law. The explanation seems to lie in the applicability of *Aldred's* logic of land use separation (and its associated absolute liability standard) to the case at hand. The proper solution for out-of-place industrial facilities like the lead-smelter and the fertilizing company was relocation, just as it had been for the offending pigsty in *Aldred's Case*.

The likelihood that lead-smelting would be found to constitute a nuisance and subsequently enjoined thus depended less on the danger or injury that it posed as such (and still less on the feasibility of abating the pollution) than on the environmental conditions prevalent within its surrounding community. While it protected upscale residential areas against industrial encroachment, the "locality doctrine" evident in *Huckenstine's Appeal* effectively closed the door to plaintiffs who resided in industrial locales.[31]

VERSAILLES BOROUGH (1935) AND WASCHAK V. MOFFAT (1954): "ONE WHO VOLUNTARILY GOES TO WAR. . ."

The case of *Versailles Borough v. McKeesport Coal & Coke Co.* (1935) epitomizes the barriers that plaintiffs encountered when bringing suits against pollution in industrial locales.[32] Unlike the other cases discussed in this section, *Versailles Borough* is a trial-level decision, rather than an opinion of the Pennsylvania Supreme Court. However, it is a particularly revealing case because the same Judge Musmanno who presided over it in the Allegheny County Court of Common Pleas, was later to serve as a Justice of the Pennsylvania Supreme Court in the similar case of *Waschak v. Moffat* (1954).[33]

Plaintiffs in both cases complained of fumes and smoke deriving from the burning piles of coal-mining waste, known as gob, a common occurrence in the vicinity of most coal mines well into the 1950s. Large gob piles were constructed immediately adjacent to mining tipples as the primary means of disposing of mining by-products. When one such gob pile caught fire in the coal-mining town of McKeesport, Pennsylvania, in 1932, the city and the local borough filed a lawsuit asking the court for an order enjoining the mine from adding gob to the burning pile or constructing additional gob piles in the area.

In an effort to establish that the pollution caused injury to health, the plaintiffs introduced fifty-one witnesses, who collectively spoke of suffering irritated throats, hay fever, asthma, coughs, and other symptoms as a result of the fumes. But against this testimony the defendants produced seventy-one witnesses who insisted that the pollution caused them no ill effects. Measurements of potentially dangerous chemicals showed concentrations significantly lower than those considered harmful to health, and the plaintiffs' case was further weakened by the absence of local doctors willing to testify to the existence of a link between the pollution and disease. The court concluded it had no evidence "to warrant the assumption that the health of anyone is being imperiled"[34] and proceeded to define the pertinent injury in terms of annoyance posed by "dust," "smoke," and "odors," an annoyance "trivial in comparison to the positive harm and damage that would be done to the community were the injunction asked for granted."[35]

In addition to the question of injury to health, the court devoted significant attention to exploring the existence of feasible means of abatement. In this regard, the plaintiffs had outlined two alternative solutions to the problem: remove the gob from the area and dispose of it in uninhabited locales, or change the construction of gob piles by adding layers of clay to prevent the piles from catching fire. The court rejected the gob removal option as economically infeasible and accepted the defendant's claim that clay layers would not prevent the gob from eventually catching fire and thus "would only delay the inevitable." Building on the assumption that no feasible alternative to gob disposal existed, the court determined that an injunction would lead to the shutdown of the mine and the loss of millions of dollars and hundreds of jobs—an unacceptable outcome, especially against the backdrop of the Great Depression.

Notwithstanding these seemingly decisive economic considerations, Judge Musmanno's opinion suggested that the scales might have tipped differently had, instead of its actual location "in the very heart of one of the most industrialized districts of Allegheny County," the mine "been sunk in the midst of a residential district, utterly free of factories and mills."[36] An injunction might be justified in such a case, the court suggested, despite the lack of proven injury to health and the drastic economic losses it would allegedly entail. What doomed the lawsuit was thus neither the plaintiffs' failure to establish injury, nor the absence of feasible means of abatement, but their implicit consent to the pollution of the industrial locale in which they chose to reside. As Judge Musmanno explained,

> The plaintiffs are subject to an annoyance. This we accept, but it is an annoyance they have freely assumed. Because they desired and needed a residential proximity to their places of employment, they chose to found their abode here. It is not for them to repine; and it is probable that upon reflection they will, in spite of the annoyance which they suffer, still conclude that, after all, one's bread is more important than landscape or clear skies.[37]

To the above he vividly added that "[o]ne who voluntarily goes to war should not complain about cannon smoke."[38]

Two decades later, by then a justice on the Pennsylvania Supreme Court, Judge Musmanno had apparently changed his mind, as his dissenting opinion in *Waschak v. Moffat* suggests. The plaintiffs in *Waschak*, who lived near a large, burning gob pile like their predecessors in *Versailles Borough*, brought suit for damages suffered as a result of the fumes. They contended that poisonous and noxious gases, including sulfur dioxide and hydrogen sulfide, damaged their houses both inside and outside, in addition to affecting their comfort and health. Numerous witnesses, including the town druggist, school principal, and a minister attested that fumes from the coal banks surrounded them with the smell of "rotten egg," awakened them at night and caused headaches, throat irritation, coughing, light-headedness, nausea, and stomach ailments.

Concluding that the plaintiffs had failed to prove any injury to health, the trial court found the defendant liable only for damage to the paint on the plaintiffs' houses, and the jury awarded damages in the amount of $1,250. But consequences far beyond this sum hinged on the question of whether the Pennsylvania Supreme Court would decide to uphold this damage award. The case was one of twenty-five similar suits waiting on the Supreme Court's docket, and its precedent, as the justices explained before voting to overturn, was likely to "affect the entire coal interests—anthracite and bituminous—as well as other industries."[39]

In finding the defendants not liable for any injury that the fumes may have caused, the court invoked two lines of justification: first, that coal-deposit practices of this type were common across the industry and were thus, by definition, reasonable; and second, that in choosing to live in such a locale the plaintiffs offered their implicit consent, per Judge Musmanno's findings in *Versailles Borough*.[40] In what might seem a surprising move in light of his own authorship of the earlier decision, Justice Musmanno responded with a sharply worded dissent from the court's decision. He distinguished his present dissent from the earlier decision on three primary grounds: first, that *Versailles* was a suit for injunction rather than one for damages, and consequently different considerations ought to apply; second, that the mine it had concerned was located in the midst of an industrial district so that "it could not be said that the discomforts of the inhabitants were due exclusively to the operation of the coal mine," and finally, that in *Versailles* the court found that "the operation of the mine in no way jeopardized the health of the inhabitants."[41] In contrast, "[t]he health of the town of Taylor is being imperiled,"[42] concluded Justice Musmanno, asking "[i]s it not reasonable to suppose that if hydrogen sulfide emanating from culm banks can strip paint from wood and steel that it will also deleteriously affect the delicate membranes of the throat and lungs?"[43]

Going a significant step further, Justice Musmanno's *Waschak* opinion cut against an entire legal tradition that imposed *de minimis*, or trivializing definitions, on the "discomforts" of air pollution whose risk could not be proven. "I do not think," wrote Justice Musmanno in *Waschak*, "that there can be any doubt that the constant smell of rotten eggs constitutes a nuisance. If such a condition is not recognized by the law, then the law is the only body that does not so recognize it."[44] Ultimately, he concluded,

> [W]e are dealing with a situation where in effect the inhabitant of Taylor, Pennsylvania, awakens each morning with a basket of rotten eggs on his doorstep, and then, on his way to work finds that some of those eggs have been put into his pocket. No matter how often he may remove them, an invisible hand replaces them. This can scarcely be placed in the category of "trifling inconveniences."[45]

What led Judge Musmanno to change his mind? In part it could be the great improvement in overall economic circumstances since the depression-era case of *Versailles*, though this appears to have had little impact on the majority decision to overturn the award. More persuasive is the hypothesis that Justice Musmanno had come to reject the regulatory assumptions encapsulated in his own "[o]ne who volantarily goes to war . . ." maxim quoted earlier. Evidence of this comes from the manner in which he reconstructs in *Waschak* the reasoning that had linked the industrial character of the locale to the outcome in *Versailles*. No mention is made this time of any consent to the pollution as such. Instead, only the evidentiary difficulties inherent in tying injury to emissions from a particular source had ostensibly doomed the earlier attempt, Justice Musmanno explained, as "it could not be said that the discomforts of the inhabitants were due exclusively to the operation of the coal mine."[46]

Justice Musmanno's change of heart may also have been due in part to the realization that an injunction need not imply a shutdown, despite his opposite conclusion in *Versailles*. That case had assumed an absence of feasible means of control, based in turn on the fact that gob fires almost everywhere were left uncontrolled. This was true in England as well, where "burning [coal] spoilbanks" came under the Alkali Inspectorate's jurisdiction only in 1932. Soon thereafter necessity proved to be the mother of invention when, at the start of World War II, concerns arose that burning banks would help guide enemy aircraft. The Public Health (Coal Mines Refuse) Act of 1939 imposed a legal obligation on the owners of such banks to "employ best practicable means to prevent them from firing."[47] Notwithstanding the public health rationale implicit in the title of the act, the driving motivation was protection against danger from bombs, not fumes. The Alkali Inspectorate made coal banks its number one enforcement priority during the war years, and, as a result, the number of burning banks fell from 142 to one between 1939 and 1943. This was accomplished primarily through the use of fine water spraying and the addition of insulating layers within the piles, a technological solution discussed and rejected by the *Versailles* court in 1935.[48]

By the 1950s, gob pile fires were the object of growing public concern in the United States, too, as evidenced by the number of cases pending before the Pennsylvania Supreme Court at the time. A 1956 article published in the *Journal of the Air Pollution Control Association* notes that whereas there had hitherto been little pressure for mines to control fires from gob piles, that was likely to change in response to what that article termed "recent public concern." The encouraging news, however, was that there existed practicable means for abating the fumes, primarily through the layering method.[49] The method was clearly not a recent innovation, as it had been among the alternatives urged by the plaintiffs in *Versailles*. The novel element (if not in Pennsylvania then perhaps elsewhere) was that, in contrast to earlier decades, some mines now faced regulatory incentives to invest in this technology.

Perhaps it was in response to his firsthand familiarity with the failures of the existing regime that Judge Musmanno opted in *Waschak* for a solution that would provide the necessary prompt for industrial sources to invest in promising, albeit infrequently used and thereby insufficiently tested, control methods.[50] In doing so, he followed in the footsteps of those judges who, since the end of the nineteenth century, had forged a new, nonabsolutist model of air pollution nuisance injunction aimed at incremental abatement through available means of control as the following, by then half-century-old, Pennsylvania Supreme Court decision illustrates.

SULLIVAN V. JONES & LAUGHLIN STEEL CO. (1904): BAT INJUNCTIONS

Just after the turn of the century, the Pennsylvania Supreme Court had already granted this kind of injunctive relief. In a dispute where underlying facts bore strong resemblance to those of *Richards's Appeal*, the court fashioned a remedy aimed at incremental abatement through available technology (1869). Like the Richards family, the *Sullivan* plaintiffs lived on a bluff overlooking a large metal producer, the Jones & Laughlin Steel Company. Their complaint focused on the large quantities of ore dust that had begun to settle on their neighborhood after the company drastically expanded its furnaces' capacity in 1898. The plaintiffs attributed a decline of one-quarter to half the value of their property to damage from the greasy soot, and they successfully petitioned for an injunction. In upholding the injunction, the Pennsylvania Supreme Court distinguished this case from *Richards's Appeal, Huckenstine's*, and other decisions wherein it had declined to grant similar relief on the grounds that, in contrast to the other situations, the nuisance Sullivan complained of amounted to practical confiscation of property and was thus different in kind "from those cases in which the rule is laid down that people who live in such a city, or within its sphere of usefulness, do so of choice, and, therefore, voluntarily submit themselves to its peculiarities and its discomforts."[51] Put differently, whereas the earlier cases concerned the "trifling inconvenience" of discomforting fumes, at issue here was concrete, visible, and substantial damage to property.

As the court emphasized in *Sullivan*, its injunction was exclusively directed to the potentially abatable problem of ore dust. The lower court had discussed two alternative control measures proposed by the plaintiffs: a switch to a less polluting type of ore and the installation of dust-capturing devices. Finding the ore substitution infeasible, and concluding that the success of available pollution-control devices was not assured, "they being, to a great extent, matters of experiment,"[52] the lower court had refused to enjoin, invoking *Richards's Appeal* among other cases. In overturning the lower court's decision, the Pennsylvania Supreme Court issued the injunction for the very purpose of spurring such experimentation. If in the earlier case it had been up to the plaintiff to prove that particular solutions could work, the court now turned the argument from uncertainty on its head, reasoning that

> [i]t is, therefore, by no means certain that the appellee will not be able to obviate, as is its duty, the continuance of the great injury done to the appellants, either by substituting another ore for the "Mesaba" or by adopting appliances that will prevent the escape of dust from "slips."[53]

Four years after the injunction, the dispute returned to the State Supreme Court, after the lower court found the Jones & Laughlin Company in contempt of the injunction.[54] Its finding had followed nearly two thousand pages of testimony detailing the company's extensive efforts at abatement, on the one hand, and the continuing ore dust problem, on the other. Regarding the scope of the company's control efforts, the lower court concluded that

> [t]he evidence in this case shows most conclusively that neither trouble nor expense has been spared by the defendants to prevent the escape of ore dust from their furnaces. . . . Every known method of operation, every experiment, however costly, has been carefully investigated and thoroughly tried to prevent

the escape of ore dust . . . These defendants, we are satisfied have done every-thing human ingenuity could suggest, or human experience indicate, to prevent their furnaces from emitting ore dust.[55]

Nevertheless, since the evidence also conclusively showed that, despite these efforts, the ore dust problem remained unsolved, the lower court felt compelled to cite the company for contempt.

The State Supreme Court disagreed and returned to its familiar trivializ-ing formula, stating that "[w]hat the court found in this proceeding was nothing more than 'annoyance, inconvenience and injury' to which the appellees must submit 'as part of their lot as citizens of the 'Iron City,' from which relief cannot be given them in equity by closing the plant of the steel company."[56] Despite this apparent retreat, it was not with respect to the actual scope of the remaining injury that the two courts primarily differed, but with respect to the meaning of the injunction itself. While the lower court worked from the assumption that compliance with this injunction was to be measured in terms of air-quality results and thus, reluctantly, cited the company for contempt, the Supreme Court em-ployed criteria based on effort and available technology. Having been persuaded, as the lower court was, that the company spared no effort, the State Supreme Court was thus able to conclude that what the injunction "intended to arrest has been arrested."[57] Although this may sound as though the court had evaluated the sufficiency of the defendant's compli-ance with the injunction in terms of an improvement in local air quality and pollution reduction, such an assessment was not the actual criterion underlying the court's conclusion. Rather, the court was responding to the assertion that the company had indeed done all that it feasibly could, in effect rendering this decision a BAT injunction. Available technology may not be sufficient to the task of eliminating all pollution, but in place of complete relief, the goal of this partial injunction (in the absence of a parallel statutory regime) was to create sufficient incentive that whatever could be done, would be done.

Georgia v. Tennessee Copper is perhaps the most important example of this type of injunction. The case, which was discussed earlier in the context of differences between justices Holmes and Harlan regarding the scope of the police power, had resulted in an injunction.[58] But as in *Sulli-van v. Jones & Laughlin Steel Co.* three years prior, the Georgia injunction aimed at the implementation of incremental improvements, rather than at a shutdown or relocation. The complex decree, formulated by the spe-cially appointed masters who were to oversee its enactment for years, required the defendant to curtail its production, install emission-control devices, limit the sulfur content of its ore, and report systematically on the amount of ores processed and the emissions released.[59] Under the terms of the decree, masters and inspectors received biweekly reviews of the defendants' records and were granted unimpeded access to their facilities.[60] It was only in 1938 (three decades after the first decision in the case) that the Supreme Court finally vacated all relevant orders and decrees.[61]

The same copper-smelter pollution problem that was at issue in Georgia had reached the Tennessee Supreme Court three years before in *Madison v. Ducktown Sulphur, Copper & Iron, Co.* (1904).[62] As in the Great Copper Trials in South Wales of the 1830s, the plaintiffs in *Madison* were farmers who complained both of the devastation of their crops and of injury to their health resulting from the smelters' sulfuric smoke. As in the South Wales case, the Tennessee Supreme Court refused the request for injunction. Working from the assumption that there existed no economically feasible means of reducing the pollution further, the Tennessee Court equated an injunction with a shutdown and the relevant balance as one between "several small tracts of land, aggregating in value less than $1,000,"[63] and "property worth nearly $2,000,000, and two great mining and manufacturing enterprises, that are engaged in work of very great importance, not only to their owners, but to the State, and to the whole country as well."[64] But in a decision that harked back to the logic of *Richards's Appeal*, the Tennessee Supreme Court awarded the plaintiffs damages in lieu of the injunction. Whereas the award may have allowed the farmers to relocate, it did nothing to reduce the severe pollution problem, as Georgia's lawsuit shows. Almost seven decades later, the choice between the alternative approaches pursued by the Tennessee and U.S. supreme courts with respect to this pollution dispute was faced again by the *Boomer* court. Rejecting the managerial function inherent in issuing a technological injunction, the *Boomer* majority, like the Tennessee Supreme Court in *Madison*, restricted its remedy to damages.

A convergence of two factors appears to account for the rise of BAT injunctions: first, increased public pressure for air-pollution abatement; and second, technological improvements in the available means of pollution abatement.[65] But the extent of investment in pollution control precipitated by such injunctions cannot be properly assessed simply by counting their number, without systematic analysis of the postdecree history of each antipollution injunction handed down. Only in retrospect can one tell the difference between injunctions that yielded a shutdown or industrial relocation from those that resulted in no compliance or led to partial abatement. Although historical data on this question are sorely lacking, there are strong reasons to assume that BAT injunctions were few and far between and that the vast majority of pollution sources, especially where they did not inflict significant visible property damage, remained completely uncontrolled.

BAT injunctions fell haphazardly upon enterprises; only producers un-
lucky enough to become targets of successful litigation were made to implement potentially costly controls, which the vast majority of their competitors could avoid. The few industrial defendants facing such lawsuits
thus had every incentive to invoke any adversarial defense tactic at their
disposal, most importantly the threat to leave the area in search of friend-
lier neighbors. Finally, evidentiary impediments would have made BAT
injunctions particularly unlikely where the relevant injury from the pollution was to health and comfort rather than property. As Justice Holmes
conceded in *Georgia v. Tennessee Copper*, Georgia has "established its
right" to a remedy in the case through proof of "injury to vegetation if
not to health."[66] As discussed before, the significance of the sentence in
the opinion needs to be understood in its relation to divisions within the
court regarding the scope of the police power and as a counterpoint to
Justice Holmes's insistence elsewhere in the same opinion that Georgia's
authority to seek pollution abatement derived directly from its "quasi-
sovereign" power rather than from its response to injury suffered by private citizens under its domain.

But in its distinction between injury to vegetation and health, the statement above makes clear what was at stake in making regulatory interventions in this instance contingent upon proof of harm. In the absence of
damage to vegetation, the fumes as such would not have provided a rationale for an injunction either in *Georgia* or in most other cases. This in
part, was a problem that the Alkali Act had sought to solve. But for those
living in industrial locales in the United States, there was little hope for
mitigation of invisible fumes under the common law regime.

CHAPTER SIX

"Inspected Smoke": The Perpetual Mobilization Regime

> "Isn't it nice to have inspected smoke?"
> —*From a 1903 poem*

THROUGHOUT the nineteenth and well into the twentieth century, the term "smoke," in U.S. and British colloquial usage, referred to the mix of visible and invisible constituents currently known as air pollution. The technical and legal meaning of the term, however, was applied more narrowly to the visible particulate emissions created when coal, burning under conditions of incomplete combustion, released volatile matter in the form of sooty particles made up of unburned carbon, tar, ash, and other compounds.[1] In England, control of smoke and gases (noxious vapors) was split between two separate regimes until the passage of the 1956 Clean Air Act. Noxious vapors were the responsibility of the Alkali Inspectorate under the Alkali Act, whereas smoke remained under the control of local authorities under the Public Health Act of 1875 (and subsequent legislation).[2] In the United States the beginnings of administrative regulation of gases would not come until the early 1950s. Instead, air-pollution regulation (outside of common-law nuisance suits) was applied exclusively to smoke between 1867, when the first municipal antismoke ordinance was passed in the United States, and the post–World War II era.

Enacted by St. Louis, that ordinance required all chimneys to rise twenty feet above surrounding buildings. A Pittsburgh ordinance two years later prohibited locomotives operating within the city from using bituminous coal.[3] Types of coal vary in the relative amount of volatile matter they contain and, consequently, in their smoke-producing potential. Whereas the amount of volatile combustible matter is quite low in anthracite (hard) coal, bituminous (soft) coal is high in these substances, and hence in the emissions it causes. Western Pennsylvania's vast bituminous coal fields were the reason that Pittsburgh and other Midwestern cities became industrial magnets during the mid-1800s, but they were also responsible for these cities' reputations for smoky air compared to cities such as Philadelphia and New York, where anthracite coal was used predominantly.[4] *Richards's Appeal* (1868), discussed in the previous chapter, was the first in a series of air-pollution nuisance cases arising in recently industrialized states and concerning smoke from bituminous coal.[5] While the Pennsylvania Supreme Court refused to issue an injunction requiring a switch in fuels, opting instead for damages and separation, Pittsburgh's 1869 ordinance suggests that there existed a broader constituency in the city for imposing regulatory restrictions on the use of bituminous coal. Air quality conditions in the city provided ample incentive for such a move. The city, wrote a reporter for the *Atlantic Monthly* in 1868, was "just visible through the mingled smoke and mist, and every object in it is black. Smoke, smoke, smoke—everywhere smoke!"[6] Yet the 1869 ordinance appears to have been ignored: while fuel substitution would ultimately prevent this manner of pollution, this strategy would not be implemented for approximately eighty years.

The British Parliament passed its first smoke law in 1819, and U.S. municipal regulation of smoke began in the late 1860s. In both countries, however, it would take until the post–World War II era for the smoke to clear. The smoke lingered long after cities found adequate solutions to dirty water, open sewage, uncollected garbage, and other environmental problems that had plagued them earlier in the nineteenth century.[7] This was not for lack of public mobilization, or for that matter, an absence of regulation. In Chicago, Pittsburgh, St. Louis, Cincinnati, New York, and other American cities from the 1880s onward, women's clubs, business groups, and engineering societies energetically mobilized against the smoke. These campaigns produced voluminous studies and reports, sympathetic newspaper editorials, and massive petition drives. By 1920, these efforts had led to the enactment of antismoke ordinances in nearly every major American city and the creation of smoke inspection bureaus with significant administrative authority.[8] Nevertheless, the promises of these public campaigns rang hollow when all that the ordinances and inspectors were able to achieve, by and large, was "inspected smoke." The smoke subsided when cleaner, more convenient and easily available gas, oil, and electric energy sources deprived coal of its competitive advantage during the postwar era. Against this backdrop in both England and the United States, regulators finally stepped in to induce and accelerate technological change.

In this respect, the history of smoke abatement in both England and the United States differs markedly from that of Germany. In 1853, the Prussian Ministry of Commerce added a "smoke clause" to its business licensing law, making smokeless combustion mandatory for steam engines and other large furnaces. Although smoke problems in Germany at the time were nowhere as severe as those in England, the ministry explained "that Prussian officials should take precautions in case a smoke nuisance of the London type developed in Prussian cities."[9] The success of this approach was evident seven decades later when members of a 1921 British Committee traveled to learn "how the Germans abated smoke." In contrast to comparable cities in England, they reported that German "great towns like Düsseldorf were pleasant and agreeable places of residence."[10]

This happened in Germany notwithstanding the absence of a civic anti-smoke movement like those that developed in both England and the United States.[11] Rather than being the product of citizen agitation for relief, smoke abatement in Germany emerged as part of the medical policing mission of the state, and its approach relied on prescriptive licensing standards, including prohibitions on the use of bituminous coal by industrial furnaces.[12] Avoiding this approach, the laws enacted in response to public agitation in England and the United States prohibited the emission of black smoke, but in a manner that placed upon prosecuting authorities the burden of proving that the smoke was of sufficient blackness and that it could be practicably controlled. More importantly, this regulatory regime depended on the vigilance of the public to alert authorities to illegal emission of smoke, and in practice imposed nearly insurmountable requirements for perpetual mobilization on the part of citizen groups. This chapter examines the mobilization demand imposed on pollution-affected publics by such regimes, together with their associated propensity to rely on prosecution as a primary enforcement tool.

The 1853 Prussian law served as the foundation on which the contemporary German approach to regulation was built. U.S. arrangements similarly reveal their nineteenth-century roots. As chapter 7 will argue, the smoke abatement institutions that American cities put in place during the nineteenth century—particularly their perpetual mobilization requirements—would later shape the course of American regulation of localized air pollution by local and state agencies.

ENGLISH ANTISMOKE EFFORTS PRIOR TO 1880

Heavy smoke, even if it left clothes dirty, buildings sullied, and eyes smarting, was an inseparable element of the environment for most residents of industrial cities such as Pittsburgh or London. To those who had known nothing but life under its pall, smoke was as inevitable and taken for granted as inclement weather. Moreover, far from being a self-evident evil, smoke was imbued by many with positive connotations, ranging from the intimate family hearth to the strides of industrial progress.[13] The task of reformers from the sixteenth century on was thus twofold: first, to make the case that smoke was an "evil" in need of abatement; and second, to demonstrate the feasibility of this goal.

Bituminous coal, known then as "sea-coal," first drew protest in England during the time of Edward I (1272–1307), when by varying accounts a man was hung, decapitated, or tortured in 1307 for having filled the air with "a pestilential odor" from his burning coal.[14] By 1659 John Evelyn wrote of a London cloaked in "such a cloud of sea-coal, as if there be a resemblance of hell upon earth, it is in this volcano in a foggy day: this pestilent smoak, which corrodes the very yron, and spoils all the moveables, leaving a soot on all things that it lights: and so fatally seizing on the lungs of the inhabitants, that cough and consumption spare no man."[15] Two years later in *Fumifugium* or *The Inconveniencie of the Aer and the Smoak of London Dissipated*, Evelyn further described the smoke's ill effects and outlined proposals for reforms, including the substitution of wood, or charcoal, for fuel and the transfer of polluting industries away from the city.[16]

During this era, a number of inventors were already actively in search of a mechanical means of reducing chimney smoke. In 1686, a Mr. Justel read before the Philosophical Society "An Account of an Engine that Consumes Smoke," and in 1716, a Fellow of the Royal Society published a work entitled "Fire Improved: Being a New Method of Building Chimneys so as to Prevent their Smoking."[17] By the 1770s and 1780s patents for a number of smoke-consumption devices had been issued. These inventions built on the understanding that smoke resulted from incomplete coal combustion and that its prevention consequently depended upon management of the flow and distribution of air within the furnace. Accordingly, the various designs promoted more efficient stoking and better oxidation through improved drafts.[18] These devices showed significant promise, particularly with regard to reducing smoke from steam engines. Like the previously discussed Gossage Towers, they received little use due to the absence of sufficient regulatory incentives.

The common law's failure to bring existing smoke-control technology into broad use prompted the appointment of a parliamentary smoke committee in 1819. Frustrated by London's deteriorating air quality, an energetic MP named Michael Angelo Taylor, who had earlier worked for improved lighting and paving in the metropolis, moved to establish a select committee "to inquire how far it may be practicable to compel persons using Steam Engines to erect them in a manner less prejudicial to public health and public comfort."[19] Taylor's initial impulse in drafting his committee's legislative recommendations was to force furnace operators to install available but rarely utilized smoke abatement devices through "a declaratory law making the present construction of furnaces a nuisance."[20] The proposal, which was soon discarded as too radical, was nevertheless in keeping with the "nuisance per se" formula.

As discussed in chapter 4, this was a common legislative device for conferring the common law's imprimatur on prescriptive, continental-styled, regulatory standards. Laws declaring the use of flammable materials in the construction of housing a nuisance per se are among the earliest examples of this legislative technique.[21] Taylor had initially hoped for the passage of a law that would follow this model and construe failure to employ smoke-prevention means as a nuisance per se, without regard to proof of a particular harm. But this goal was hampered by the fact that smoke, unlike fire and other traditional objects of nuisance per se legislation, was not a self-evident hazard. Though impressed with the effectiveness of the smoke-prevention devices it observed, the committee enacted in 1821 a bill that moved only slightly beyond existing common law.[22] A second parliamentary smoke-investigation committee produced two reports but no legislation, because "no witness could produce hard evidence that smoke was injurious to health."[23]

The discovery that bacteria-contaminated water could spread cholera and other epidemic diseases prompted the passage of the 1848 Public Health Act and, by the 1850s, municipal investment in and control of water supplies.[24] Soon thereafter, British cities began to take responsibility for additional preventative measures, including the containment of sewage, the collection of refuse, and the cleaning of streets, which until then had been the province of various private entrepreneurs.[25] Smoke abatement fit naturally with these municipal cleanliness measures, but reformers' efforts lagged in this arena because, unlike other contemporary public health measures, smoke abatement could not rely upon the germ theory of disease for justification.

Sanitary efforts against smoke gained an important ally in Lord Palmerton, who pursued smoke abatement and other social reforms vigorously during his brief tenure in the Home Office. A short bill he brought to Parliament in July 1853 became the Smoke Nuisance Abatement (Metropolis) Act by August that year. It was, notwithstanding its title's reference to nuisance abatement, a prescriptive technological standard requiring that "Every Furnace within the Metropolitan District, and Every Steam Boat on Thames . . . shall be fitted with an apparatus for consuming Smoke or shall burn Coke instead of Coal."[26] As such, Lord Palmerton's law closely paralleled the approach adopted that same year by the Prussian law discussed earlier. But the Palmerton law diverged from the Prussian model in its inclusion of what came to be known as a Best Practicable Means (BPM) clause.

As enacted, the 1853 law included an exemption allowing judges to remit penalties where defendants' furnaces "consume and burn as far as possible all the Smoke."[27] Exemptions of this nature had appeared in earlier smoke legislation: an 1842 City of Leeds ordinance imposed a fine of

42 shillings for smoke offenders who failed to use the best practicable means (BPM), and other cities soon followed suit.[28] Because defendants typically argued that they already employed the best practicable means, judges tended to place the burden of proof as to the superiority and practicability of alternative measures upon prosecutors. Their situation was thus parallel to that of private nuisance plaintiffs and yielded similar, generally unsuccessful, results. The ubiquity of BPM clauses, an 1846 parliamentary report concluded, made convictions under the local antismoke laws almost impossible to obtain.[29]

Lord Palmerton's undersecretary "felt obliged to remind his master that it would not be proper for him to give orders to a magistrate." Yet even without such direct pressure, the large crop of convictions in the years immediately subsequent to the passage of the 1853 law suggests that judges understood and complied with what the Home Secretary expected them to do.[30] In the absence of similar political engagement by subsequent Home Secretaries, however, persuading judges that all practicable abatement means were already in place was an easy task for many defendants. BPM clauses gave judges discretion to decide on the practicability of technological means of abatement, the most important of which at the time was a switch in fuels. The Alkali Act, in contrast, transferred that discretion from the judges to the Alkali Inspectorate.

As chapter 3 showed, beginning with the Alkali Act of 1874, the Inspectorate's mandate defined its authority through reference to BPM. In contrast to smoke regulation, where BPM clauses tended to impede abatement, the same formula became the key to the Alkali Act's success. The difference followed from the Alkali Inspectorate's avoidance of prosecution and its reliance, for the most part, on voluntary compliance. Under this cooperative regime, BPM transformed from a legalistic evidentiary burden into a consensual administrative guideline.[31] This might well have worked with respect to smoke, but the Alkali Inspectorate did not succeed in adding that component of pollution to its mandate.

A number of elements contributed to this failure to expand the domain of the inspectorate. A crucial factor in the initial passage of the Alkali Act had been the support of the alkali industry itself, given the availability of the Gossage Towers. In contrast to the hydrochloric acid that prompted the Alkali Act, smoke was produced by a vast number of diverse industrial and residential sources, each of which had much less capacity or incentive to cooperate. Furthermore, the main technological option of switching from bituminous to anthracite coal directly threatened the interests of powerful bituminous coal mine owners' in northern England.[32] Finally, unlike noxious vapors, smoke had been the purview of local authority regulation through a variety of earlier sanitary acts. The Local Government Boards came out strongly in support of maintaining this practice and in opposition to shifting control of smoke to the centralized authority of the Alkali Inspectorate. Their view prevailed, and the Public Health Act of 1875 relegated smoke, together with other sanitary nuisances, to local authority control.[33]

The limitations of this decentralized regime became increasingly evident during the 1870s and 1880s through a series of severe fogs. F.A.R. Russell's 1880 book, *London Fogs*, analyzed deaths during intense fog incidents in 1873 and 1880 in comparison to average death rates. Russell attributed an excess five hundred deaths to the former and no fewer than two thousand to the latter.[34] For the first time, smoke was cast by these numbers as a threat as potentially catastrophic as that posed by long dreaded epidemics.[35] The study invigorated the efforts of an already growing antismoke movement in London and other British cities during the early 1880s. At the center of this movement was the Fog and Smoke Committee (later the National Smoke Abatement Institution), a lobbying group whose members came from the upper echelons of London society. The group focused on the need to subject the hitherto exempted smoke from private dwellings to control. Hoping to demonstrate that practicable means for abating the smoke were already at hand, the Fog and Smoke Committee mounted a major exhibition of smoke abatement appliances in 1880. More than 100,000 people visited the exhibition in London before it moved to Manchester in 1882.[36]

SMOKE IN AMERICA: 1881–1948

News of London's emergent antismoke movement helped spawn antismoke efforts in the United States. The late 1800s were a time of intense trans-Atlantic exchange, and Progressive-era American reformers were especially cognizant of and influenced by contemporary developments in England.[37] American cities followed the British lead regarding numerous municipal sanitary reforms, and it was probably not by coincidence that Chicago, parallel to London, enacted an antismoke ordinance in 1881.[38] During the 1890s, the American antismoke movement gained real momentum with the rise of grassroots efforts in Pittsburgh, St. Louis, Cincinnati, New York, and other cities. As in England, these groups were largely comprised of and supported by the well-to-do and politically influential segments of the community, but in the United States the prominence of women groups, such as The Women's Organization of St. Louis, the Ladies' Health Association of Pittsburgh, and The Women's Club of Cincinnati, added a distinct configuration to the antismoke campaign.[39]

Women's groups often justified their antismoke activism in "municipal housekeeping" terms compatible with contemporary constructions of women as guardians of the cleanliness of their homes and the health of their families. Thus members of the Wednesday Club, an organization of top-drawer St. Louis women, offered both health and cleanliness in 1892 as their justification for taking up the fight against smoke, explaining,

> We feel that the present condition of our city, enveloped in a continual cloud of smoke, endangers the health of our families, especially those of weak lungs and delicate throats, impairs the eyesight of our school children, and adds infinitely to our labors and our expenses as housekeepers, and is a nuisance no longer to be borne with submission.[40]

Opponents were quick to attack both aspects of this argument. Where the smoke's alleged injury to property, cleanliness, or aesthetics was concerned, they countered with images of smoke as a praiseworthy symbol of industry and economic progress. For example, coal dealer William P. Rend argued in an 1892 speech before the Union League Club of Chicago that "[s]moke is the incense burning on the altars of industry. It is beautiful to me."[41] With respect to smoke's purported ill effects on health, these same opponents condemned any such claims as mere speculation. Thus, when a Pittsburgh physician argued later the same year that the fact that smoke killed trees and other plants suggested that it harmed humans as well, the same coal dealer interjected, "Now, I am not a doctor, but if I was, I probably would differ with that gentleman. I believe that smoke is healthy. I challenge the doctor to prove that it is unhealthy."[42] When answered that the presence of carbon deposits in the lungs of cadavers indicates smoke-induced injury to health, Rend turned to the argument that pulmonary carbon could help to purify air as it passed into the blood. Rather than a hazard, smoke was, in fact, beneficial to health. Although such characterizations of air-pollution fumes as salubrious disinfectants declined in influence as the nineteenth century progressed, they remained part of the debate until the start of the twentieth century.[43]

As Rend correctly perceived, the political burden of proving smoke's harm fell upon those who advocated its abatement, a task made all but impossible by the rudimentary state of the relevant science. In 1897, the best that the president of Philadelphia's Board of Health could offer on this matter was the equivocal statement, "[F]rom the evidence collected there can hardly be a reasonable doubt that there is from this cause a possibility of injury to health."[44] By the early 1900s, however, scientific research, largely coming out of Europe, was beginning to yield more systematic evidence about the detrimental effects of smoke. In 1905, the German physician Louis Ascher reported on an experiment that exposed animals infected with tuberculosis to varying levels of smoke. He discovered that small infected animals died faster when exposed to the smoke. Ascher's finding, together with additional scientific progress in the study of smoke, finally led the American Medical Association to abandon its neutrality on the issue and to advocate making smoke control part of the larger campaign against tuberculosis and pneumonia.[45]

During the first decade of the twentieth century, physicians assumed an increasingly visible role within the antismoke campaign, and their presence revived and enhanced the legitimacy of the movement, which had lain dormant during the economic depression of the mid-1890s.[46] Despite the medical profession's growing commitment to the cause, understandings of how and why smoke injured health continued to lack scientific rigor. While physicians repeatedly observed a correlation between levels of smoke and various diseases, the causal forces underlying this observation remained unclear. One influential theory emphasized the impact of reduced sunlight on resistance to disease. Thus in a twist on earlier assertions regarding smoke's antiseptic benefits, a 1922 book argued that "[t]hose towns which have their sunlight diminished through smoke are deprived to a greater extent of a powerful, natural germicide, and in such places man's bacterial enemies have every opportunity to lead prolonged and mischievous lives."[47] More persuasively, lack of sunshine was likewise blamed for increased depression, suicide, and crime in smoke-affected areas.[48]

As had been the case throughout the nineteenth century, those opposing the regulation of smoke stressed the need for further scientific investigation of smoke's impact on health. For example, the authors of a 1911 railroad-funded report criticizing earlier recommendations for the electrification of Chicago's trains wrote,

> The contrast which appears, for example, between the frequency and vehemence with which smoke is denounced and the amount of experimental or statistical evidence as to the effects of smoke upon human health, is rather striking. . . . Numerous detailed observations, experiments and analyses have yet to be made before the general subject of smoke abatement can be said to have attained a truly scientific form.[49]

The need for better data on smoke's effects was the only conclusion shared by both sides of this debate prior to World War I. A plethora of studies conducted around that time variously sought to measure, quantify, analyze, and define all dimensions of the smoke problem. The most important of these was an extensive study undertaken by the University of Pittsburgh between 1912 and 1914 using a grant from Richard B. Mellon. The project brought together a large, interdisciplinary team and resulted in the publication of nine bulletins devoted to the effects of smoke on health, vegetation, weather, building materials, human psychology, and the economy. Only one of these bulletins, entitled "Some Engineering Phases of Pittsburgh's Smoke Problem," moved from the study of the problem to possible solutions. It began by declaring that "[t]here is nothing impossible or wonderful about the smokeless combustion of even Pittsburgh coal."[50] Smoke, in other words, was amenable to technological controls given the right regulatory incentives.

SMOKE ABATEMENT AND THE POLICE POWER

Smoke reformers encountered two separate challenges in their campaign to implement such incentives. First, they had to overcome powerful political opposition and persuade cities, and later states, to enact smoke abatement laws. Second, these reformers met an even more formidable challenge in the courts. The first smoke ordinances (in St. Louis and Pittsburgh) were in essence technology standards restricting the use of bituminous coal and requiring tall stacks. There is no record to suggest that the laws were ever enforced, either because they were intended from their inception to be only symbolic gestures, or because it was feared that the laws would not withstand judicial review.

Introducing a different model, Chicago enacted an ordinance in 1881 declaring the emission of "dense smoke" from places other than private residences to be a public nuisance. The ordinance imposed a fine of no less than five and no more than fifty dollars, and delegated its enforcement to the Commissioner of Health and the Superintendent of Police.[51] In contrast to the technology standards of the earlier ordinances, the Chicago law required no specific means of control and gave judges authority over whether prosecutors proved that the source emitted smoke of sufficient density to justify conviction. After an initial spurt of successful prosecutions, public pressure waned, and little smoke abatement action ensued.

Smoke reappeared as a major political issue in Chicago and other Midwestern cities during the early 1890s.[52] In 1892 Pittsburgh passed an ordinance making it "unlawful for any chimney or smoke stack used in connection with a stationary boiler to allow, suffer or permit smoke from bituminous coal to be emitted or escape therefrom, within a certain district."[53] The following year, St. Louis passed an ordinance declaring emission of dense black or gray smoke a nuisance and creating a commission to conduct practical tests of all devices claimed to prevent or suppress smoke and to notify the public when these devices were found satisfactory.[54] In all of the above examples, enforcement depended on proof of the emission of dense or black smoke, a vague and thus legally vulnerable standard when it came to securing convictions in court.

Enforcement efforts were aided in this regard by the 1897 arrival in the United States of the Ringelmann chart, a tool for describing and comparing the density of particular smoke plumes. It consisted of six boxes in a spectrum from white, through steadily increasing shades of gray, to black.[55] Municipal ordinances in many American cities subsequently relied on this method, usually through a prohibition on smoke exceeding a reading of no. 2 (or 40 percent shade) on the Ringelmann chart.

The approach greatly eased the evidentiary burdens on which the enforcement of smoke laws depended. The standard offered an objective measure, thus diminishing judges' discretion over the density of the smoke or the practicability of abating it. But in late nineteenth-century America these very limitations on judicial discretion made such smoke-abatement laws vulnerable under constitutional judicial review. In 1895, Pittsburgh made the emission of more than 20 percent black or dark gray smoke a public nuisance and imposed a fine on all who emitted such smoke for a period exceeding three minutes. This law was overturned in 1902 as an invalid exercise of the police power.[56] Pressure from the Pittsburgh Chamber of Commerce (revealing conflict within the business community regarding the need for smoke abatement) gave rise to another ordinance in 1906. That law allowed eight minutes of exemption per hour but was, like its predecessor, successfully challenged in court. This 1911 opinion deemed the ordinance unreasonable because it implicitly required all coal consumers to install mechanical stokers, of which there were only five hundred at the time in Pittsburgh (although the court did not explain why more stokers could not be imported to satisfy demand once the law passed).[57] The court also suggested that the city lacked the authority to pass smoke-abatement legislation of this nature under the terms of its state-enacted charter. The latter argument had previously prevailed against other municipal smoke ordinances, most notably in St. Louis, where the Missouri Supreme Court overturned the City's 1893 ordinance in 1897. The scope of cities' legislative authority had already been the subject of debate earlier in the century when cities sought to enact municipal fire-prevention measures. Critics claimed that cities could not validly move beyond what common law had traditionally defined as a public nuisance; that is, they could not undertake preventative, nuisance per se, regulatory measures. Since the institution of innovative nuisance per se ordinances aimed at fire prevention (and a host of other safety-related measures), courts had tended to ignore the critics and to uphold the municipal authority to enact them. But the critics' line of argument was to prove much more successful in challenging laws concerning municipal smoke abatement.[58]

Courts in Missouri, Minnesota, Ohio, and other states decided that proactive municipal smoke legislation required the passage of enabling state statutes. Without them, the Missouri Supreme Court explained, cities could not target smoke for abatement and regulate it preventively, but could only consider its injurious nature, that is, regulate it as nuisance-in-fact.[59] St. Louis responded by enacting a revised ordinance in 1899 forbidding only smoke that caused damage, injury, annoyance, or detriment to any inhabitants or property in the city.[60] Enforcement consequently required concrete proof that the particular smoke source in question caused such injury. A massive petition drive led to a 1901 Missouri statute that specifically enabled cities of 100,000 or more to declare smoke a nuisance per se, and other states soon followed this model.[61] A Missouri court upheld this law in 1904, and courts in other states soon concurred with this decision.[62]

As the author of a 1905 law review article observed, the focus of pertinent judicial review thus changed from the question of whether states and cities possessed the authority to regulate smoke to the *reasonableness* with which they exercised this authority—in other words, from judicial review of legislation to judicial oversight of administration.[63] Where judicial review of legislation was concerned, as the *Lochner* decision argued that same year, reasonableness depended upon a balance between regulatory means and (common-law-compatible) governmental ends.[64] The same principle, "namely moderation and proportionateness of means to ends," Ernst Freund argued a year earlier in his *Treatise on the Police Power,* is what distinguishes reasonable from unreasonable statutory administration. As to what would be likely to constitute unreasonable, or disproportionate administration, Freund added, "The question of reasonableness usually resolves itself into this: is regulation carried to the point where it becomes prohibition, destruction, or confiscation?"[65]

Doctrines of this nature cast a pall of uncertainty over the constitutionality of costly regulatory measures intended to abate smoke, especially if they could be construed as likely to shut down the offending source. In 1916, this question came before the Supreme Court in *Northwestern Laundry v. City of Des Moines.* The court explained,

> So far as the Federal Constitution is concerned, we have no doubt the State may by itself or through authorized municipalities declare the emission of dense smoke in cities of populous neighborhoods a nuisance and subject to restraint as such; and that the harshness of such legislation, or its effect upon business interests, short of a merely arbitrary enactment, are not valid constitutional objections. Nor is there any valid Federal constitutional objection in the fact that the regulation may require the discontinuance of the use of property or subject the occupant to large expense in complying with the terms of the law or ordinance.[66]

Standing on its own, this statement suggests no particular due process or any other constitutional constraint on the scope of antismoke legislation. The actual ruling in the case, however, was significantly narrower. The court ultimately concluded "[t]hat such rules and regulations are valid, *subject as they are to final consideration in the courts*, to determine whether they are reasonably adapted to accomplish the purpose of a statute [emphasis added]."[67] In other words, although a smoke ordinance is not invalidated by the mere possibility that its enforcement would result in shutdowns, the authority to legislate in this arena is affirmed only to the extent that the final decision regarding the reasonableness of any such measures remains with the courts.

Northwestern Laundry concerned an ordinance that, in addition to declaring smoke a nuisance, required permits for newly constructed furnaces and authorized city inspectors to demand the remodeling of any existing furnaces not in compliance with the standards. The Des Moines ordinance typified a new generation of antismoke laws that reflected the growing influence of engineers within municipal smoke departments. By the time of the court's decision in *Northwestern Laundry v. City of Des Moines* (1916), seventy-five American cities had passed antismoke ordinances of various types.[68] After decades of intermittent activism dating back to the efforts of women's and other civic groups during the 1880s and 1890s, the American antismoke movement was more visible and influential in the summer of 1916 than ever before. To its credit, it could claim both increasingly complex legislation and a more professional bureaucracy, but little in the way of cleaner air.

Perpetual Mobilization and Nuisance Per Se

In city after city, mobilized publics pushed for the enactment and tightening of municipal antismoke ordinances through highly organized campaigns. In St. Louis, smoke was prominent on the city's political agenda in 1893, 1901, 1906–7, and 1911, and in Pittsburgh in 1892, 1899, 1906, and 1912.[69] Other cities such as Chicago, Cincinnati, and New York showed similar patterns of recurrent antismoke mobilizations during that era and between the two world wars. In between such campaigns, however, little smoke abatement action ensued. In 1950, Raymond Tucker, who led St. Louis' final assault on the smoke, offered the following interpretation of this pattern: "After each unsuccessful attempt a feeling of apathy descended on the community. For a period of 3 to 5 years nothing would be done, then conditions would become so severe that small groups of citizens would again become aroused and a new attempt would be made."[70]

The failure of municipal agencies to achieve better smoke abatement results was explained in 1923 by Osborn Monnett, formerly Chicago's Chief Smoke Inspector: "Communities," he argued, "get just as much law enforcement as they desire. Until the public is thoroughly roused, demands smoke abatement, and shows *continued interest* in it, no permanent improvement is possible [emphasis added]."[71] Echoing this sentiment, the author of a 1933 book entitled *Stop that Smoke* put the blame for the smoke's persistence on the public's doorstep:

> Much of the public's inertia in the face of continued and obvious pollution of the atmosphere is due to an attitude of resignation, we believe, rather than to absolute indifference. . . . No wonder we see so many instances of sudden, hopeful spurts of activity against smoke relapsing into the customary desuetude. If results are immediately apparent, the citizenry pats itself on the back—and promptly disbands. If they are not, they soon tire of the effort.[72]

Common to the three accounts is the view that the key impediment to better smoke control was not lack of technological know-how, economic means, or adequate laws. It was the failure of the public to maintain the pressure necessary to ensure that the laws would be enforced. It was not enough for the public to mobilize on behalf of antismoke legislation and then to expect professional inspectors independently to tend to its administration. Instead, a burden of showing "continued interest" via perpetual mobilization fell on those who wanted to see the laws move from the books into active practice. Rather than questioning the logic of a regime that would demand such public involvement, all three accounts seemed, to varying extents, to fault the public for its lack of sustained mobilization.

Smoke abatement demanded perpetual mobilization in England as well, as the following account, published in 1922, suggests:

> During the past 30 years smoke abatement societies have arisen in this country in large numbers. They have rarely survived more than a few years. They failed in their earlier days to recognize the complexity and the difficulty of the problem, and have thought that it could be dealt with by enthusiastic propaganda, combined with larger fines and more active prosecution of manufacturers. As they gained experience, they began to appreciate the hopelessness of the problem when tackled along these lines, the members gradually lost interest, and after a time the society died, to be succeeded in a few years by another one which duly went through the same cycle.[73]

In contrast to these recurrent patterns of stop-and-go smoke regulation in both England and the United States, public mobilization appears to have been virtually irrelevant to the Alkali Inspectorate's enforcement of its mandate. The legacy of the alkali regime from its founding inspector, Angus Smith, onward was one of consistent, if incremental, regulation. This regime was conducted in an insulated fashion, away from the public eye, in a process independent of any popular mobilization. Instead, the key to this regime was cooperative relations between industry and the inspectorate.[74] In fact, during its first twenty-five years the Inspector brought a total of four prosecutions.[75]

Looking at the Alkali Inspectorate alone, it might seem that differences in organizational culture and leadership style account for the divergent trajectories of the smoke and alkali pollution control regimes within Britain. But parallels between the Alkali Inspectorate and the German experience in controlling smoke suggest that something other than internal organizational culture alone is at play. In contrast to the perpetual mobilization demanded by British and American smoke-abatement regimes, the German regime was marked by consistent implementation with minimal public participation or pressure.[76] As with the Alkali Inspectorate, the key, once again, was a cooperative relationship between regulators and industry, evident in a paucity of prosecutions. These similarities suggest that more than the particular organizational culture of the Alkali Inspectorate was at work in producing effective pollution control based on cooperative relationships with industry, and without the need for perpetual mobilization.

In similar fashion, a focus on the German regulatory regime alone could lead to the conclusion that its outcomes derived from a statist regulatory culture. But an explanation rooted solely in national culture is not supportable, given the similar avoidance of prosecutions on the part of the English Alkali Inspectorate (in contrast to the English smoke regime). Thus the German experience suggests that a lack of prosecution is not strictly a function of the internal organizational culture of the Alkali Inspectorate, and the cooperative attitude of Alkali Inspectorate suggests that the German pattern is not strictly the result of national regulatory culture. The proliferation of litigation under the English smoke regime, together with its near-absence under the Alkali Act, establishes significant variation within a single national culture. This suggests that industrial cooperation emerged not only as a function of national traditions, but also as a response to the imperatives of the type of pollution regime a firm found itself governed by.

The common denominator linking the Alkali Act and the German smoke regime, and separating both of them from British and American smoke-abatement, regimes, is the use of some manner of technology-based standards. Smoke in the United States and England was subject to nuisance per se standards as noted above; these were strictly defined as prohibitions on dense smoke without reference to the feasibility of technology to be used in its abatement. In contrast, both the German smoke and British Alkali regimes tailored regulatory interventions to the use of feasible and available means of control, in the German case through licensing.[77] If technology standards indeed were to constitute the common element of pollution regimes able to secure cooperation from industry and avoid imposing requirements of perpetual public mobilization, the mechanisms by which they achieve these results are not immediately apparent.

The argument made here is that the absence or presence of regulatory discretion in nuisance per se or technology regimes, respectively, lies behind the patterns identified above. Violations of a nuisance-based emissions standard—such as the smoke density standard employed in England and the United States in the late nineteenth and early twentieth centuries—demanded abatement, regardless of feasibility, and left no discretion to the enforcing agency. This lack of discretion was exacerbated by the fact that defining the standard in terms of visible emissions made professional or scientific expertise all but irrelevant to the detection of violations; any citizen could quickly assess the apparent density of smoke emissions and demand enforcement action by the agency, which had little autonomy in its choice of response. Limiting discretion on the part of agencies would have tended to reduce incentives for voluntary cooperation on the part of regulated firms because it decreased the capacity of agencies to seek solutions that stopped short of absolutist abatement demands that took no account of feasibility.

In the absence of voluntary cooperation, agencies were left with virtually no enforcement alternative other than prosecution. Prosecution, on the other hand, was costly in terms of both human resources and political capital. Chronically understaffed pollution agencies had to be quite selective about cases they brought to court. Citizen mobilization had the potential to alter this outcome by changing the agency's internal calculus regarding prosecution in two ways. First, it worked to alter the political landscape by lowering the political costs of prosecution and raising the penalty for inaction. Second, by identifying and documenting pollution sources, citizen mobilization lowered the material costs of prosecution as citizen-inspectors served effectively as gatherers of evidence that strapped agency personnel could not assemble. Thus the nuisance regimes of England and the United States relied on prosecution because lack of agency discretion tended to restrict the cooperation-based route of abatement; in turn, a prosecution-based regime demanded perpetual mobilization of pollution-affected populations because, in the absence of such mobilization, agencies frequently found it more appealing to turn a blind eye to mandates that may have been infeasible in the first place.

In contrast, the technology-based regimes, such as the Alkali Inspectorate and the German pollution regime, began first and foremost with agency discretion as to the feasibility of mitigation technology. Rather than absolute abatement, these regimes demanded only the application of technology that had already been judged to be feasible, and even the imposition of these technologies was typically handled on a case-by-case basis. Both factors tended to secure firms' cooperation, reducing the need for prosecutions as an enforcement mechanism. Citizen mobilization in this process was both more difficult and less necessary than in the nuisance-based regimes. The difficulty attending citizen involvement stemmed from the complex nature of the engineering judgment needed; rather than a capacity to assess the density of visible smoke, these regimes required professional knowledge of the relevant control technologies and the production processes they were designed to abate. Since this technical judgment was rarely accessible to the layperson, the scientifically trained professional was left with greater independent discretion in this realm. By the same token, the fact that the system was run according to the logic of a professionalized, technocratic cadre rendered grassroots political mobilization virtually irrelevant to the process.

Differences observed in the two types of regulatory regimes are in part a product of the greater acceptance in Germany of the state's right to regulate; the vast majority of industrialists viewed it as their duty to comply, and those that did not exposed themselves to censure by their colleagues. For example, in the early twentieth century, the *Bund der Industriellen*, the second largest association of industrialists in Germany, publicly criticized the technological ignorance of entrepreneurs who allowed their companies to emit smoke.[78] In contrast, American industrialists had no compunctions about mobilizing against requirements for abatement. In Chicago, the representatives of twenty manufacturing interests formed "a defensive association against the city smoke inspectors," in order to ask the City Council for "relief from the injustices of the smoke ordinance."[79] Hence culture, in the sense of national traditions regarding the role of the state is clearly operative here, though its primary route of influence appears to be via the selection of the relevant regulatory regime.

As previously noted, nuisance per se differed from traditional common law nuisances doctrines in that it did not require proof of harm to establish liability or trigger administrative enforcement. Rather, smoke as such was the relevant offense, a factor that greatly reduced the evidentiary burdens associated with this regime, and in this it represented a policy move in the direction of the continental model. But, as the following section explains, the American smoke regime retained distinctively reactive characteristics in its de facto modes of enforcement. This was most evident in the important role of private citizens in the smoke bureaus' enforcement efforts.

During the late nineteenth and early twentieth centuries, most cities had no more than a handful of inspectors to oversee thousands of potentially smoky stacks. Since the beginning of antismoke efforts in America, lay activists had helped fill the gap by gathering the evidence necessary to support legal enforcement. As early as 1874, the Chicago Citizen's

Association "undertook to determine some of the legal aspects of the problem of smoke prevention, and to aid smoke inspectors in their work by assisting in the prosecution of the more conspicuous offenders."[80] In 1904, the Municipal Art League's Committee on Smoke Prevention submitted a report urging "[e]very citizen who sees a chimney habitually smoking should be a voluntary inspector, and register complaints at the City Hall. Public opinion can be expressed by personal condemnation of smoke offenders."[81] St. Louis, New York, and other cities also relied on members of the public during this period for registering complaints against offending sources and offering testimony regarding the damage and annoyance caused by smoke.[82] After a while, people who devoted themselves to this endeavor would tire and give up, probably hoping that others would carry the torch. However, it was always difficult to find enough bodies to keep carrying the torch, and the classic "free-rider" problem gave mobilization efforts a sporadic character and thus effectively gave agencies license to retreat into inaction.

This mode of reliance on citizen enforcement was not the exclusive domain of smoke abatement. Lawrence Friedman describes early-nineteenth-century regulation, in a variety of spheres, as tending to be "local, self-sustaining—as in the fee system—and conservative in the use of staff."[83] A narrow tax base and its ensuing fiscal constraints are the most immediate explanation as to why this reactive regulatory model evolved. But as Friedman suggests, the result conferred a distinctly reactive cast to the early American administrative state. In practice, this method meant that "[b]asically, the law let private citizens enforce what regulation there was. If no one brought a lawsuit, or complained to the district attorney about some violation, nothing was done. The state did not seriously try to administer, or carry through independently, what the statutes decreed."[84] Thus even as nuisance per se structures removed the legal necessity of proving harm, understaffing and reliance on public mobilization tended to restore the common law's customary reactivity to the regulatory regime.

For some time during the 1910s and 1920s it seemed as if the German and American models might be moving toward convergence. The period was marked by the growing influence of engineers within smoke inspection departments and a shift toward a cooperative, rather than a prosecutorial, style. Where the women's groups who had pushed early smoke legislation in most cities had tended to favor solutions based on legal prosecutions, most engineers chose strategies of cooperation.[85] A cooperative relationship developed, based on shared sensibilities and expertise between the engineers who staffed municipal inspection departments and those who worked for the manufacturers that these departments oversaw.[86]

To this extent, the American approach began to resemble the technology-driven pollution regime of Germany. Nevertheless, there remained a fundamental difference in the underlying rationales as to why business ought to cooperate in abating the smoke. The cooperative regime in America was created in tandem with the rise in efficiency rationales that attributed smoke to the inefficient burning of coal; abatement was thus cast as serving the direct interest of smoke emitters because of fuel efficiency concerns.[87] Familiar from the nineteenth century, this notion was advanced much more strongly in the 1910s and 1920s by engineers attracted to the definition of smoke as an economic waste, rather than a public health problem, especially since this win-win construction suited their professionally socialized preference for cooperation. This rationale was generally absent from German regulatory discourse around the same time. Business there was obligated to control smoke out of duty, not self-interest, whereas "fuel economy" was understood as a "burgeoning field of engineers which the state left to the judgment of entrepreneurs."[88]

The fuel conservation rationale succeeded in spurring a more cooperative U.S. regime, but this regime was vulnerable because of weaknesses in the rationale itself. Energy savings proved an insufficient incentive for voluntary smoke abatement because coal was simply too abundant and inexpensive an energy source to make significant investment in smoke control economically worthwhile.[89] Coal prices in the post–World War I era dropped, and with them the incentive to abate smoke as means of fuel conservation.[90] By casting coal savings as a central smoke-abatement rationale, municipal smoke departments in the decades before and after World War I assumed a consultative posture built on interests shared by both manufacturers and administrators. Once it became apparent that more than self-interest would be needed to abate smoke, these departments were left with a cooperative orientation but lack of authority to demand sacrifices (in contrast to Germany). As David Stradling writes, "As the salience of coal conservation waned in the 1920s and 1930s, the postwar antismoke efforts proved no more successful than those before the war, and perhaps even less so."[91]

The result was a shift to a regime that added perpetual measurement to perpetual mobilization as salient elements of its regulatory repertoire. Administrative effort focused on the quantity of smoke, rather than the ease or difficulty of its abatement. These investigative efforts gradually took an increasingly scientific turn with the invention during the 1930s of a complex mechanical lung-like device designed to quantify hourly fluctuations in smoke. Administrative investment in such arcane technology led some members of the public to view the preoccupation with smoke measurement as an impediment to actual regulation, "a somewhat unnecessary refinement, designed to give work to a lot of fussy pedants and professors. Anybody can see the smoke, and even a child can usually tell where it is coming from."[92] Similar sentiments prompted F. L. Rose's satirical encomium to "inspected smoke" in this chapter's epigraph.

By demanding perpetual mobilization and measurement, smoke-abatement regimes served to reinforce the reactive suppositions of the common law. Public nuisance mandates made intervention contingent upon citizen demands for government action but offered no regulatory rationale if these faltered while the problem continued. Although antismoke legislation explicitly moved beyond this reactive model, these laws did not result in an independent administrative mission. Instead, smoke regulation continued to depend, de facto if not de jure, on proof of public injury. Perpetual mobilization proved nearly impossible to sustain; the energy and resources brought by antismoke advocates into their campaigns inevitably dwindled due to frustration, fatigue, or a false sense of victory.

BEYOND SMOKE

By and large, "inspected smoke" was all that this "perpetual mobilization regime" was able to produce in half a century of operation. The turning point for the country's notoriously smoky cities came during the 1940s, when St. Louis, abandoning the nuisance per se approach, adopted an ordinance with an explicit technological standard requiring all consumers of high-volatile fuel to install stokers. Intended to encourage coal consumers to switch to hard coal, the ordinance likewise empowered the city to take measures to ensure the supply of such coal, which the city soon did by arranging for cheaper rail transportation of cleaner Arkansas coal.[93] Impressed by the program's success in St. Louis, Pittsburgh followed suit with a similar ordinance a year later.[94] Both World War II and strong opposition from the coal industry delayed implementation of Pittsburgh's 1941 ordinance, but starting with the winter of 1947–48, the city began to see a steady and ultimately dramatic reduction in its smoke. By that time, the availability of more convenient and reasonably priced gas, oil, and electric alternatives greatly diminished soft coal's economic appeal.

The solution, as both the plaintiff in *Richards's Appeal* (1868) and the authors of the 1869 Pittsburgh ordinance had already understood, lay in the substitution of cleaner fuels for smoky, bituminous coal. But neither they nor the many activists who for many decades had sought to bring this about would see the smoke lift during their lifetimes. A century after Germany adopted its technology-based regime, American cities, finally, conquered the smoke through the same means.

When the smoke finally dissipated, the profound sense of relief was marred by a dawning realization that smoke had never been the most important air-pollution problem; rather, many invisible and virulent pollutants had been left untouched. A 1948 incident in the Pennsylvania town of Donora, only thirty miles south of Pittsburgh, left little doubt as to the dangers indeed posed by long-ignored industrial gases. Situated within a river valley surrounded by high bluffs, Donora was particularly vulnerable to pollution during times of atmospheric inversion, when a layer of cold air kept air from circulating and thereby diffusing pollution. When one such inversion lingered for a week in October 1948, the town was engulfed in "the bittersweet reek of sulfur dioxide."[95] Complaining of headaches, nausea, and difficulty breathing, residents began to flood emergency rooms and doctors' offices. A U.S. Public Health Service Survey later put the episode's toll on life and health at twenty deaths and approximately three thousand severely and moderately affected individuals.[96]

These numbers dramatically demonstrated that far from being "trifling inconveniences," chemical fumes could shorten lives and severely injure health. In response, municipalities and states began enacting laws directed at the control of invisible as well as visible forms of air pollution. But these laws changed neither the reactive regulatory patterns nor the perpetual mobilization demands associated with the earlier smoke regime, both because they tended to rely on traditional public nuisance mandates and because their implementation fell to the same agencies or to ones modeled upon those that had earlier failed to stop the smoke.

CHAPTER SEVEN

"Odors," Nuisance, and the Clean Air Act

"ODORS" is the regulatory classification to which municipal and state agencies have assigned localized air-pollution concentrations since the early 1950s, when these bodies' jurisdiction was extended beyond smoke to the broader category, "air pollution." This chapter follows the history of this regime during the two decades prior to and subsequent to passage of the 1970 Clean Air Act (CAA), focusing on how and why localized pollution came to be defined as "odors" and on the regulatory consequences that followed from this problem definition. Most importantly, as the chapter highlights, the term "odors" imparted an aesthetic and subjective meaning to the pollution problem in question. The term rendered toxicological worry—the most pressing concern behind citizens' appeal for air-pollution abatement—largely irrelevant to regulatory policy toward these concentrations. At the same time that this approach trivialized the meaning of the problem, it also held the potential for incremental implementation of pollution controls independent of specific scientific proof that the pollution caused disease.

Congress twice put before the EPA the option of incorporating odors within the category of pollutants regulated under the CAA. Doing so would have provided the EPA with a mechanism for achieving incremental reductions of Hazardous Air Pollutants (HAPs), which are often odorous as well. But the EPA rejected this course under the argument that differences in communities' sensitivity to odors render the reactive suppositions of local and state-implemented nuisance law a more appropriate regulatory framework. Ironically, it was the CAA's absolutist—if unimplemented—promise of complete protection against risk from HAPs that allowed for the entrenchment of nuisance law in this domain. This occurred through the creation of a false distinction between HAPs (ostensibly subject to complete control) and residual aesthetic annoyances from "odors."

AN EMERGENT AIR-POLLUTION REGIME: 1947–55

Coal smoke was never much of a problem in Los Angeles, where there was little industrial development prior to Word War II. The war brought rapid industrialization and severe air-quality deterioration to an area where citizens had been accustomed to clean air, and by 1946 the issue had come to a head. Air-quality concerns of the era were divided between two categories of pollution: localized smoke and fumes in the vicinity of many refineries, chemical manufacturers, and other heavy industrial sources new to the area; and a second type of pollution that affected not only people in immediate proximity to industry but across the region. It appeared as intermittent episodes of brownish haze that settled over the Los Angeles basin, lowering visibility, irritating eyes, and leaving some residents short of breath. Beginning in 1945 the *Los Angeles Times* published a series of articles "on the smoke and fumes nuisance—the 'smog' in the Los Angeles area."[1]

The source of the "smog" problem was poorly understood but the governing assumption, at least at the start, was that it derived from overall growth in stationary industrial emissions in the area. In January 1947, the *Los Angeles Times* published a report attributing the city's growing air-pollution problem to "fumes, smoke, odors and dust" produced by a long list of industrial sources: chemical industries, refineries, food product plants, soap plants, paint plants, building materials, nonferrous reduction refining, and smelting plants. The author of the report was Raymond Tucker, the man who a few years earlier had led St. Louis's finally successful battle with smoke. Tucker came to the Los Angeles at the behest of the *Los Angeles Times* to help find similar solutions for the city's air-quality problems, ultimately recommending across-the-board reductions in discharges of "sulphur dioxide, smoke, dust, aldehydes and other noxious gases."[2] The approach was directed simultaneously at problems of localized pollution and the larger regional problem that they were thought to cause. The method, following Tucker's approach in St. Louis, was to be based on the implementation of available technological means.

Because many of the industrial sources were located outside of Los Angeles's city limits, implementing pollution controls required a regional, rather than municipal regulatory body. Enacted for this purpose, California's Air Pollution Control Act of 1947 authorized the creation of countywide air-pollution districts. The statute further authorized the district to promulgate pollution-control rules and regulations. Most importantly, the law authorized the districts to implement a permitting system under which industrial sources would be required to install pollution-control equipment, and their permit could be revoked for lack of compliance. The rationale behind this approach was ease of enforcement stemming from freedom from demands for proof of injury and simplicity of compliance monitoring.[3]

The Los Angeles County Office of Air Pollution Control—later to be renamed the Air Pollution Control District (APCD)—was established in October 1947 as the first air-pollution agency in the United States whose jurisdiction extends beyond smoke to gases. The approach it adopted initially was reminiscent of the technology regimes implemented in England, under the Alkali Inspectorate, and in Germany. The district made extensive use of this permitting authority, setting out to implement a regime that used standards derived from judgments on engineering feasibility rather than scientific evaluations of harm.[4] Showing little interest in investigating the threat to health or offering scientific justifications for pollution reduction, the district moved to require the deployment of technologically feasible mitigation measures. The policy was one of source-by-source controls across the thousands of industrial facilities in the area, with a particular emphasis on "smoke, fumes, and sulfur dioxide, from oil refineries, chemical plants, oil burning industries, and rubbish dumps."[5] At the same time, the district took the economic constraints of particular facilities into account, and "[v]ariances from the strict requirements of the law were commonly granted where control technology did not exist, was not good enough, or was unduly expensive for a particular source."[6] Both sides of this approach soon became lightning rods for political controversy.

The district's failure to produce quick and visible reductions in levels of smog resulted in public frustration. As Harold Kennedy, the attorney for the APCD, conceded in 1954, "Seven years after the creation of the Los Angeles County Air Pollution Control District . . . the problem in the Los Angeles region remains approximately the same from the viewpoint of the public. While large tonnages of air pollutants have been removed by the various activities [of the district], Los Angeles still has smog and people generally do not know all that has been accomplished."[7] On the other hand, industrial sources, most notably the oil companies, considered the policy overly strict, inequitable, and lacking in sufficient scientific rationale.[8] A 1952 report issued by the California Assembly Committee on Air and Water Pollution faulted the APCD for setting standards based upon "the ability of industry and others to meet the standards," rather than "the effects of the pollutants on the public health."[9] In particular, the committee expressed its concern regarding the specification of control technology under the district's permitting policy and its potential to impede the development of newer and better pollution-reduction measures. Presaging later critiques of the CAA's BAT provisions, a central charge of the committee was that the APCD's "blanket approach" might be "be too lenient for some and too harsh for others."[10]

While recognizing the paucity of necessary scientific knowledge for better-tailored reductions, the committee criticized the low priority, and even lack of interest, that the APCD showed in developing a better scientific foundation for its program. Whereas feasibility might be an acceptable stop-gap substitute for health-based standards, it ought not take the place of scientifically tailored regulation in the long run, according to the report. Importantly, the relevant public health problem demanding greater research, according to the committee, was that of smog. Knowledge was lacking both in terms of the pollutants and pollution sources that were responsible for smog, and of its health impacts at various concentrations. The initial presumption regarding the former question was that stationary industrial sources were at fault, but by the mid-1950s, attention began to focus on the automobile. This discovery undermined the rationale for across-the-board reductions in stationary source emissions at the same time that it separated the antismog measures from those that would reduce localized fumes in proximity to industrial sources. Thus the oil companies were able to argue against the APCD's efforts at controlling sulfur emissions from refineries on the basis of lack of "sufficient proof that the removal of the sulfur would cure the overall smog problem."[11] This criticism was echoed in the committee report where an acknowledgment of the APCD's success in reducing sulfur dioxide emissions was followed with a reference to the fact that SO_2 was "one of the least important contaminants in the Los Angeles smog."[12] Following the committee's report, a panel of scientists was appointed to review the district's research to date and to recommend enforcement priorities. Reflecting improved understandings of the sources of photochemical smog, the scientists recommended targeting two primary sources of pollution: gasoline vapors (hydrocarbons) and automobile exhausts.[13]

The emphasis, beginning in California during the 1950s, on regional pollution rather than on localized pollution "hotspots" in framing the meaning of air pollution and the rationale for its control would subsequently have a profound affect on the course of air-pollution interventions under the federal Clean Air Act regime. This regional focus was not consistent with the role that concern over acute localized pollution had played in pressuring the creation of a federal regime. The 1948 Donora incident discussed in the previous chapter helped catalyze demands across the country for greater attention to air pollution both at the state and the federal level with a floodgate of pent-up concern over chronic localized air-pollution problems, together with worry about incidents of the more acute variety. In the two years following Donora, the U.S. Public Health Service received more than thirty official requests for help in evaluating localized pollution risks in response to worried and often angry complaints from citizens.[14]

This pressure led President Truman to convene in 1950 the first United States Technical Conference on Air Pollution. The purpose of the meeting, President Truman explained in his speech to the delegates, was "to bring to bear on the problem of air pollution all the scientific knowledge at the command of industry, government, and scientific institutions" so as to "find out all we can about the relationship between air contaminants and illness."[15] Fourteen of the papers presented during the conference high-lighted possible connections between exposure to airborne pollutants and a number of diseases, including cancer.[16]

In 1955 Congress took a first cautious step toward greater federal involvement in this area. In a statute officially recognizing the existence of a nationwide air-pollution problem, Congress authorized the Department of Health, Education and Welfare (HEW) to conduct research on the health effects of air pollution and to provide technical support on air-pollution abatement, even as it emphasized that "the prevention and control of air pollution at its source is the primary responsibility of states and local government."[17] In practice, this meant that air pollution would remain under the domain of nuisance law, even if, by the mid-1950s citizens could direct their air pollution complaints to local agencies, in addition to courts.

THE PROBLEM OF "ODORS"

An article published by two Los Angeles air pollution officials in 1952 started with the following: "Malodors in any air pollution picture are likely to incur more public vexation than any other class of atmospheric contaminants."[18] The statement is significant for two reasons. It suggests that notwithstanding the growing political preoccupation with smog (evident in the legislative committee report published that year), problems of localized pollution remained a source of far deeper concern. Los Angeles was not unique in this regard. By 1955, 78 percent of sixty-seven air-pollution agencies surveyed nationwide indicated that their agencies received and handled odor complaints. The long list of sources implicated in these complaints included paint and varnish, chemical manufacturers, food processing and rendering plants, plastic and oil refineries, and producers of rubber, steel, and coke.[19]

But equally significant was the use of the term "odors" as a reference to fumes or gases. As this list suggests, "odors" was a term that lumped pollution associated with chemical manufacturers together with that of various animal and food processing-plants. The ostensible logic behind the combination of chemical and nonchemical pollution under the overarching category of odors stems from the fact that sensory perception, in both instances, occurs largely via the nose. However, both the sensations and the concerns that led to complaints against chemicals differed qualitatively.

The nose contains two distinct sets of chemically sensitive nerves, each connected to a different region of the brain. The first is the olfactory organ or bulb associated with the perception and recognition of smells, and the second is the trigeminal nerve. The discomforts associated with overstimulation of each of those nerves differ. Putrid smells are most commonly associated with nausea, and their impact is primarily olfactory. "Irritating," "tickling," or "burning" sensations characterize trigeminal exposure.[20] This is a distinct set of physiological responses sometimes known as the "common chemical sense."[21] Yet the shared terminology of "odors" eliminates this distinction, lumping together what are in practice not only very different sensations but also, more importantly, underlying concerns. Whereas some bad smells, such as sewage, can trigger deep revulsion, the concern they generate is with their immediate impact. In contrast, the worry associated with trigeminal chemical exposure often includes, and is at times predominated by, worry that caustic sensations are but warning signals against greater dangers. The list of symptoms long familiar from nuisance lawsuits—smarting or irritated eyes and stinging throats—is characteristic of trigeminally mediated sensations, the very sensations that came to be dismissed as "trifling inconveniences" under nuisance law. In similar fashion, the terminology of odors likewise minimized the injury associated with exposure to chemical fumes. Thus Governor George Wallace upon encountering the smell of a paper mill in a poor black county in Alabama reportedly exclaimed, "Yeah, that's the smell of prosperity. Sho' does smell sweet, don't it?"[22] The expression "the smell of prosperity" (or in alternative formulations, the smell of money, jobs, or success) here and elsewhere stood for a view of air pollution as part of a voluntary, reciprocal, and ultimately harmless bargain between industries and their neighbors.

The rush of "odor complaints" that local and state air-pollution agencies received with the expansion of their jurisdiction beyond smoke challenged these assumptions of consent and exerted strong pressure for pollution abatement. But the applicable "odor" framework provided a useful rhetorical device for those who sought to question the need for greater controls. In a typical example, an employee of one chemical company asked during a talk he delivered at the 1958 National Conference on Air Pollution: "Should the ultimate consumer have to pay the relatively high cost of preventing an occasional odor which is only a nuisance and has no health or property damaging effects? After all, many of us will rush to turn on the kitchen exhaust fan to keep the odors of cooking onions from permeating the house. Thus, we expect, just as in the case of the chemical plant with its high stack, that the great outdoors will disperse this nuisance before it reaches the neighbors. While this dispersive action of the atmosphere is adequate, we occasionally know that the Joneses next door are having fried onions with their steak."[23] The 1958 National Conference on Air Pollution included a long list of papers on the health effects of air pollution, with four devoted to the growing concern over carcinogenic pollutants. But these concerns could not dislodge the by-then entrenched odor definition or the reactive nuisance regime that this exclusively aesthetic construction sustained.

Since "odors" are fumes and gases by another name, it should come as no surprise that the technological solutions applicable to the control of gases generally applied to odors as well. By the mid-1950s, available technological means of reducing gases (odorous or not) included combustion (incineration), absorption in water or chemical solutions, adsorption in activated carbon, and prevention through changes in the industrial process itself.[24] But in addition there emerged during that time an additional method applicable only to "odors": the use of various chemical odorants or masking agents as means of altering, or covering up their smell. Consistent with the definition of the pertinent pollution problem as a "malodor," this method aimed at making the emissions more palatable rather than reducing the pollution.

In testimony both to the persistence of public pressure for localized pollution abatement and to the pervasiveness of the "odor" problem definition, masking and odor counteracting gained significant acceptance in the later 1950s.[25] Issues of the *Journal of the Air Pollution Control Association* from that era contain various commercial advertisements by companies selling essential oils and fragrant chemicals promised to impart "pine" or "floral" odor to industrial fumes. One 1957 example carried the following caption over a picture of a helicopter hovering over a company's smokestacks: "Airkem's flying odor researchers solve one of your toughest industrial relations problems. . . . To determine the odor source and type, and to cure it," the advertisement further explains, "Airkem field engineers even take to the air."[26] Two decades later, a National Research Council report on odors concluded that "[t]he reduction in intensity, although hardly dramatic in the cases reported so far, lends credence to claims of odor counteraction."[27]

The appeal of this method for industry is clear: it was much cheaper to perfume the emissions than to control them. More surprising was the capacity of this system to gain acceptance by regulatory bodies and the scientific community. This need not be seen as a cynical expression of regulatory capture; once pollutants were defined as odorants the masking solution assumed a logic of its own, forcing all localized pollution complaints into the "odor" administrative box, and the underlying toxicological concerns became irrelevant to the administrative task at hand.

ODORS AND NUISANCE LAW

Nearly everywhere, agencies regulated "odors" under statutory mandates that prohibited air-pollution emissions constituting a "nuisance."[28] In keeping with the traditional common law public-nuisance doctrine, this approach left the final decision on what constituted a nuisance to the courts on which administrative agencies must rely to approve enforcement actions. Use of this statutory model to regulate gaseous air pollutants began in California, whose law was one of the more carefully worded examples of this type of mandate: "A person shall not discharge from any source whatsoever such quantities of air contaminants or other material which cause injury, detriment, nuisance, or annoyance to any considerable number of persons or to the public."[29] In contrast to common law doctrines dismissing air pollution "annoyances" as falling below the threshold of legal injury, this and other nuisance statutes did not condition pollution regulation on a scientific link between exposure and a particular disease. Annoyance, under this law, would suffice. But in keeping with the distinction between private and public nuisance, evidence of annoyance to a considerable segment of the relevant community was required to trigger pollution abatement under these statutes. These statutes, however, offered no help regarding evidence or the number or proportion of individuals sufficient to establish such a claim.

As noted, air-pollution regulation began in California with the Air Pollution Control Act of 1947. The law distinguished between smoke, which was to be regulated as a nuisance per se (under a specified Ringelmann standard), and all other air pollutants whose emission was prohibited above levels constituting a nuisance. The distinction followed from the availability of an objective scaling method where smoke was concerned, and from the absence of a parallel method applicable to the regulation of gases. Although there already existed means of measuring the concentration of various pollutants in the air, these were of no assistance in enforcement without standards specifying allowable levels of pollution. Instead, what was thought to be needed was a device that could measure the sensory impact of the pollution while avoiding the vagaries of subjective perception. In the absence of such a device, vaguely worded nuisance standards delegated the decision on the line separating legal from illegal pollution to agencies and overseeing courts. But the drafters of the law hoped that this would be a temporary deficiency, as they viewed a "a statute based on some simple objective test" to be "highly desirable."[30] The temporary solution became entrenched as a regulatory principle, since nuisance law's attention to variations in local conditions was thought to render it the appropriate regulatory framework for managing the subjective and locally contextual problem of "odors."

This is most evident in the later rejection of various "odor measurement" instruments on the ground that by virtue of their very objectivity they deviated from the reactive logic of nuisance law. Throughout the 1950s, some air-pollution agencies searched for means of setting and enforcing more objective odor standards. This effort met with some success by the end of the decade with the invention of the "scentometer." Its creators, a group of Cincinnati pollution-control officials, offered the following description of the state of odor enforcement at the time to explain the need for their device: "In such [odor] investigations, the position of the inspector is that of an arbitrator between management and citizens. This position must be changed to one of a true enforcement officer through more adequate methods of investigation."[31]

The scentometer relied on the proportion of clean air needed to dilute an odorous sample to below the threshold at which the odor can be detected, to provide a quantitative standard for comparing odors.[32] The mechanism created for this purpose was highly cumbersome. It consisted of a rectangular box with separate panels, some of which were designed to hold odorous samples of air, while others served to create and hold odor-free air to be used for dilution. Attached to the box were two tubes, one for bringing ambient air into the device and the other to draw the variously diluted air from the device into the operator's nose. The measurement test relied on a process in which an operator gradually increased the proportion of clean air within the untreated odorous sample until he or she could no longer detect any smell. The device was intended to enable the objective setting of regulatory standards on the basis of the dilution required to bring the odor in the air sample below the threshold of detectability.

As agencies set to implement this approach they encountered three sets of problems. The first followed from the device's tendency to "undermeasure" odors, primarily because of difficulties in capturing representative odor samples. Because of the tendency of gases (and thus odors) to travel in transient plumes, positive readings depended upon the particular timing of individual sniffs in relation to recurring fluctuations in odor intensity. This problem was compounded by the fact that because the evaluation was conducted in the field, the inspectors' own olfactory perception was desensitized in a manner that diminished their ability to detect odor within the diluted samples.[33] The likelihood of "false negative readings" was coupled with the possibility of false "positive readings." Because of the absence of reliable separation between the operator and the ambient air, odorants could bypass the instrument and be detected directly by the nose, resulting in this case in false "scentometer readings." The latter rendered the scentometer-based enforcement vulnerable in court and consequently undermined its capacity to support enforcement actions.

More fundamentally, however, the legal validity of scentometer-based pollution standards was called into question because the method was said to be inconsistent with the reactive logic of the governing nuisance law. The scentometer substituted a measure of "odor strength" for that of "odor annoyance."[34] This substitution fit with a "nuisance per se" assumption on the need for abating strong odors, but conflicted with the requirement under the governing nuisance statutes for evidence on injury or annoyance that the fumes caused. Attempts to improve on the process in response to these objections relied on panels of observers who were trained to compare the smells they experienced in the field with a spectrum of odors with various negative and positive characteristics. But the effort to account for the subjective quality of odor and the contextual nuisance-based definition of the relevant policy problem inevitably conflicted with the goal of bringing greater precision and legitimacy to this regulatory process.

By 1969 only six out of a hundred agencies responding to an odor enforcement survey indicated that they relied on scentometers or other scientific devices in the definition of odor problems.[35] In 1980, an EPA report attributed the scentometer's failure to the impact of technical problems on the scentometer's accuracy and its capacity to "sustain enforcement actions where millions of dollars in control costs may be at stake," and to the absence of a direct correlation between scentometer readings and "community odor nuisance."[36] To begin with, at least in California, it was the absence of an adequate measuring device that forced air-pollution reformers to build their regime on nuisance law. Once this regime was in place, however, it became an impediment to moving beyond the reactive framework of common law even as measuring technologies, however imperfect, became available.

"Odors" and the Road to the CAA

The agencies in charge of air pollution prior to the 1970 CAA were, with few exceptions, understaffed and underfunded. For the most part they were local (municipal, county, and multijurisdictional) rather than state agencies. In 1965 there were approximately 130 local agencies of this type with a budget over $5000, and only 42 with a budget over $50,000.[37] Yet the total amount of funds available to these agencies was by then 5.5 times greater than in 1952.[38] As these numbers suggest, in the vast majority of American cities there was no air-pollution regulatory presence to speak of during this period.

Under the 1963 Clean Air Act, Congress took a number of steps directed at strengthening local and state regulatory capacity in this area, primarily by authorizing federal research as well as technical and financial assistance to state and local air-pollution control programs. But the act included an additional provision allowing for federal conferences geared at voluntary pollution abatement and enforcement procedures in instances of interstate pollution disputes. Of the ten conferences held under this provision, at least three were framed as interstate odor disputes. The facilities involved included an animal reduction plant, and two pulp mills, one in New York (near the Vermont border) and one in Lewiston, Idaho.

The Lewiston pulp mill opened in 1950, giving rise almost immediately to air pollution complaints. The wind carried the fumes across the state border to Clarkston, Washington, whose mayor wrote in 1960 to the federal Public Health Service with a request for its assistance in abating this interstate pollution problem. Seven years later, the Public Health Service held a formal Clean Air Act conference in the area. In this connection 495 residents joined in a petition stating that "[t]his contamination of our air and its odor affects us from headaches, watery eyes, runny noses and breathing difficulties, to paint corrosion or other property damages. This area has put up with this problem for 17 years, which is long enough."[39] In contrast to Governor Wallace's "smell of prosperity" aphorism mentioned earlier, one resident wrote: "How many times have I heard it said 'it smells like money.' This stupid silly joke is not funny. To me it 'smells like death.'"[40] Anger and frustration at the failure of local governments to take action against chemical fumes were by that time a common refrain in citizen letters to federal officials and congressional representatives such as Senator Muskie.[41]

The 1967 Air Quality Act marked another step in the creation of a national federal air pollution regime, requiring the states, for the first time, to regulate air pollution. Among its major provisions, the act provided for the designation of specific air-quality control regions by the Department of Health, Education and Welfare, and the development and publication of air pollution criteria indicating the extent to which particular pollutants are harmful to health and damaging to property, as well as providing information on the costs and effectiveness of prevention and control measures. These were to serve as guidelines for the development of air quality standards by the states and were to be implemented on a regional basis. The central emphasis was on the setting of regional ambient standards, rather than on control of localized pollution at the source. A potentially important exception to this focus derived from the inclusion of odors among the categories of pollutants for which criteria documents were to be developed, because the olfactory definition facilitated the setting of control standards on the basis of sensory impact, rather than evidence of risk to health through exposure to particular levels of specific chemicals in the environment.

To create its odor criteria document, the National Air Pollution Control Administration (in charge of implementing the 1967 act) contracted with the Copley International Corporation (CIC) to undertake a three–phased study of the social and economic impact of odors.[42] As part of its investigation, CIC conducted a national survey of 184 local air-pollution control agencies (coupled with an in-depth study of odor abatement in seven major metropolitan areas). The study concluded that "odor problems exist in many cities and counties throughout the nation" and that the "odor problems ... affected a very large number of people."[43] At the same time the study found little evidence of odor-directed enforcement action. Of the seven major air-pollution control agencies whose records were examined in the CIC study, none could claim "significant control of odorant conditions in their areas even though the sources were fairly well pinpointed and identifiable."[44] The authors of the report put the blame for this on the combined impact of budgetary constraints and the evidentiary burdens of nuisance law: "Due to staff limitations in air pollution control agencies as well as the general requirement that a considerable number of persons perceive an odor situation as a nuisance, nuisance laws have been ineffective tools in abating odors. To the extent that this study could determine, none of the metropolitan areas investigated had a record of a substantial fine or other judicial penalty levied against an odor pollution violator."[45] In view of this finding, it is hardly surprising that the study likewise found that although people living within areas affected by odor problems were disturbed by the pollution, they rarely took action as "many of them appear to have a feeling of hopelessness, believing they have little power to change the situation."[46] Nevertheless the CIC study refrained from linking the nuisance regime's evident failures with the seeming gap between citizen concern and action in this regard. Instead the study followed its conclusion that of the large number of Americans who "perceive odors as a problem ... only a small percentage are motivated to seek recourse" with the painstakingly cautious statement that "[t]he reasons for this apparent apathy cannot be inferred from the public opinion survey findings. Instead, additional study of attitudes is required to develop meaningful conclusions."[47] CIC submitted the first phase of its study to the National Air Pollution Control Administration in January 1970. By that time Congress was in the midst of drafting the bill that, supplanting the 1967 Air Quality Act, would become a new Clean Air Act that year. In the report that accompanied that bill, odors were among the six pollutants that Congress highlighted as candidates for listing as "criteria" pollutants, in addition to the five prevalent pollutants for which quality criteria had already been issued at the passage of the 1970 act.[48]

ODORS AND THE EPA: 1970–92

The EPA quickly moved to regulate one category of "odorants": reduced sulfur from Kraft pulp mills, relying on its authority under section 111 (d) of the 1970 act. As the pulp mills standard showed, section 111's technology-based approach could have been applied to a broad range of "odor-ant emitting" industrial sources.[49] But the EPA opted not to issue any other such odor-directed rules subsequent to the pulp mills standard. Instead, its efforts focused on reduction of regional concentrations of the six criteria pollutants for which it set National Ambient Air Quality Standards (NAAQS). Pushed to the sidelines were not only "odors" but the regulation of Hazardous Air Pollutants (HAPs) under section 112. The result was a federal regulatory regime that paid scant, if any, attention to problems of localized pollution.

Yet pressure from those impacted by such localized pollution did not abate. In response Congress, once again, pointed the EPA's attention to the odor problem under the 1977 Clean Air Act Amendments. In a specific legislative directive to the agency, under section 403 (b), the act required the EPA to study the effects on public health and welfare of odor or odorous emissions and the availability and cost of technology or measures capable of odor control; and to issue a report evaluating regulatory options for the control of odors under the CAA.[50] The EPA contracted with the National Research Council (NRC) for the study that the congressional directive required, and the NRC's Committee on Odors from Stationary and Mobile Sources issued its report in 1979.[51] The EPA followed the next year with a report that, as noted before, opted not to make odors an object of federal Clean Air Act controls. The arguments put forth in support of this decision offer an especially illuminating example of the ongoing impact of common-law problem definitions and conceptions of proper regulatory authority within contemporary American administration.

In its 1980 report the EPA concluded, after reviewing the various regulatory options available to it for controlling odors under the CAA, that the problem was best left to the administrative nuisance regime and the local and state agencies. The report explains that the primary benefit that nuisance law brought to odor regulation—which none of the available regulatory options under the CAA held—was a sensitivity to the varying environmental standards of different local communities. The need for such sensitivity, the report explained—without making reference to the agency's failure to control HAPs—derived from the inherent subjectivity of odor problems:

> Odor pollution, unlike most other forms of air pollution, is a problem only to the extent that affected individuals perceive it as a problem. Uniform national standards . . . leave no room for variable community sensibilities and preferences. Reactions to odors vary, not only between individuals, but also among different localities. . . . It is certainly logical to argue that an odor regulatory strategy should be flexible enough to accommodate such local sensibilities.[52]

As chapters 3 and 5 discussed, the assumption that the meaning of legal injury, or nuisance, caused by pollution ought to differ by the nature of the locale was the organizing principle of the land-use separation regime that common law judges aimed to implement. Confronted with air pollution lawsuits from residents of industrial locales, judges in cases such as *Huckenstine's Appeal* (1872) or *Versailles Borrough* (1935) relied on assumptions of local consent to pollution to deny a remedy to the plaintiffs. The EPA report does not invoke such assumptions of consent. Instead it speaks of "sensibilities," "preferences" and "reactions to odors." The argument is that since "[s]ubjective reactions to odor differ between individuals and between communities" there is little logic in abating pollution that does not cause injury. It is for that reason, the report concludes, that nuisance law (which depends on proof of injury to trigger interventions) "is an appropriate mechanism for addressing odor problems."[53]

On the core assumption that "reactions to odors vary not only between individuals but also among different localities" the report offers no evidence, beyond conventional wisdom. Significantly, also absent from the EPA report is any mention of the CIC report submitted to the National Air Pollution Control Administration (later to be joined with the EPA) a decade earlier. The CIC study, which had provided the only systematic investigation of the "odor problem" to date, confirmed the EPA's assumption that in many locales citizens are indeed passive in the face of odors. But, contrary to the EPA, the CIC found in this passivity evidence for the failure of the nuisance regime, rather than a reason for maintaining its hold.

The EPA report made no secret of the "substantive, procedural and evidentiary shortcomings" of the existing nuisance regime.[54] In fact, a footnote in the report all but conceded the long-shot odds of securing odor abatement under nuisance law, since

> Under the most widely recognized view, an odor problem must cause substantial annoyance to qualify as a nuisance. Unusually sensitive individuals are at a distinct disadvantage since annoyance is judged on the basis of the ordinary person living in that locality. Technical legal defenses and burdensome evidentiary problems also detract from the usefulness of nuisance actions and in most cases courts will not issue prohibitory injunctions even if the plaintiff prevails on the merits of his claim.[55]

The report offers no explanation as to why it endorsed the regime despite these obstacles. But the thinking seems to resemble that of common law judges who denied nuisance complaints: those who bring nuisance lawsuits and odor complaints are seen as deviants from prevailing community norms of pollution tolerance. The deficiencies of that regime propelled the regulatory reform process that culminated in the CAA. But with the EPA's 1980 decision to leave localized pollution to local nuisance control, a fundamental continuity between the two regimes was entrenched.

As the EPA report explained, this was not a decision based on the lack of regulatory authority to regulate odor. There were a number of possible means of intervention, most obviously through the New Source Performance Standards. Rather, this decision was based in a particular regulatory philosophy on the proper goals and ends of the agency's regulatory mission. Its decision might have been different, the EPA explained, if the act's technology-based standards had included means of assuring that intervention was desired by the local community. In this connection, the report drew an example from Pennsylvania where (in deviation from the prevailing nuisance approach) odorous emissions from a long list of sources were subject under state law to the requirement that they be incinerated at a minimum of 1200 degrees F for at least 0.3 seconds or that an approved equivalent control technology be used.[56] This approach was deficient, the EPA report argued, because it applied to entire industrial categories in uniform fashion "regardless of the fact that a community odor problem may not be caused or threatened by the source."[57] In response to this criticism, Pennsylvania later amended this process administratively by conditioning actual enforcement of the law upon prior proof that odors from the industrial source in question were a matter of sufficient concern. This type of complaint-triggered screening device, the EPA report noted, would not be consistent with the proactive and uniform mandate of the applicable technology-based provisions of the CAA.[58] Echoing the absolute liability suppositions of nuisance law, the EPA observed that the "application of best available control technology does not guarantee that community odor annoyance levels will not be exceeded."[59] "In the final analysis," the EPA report summarized, "the basic structure of the Clean Air Act makes it difficult to tailor odor regulations to the needs and sensibilities of our nation's local communities. Therefore, it is concluded that specific federal odor regulations are not warranted."[60]

By 1980, a decade after the enactment of the CAA, the EPA could only have been aware of its failure to regulate HAPs and of the general inattention of the CAA to problems of localized pollution. Its decision not to utilize the opportunities that the CAA granted it to implement available and feasible technologies so as to reduce localized pollution burdens— "odors"—is curious. The most obvious explanation for the EPA's decision not to extend the federal CAA is its desire to avoid a regulatory task of potentially immense size, complexity, and political consequence. Promulgating and implementing a national odor control regime would no doubt have demanded extensive administrative energy and resources.

It also might have detracted attention and resources from the EPA's primary concern with reduction in levels of criteria pollutants at the regional level. Yet this explains neither the priority placed on regional pollutants to the exclusion of local concentrations, nor EPA's choice to reject the Clean Air Act's proffered tools for treating local pollution, especially in the face of continuing pressure including from Congress.

A more cynical line of explanation would focus on the influence of industrial sectors opposed to such regulation on the EPA decision. The only evidence for such influence appears in the prominence that the EPA report accorded to one that the Air Pollution Control Association's Committee on Odors (T-4 Committee) published in 1978.[61] The origins of the Air Pollution Control Association, as discussed in the previous chapter, evolved out of the Smoke Prevention Association that was established in 1906. Over time, what began as a professional organization for smoke abatement officials, integrated representatives of industrial interests in an important arena for interaction and cooperation between industry and the air pollution bureaucracy.[62] The composition of the T-4 odor committee attests to the continuing power of this tradition well into the 1970s. Of the T-4 Committee's seventeen members, ten were from industry, five from academic or research institutions, and two from regulatory agencies. William H. Prokop, the committee's vice chairman and the author of the report was himself associated with the National Renderers' Association, which represents an industry engaged in utilizing meat by-products for the production of animal feeds and other uses.

The timing of the 1978 report suggests a desire on the part of the Air Pollution Control Association to influence the EPA's deliberations on the odor issue. They appear to have succeeded in this respect. The EPA report made approximately seven separate citations to the T-4 position paper in addition to incorporating the T-4's conclusions directly into its text, in a quotation almost two pages long.[63] The committee's conclusions were virtually the same as those that the EPA came to adopt.

1. [T]he the existence of a community odor nuisance should be established *before* regulatory limits are applied to a specific odor source to obtain compliance. The procedure for establishing a community odor nuisance would require a specific number of valid complaints received from separate households during a fixed time period. The Committee also concluded that there should be specific procedures and guidelines provided to establish the existence of a community odor nuisance which take into account the community's characteristics: population distribution, socioeconomic activity, and land use zoning.

2. The Committee agreed that odor problems are basically related to the local community and should be regulated by the appropriate local agency.[64]

In addition to the T-4 Committee, the EPA report placed significant importance on the opinion of state and local air-pollution control officials who had responded to an EPA survey on this issue. As the EPA reported, these officials "believe that, while existing regulatory approaches need to be improved, they are generally adequate to solve major community odor problems. The combination of citizen / agency pressure and threatened legal action is generally sufficient to encourage problem sources to undertake voluntary compliance and abatement programs."[65] This ultimately optimistic conclusion contrasts sharply with those reached ten years earlier by the CIC study, which was ignored by the EPA report. It also contradicts the EPA's own concession in the report on the scope of the obstacles that those who wish to bring about nuisance-based enforcement encounter.

The responses of both these air pollution officials and of the EPA itself suggest, at some level, industrial influence. But offering regulatory capture alone as explanation ignores the role of ideas, pertaining both to the meaning of the relevant regulatory task and to the criteria for reasonable intervention, by which EPA officials could justify this decision to themselves. To understand the EPA's decision to uphold a regulatory regime that it knew was incapable of yielding any meaningful abatement we must recognize the extent to which the trivializing definition of odors became the reality for the implementing agencies, and ultimately those in the EPA who made the decision not to regulate.

Paradoxically, the CAA's absolutist (albeit unimplemented) HAPs regime served to rationalize subjective constructions of odors as phenomena whose meaning, and thereby control rationales, correctly depend on "local sentiments," "values," and "aesthetics."[66] The tension between the subjective aesthetic definition inherent to the terminology of odors and the toxicological concerns triggered through exposure to odorous industrial chemicals was ostensibly resolved with the creation of the 1970 act's HAPs regime. Whereas the prior air pollution regime had lumped both potentially toxic and nontoxic pollution concentrations under the odor rubric, in the CAA regime "odors" became a residual category of pollutants that were deemed safe as a matter of law, notwithstanding the fact that hazardous air pollutants remained largely uncontrolled.

This was the assumption with which the 1979 NRC report began its discussion of the public health aspects of odors: "*By definition*, chemicals hazardous to human health are considered to be toxic; hence, they are subject to control in accordance with existing laws or regulations[emphasis added]. . . . Toxic odorous substances in the atmosphere are automatically subject to standard-setting under the Clean Air Act of 1970 and its amendments, and reduction of their presence to below toxic thresholds is mandatory."[67] In similar fashion, the Air Pollution Control Association T-4 Committee report explained: "Odor control regulations usually are concerned with objectionable type odors which are not harmful to health. Hazardous or toxic odorous vapors and gases require a separate type of regulation. In this case, measurement and control of a specific chemical compound is required to maintain its concentration in the ambient air below an established physiological danger level."[68] With that assumption in place, the committee then proceeded to recommend an exclusively reactive local-community-based regulatory approach in which interventions came only in response to "valid complaints" from a "significant number of people" and where "what exactly is 'significant' is dependent upon the community's characteristics."[69]

In endorsing this recommendation, the EPA report did not make a similarly explicit distinction between odors and air toxics. Well aware of its own difficulties in implementing section 112, the agency could hardly claim, as the NRC report did a year earlier, that emissions of toxicological concern are by definition subject to regulatory control under the CAA. Nevertheless the distinction between odors and air toxics is the foundation of the EPA decision in favor of the nuisance regime. Seeing this as strictly a capitulation to industrial pressure would miss the manner in which the odor definition had assumed a reality of its own. The definition framed the debate in a way that rendered plausible the assumption that the generally poor communities living in industrial locales do not suffer from the fumes. The policy choice was a natural outgrowth of this assumption.

Throughout the 1980s, concern about air toxics mounted in communities across the country, leading to increased pressure on agencies in the form of accumulating "odor" complaints. A 1989 book entitled *Odor Control: Including Hazardous / Toxic Odors* offered the following account of the typical state of odor regulation around that time:

> Occasionally, an inspector from the pollution control agency may visit the site of the complaint. The officer may or may not be able to detect the odor, depending upon the frequency of the emissions and changes in meteorological conditions. Even if he is able to detect the odors at the site of the complaint, he is not in a position to objectively determine the impact of the odorous emission on the complainer. . . . The process continues to the point at which the complainers give up filing complaints.[70]

It is the specific reference to "Hazardous / Toxic Odors" in this book's title that is of particular interest. This wording is an explicit attempt to counter prevalent aesthetic definitions of the problem and especially the false dichotomy subsequent to the CAA between HAPs and odorants.

The following year, the 1990 Clean Air Act Amendments responded to the federal failure to control air toxics with a drastically revised approach to the regulation of HAPs, shifting the HAPs regime in a technology-based direction. This is the course that the EPA rejected a decade earlier in its odor report. The contradictions inherent to the agency's policies and odor definition itself had been clearly revealed with the 1992 publication of what the EPA named a "Reference Guide to Odor Thresholds for Hazardous Pollutants listed in the Clean Air Act Amendments of 1990." The report aimed at assisting state and local agencies faced with odor complaints "that are associated with safety concerns due to chemical exposure." Adequate response to these complaints, the EPA explained, depends upon "knowledge of odor threshold values, together with a variety of background information, toxicity data, and analytical data."[71] Odorants and HAPs, after all, were often the same.

Among the industrial categories whose HAPs emissions were targeted for control under the 1990 CAA were foundries, a source of long-standing odor complaints and toxicological concern in communities across the country. The story of four such foundry "odor" disputes, spanning the early 1970s to the mid-1990s, is at the heart of the following chapter.

CHAPTER EIGHT

Regulating "Odors": The Case of Foundries

THE EPA DECISION not to regulate odors had far-reaching consequences for the experiences of firms, their surrounding communities, and state regulatory agencies. This chapter explores these implications through an examination of four disputes surrounding iron and steel foundries and their pollution-affected communities.

Foundries melt and shape metal into parts used in 90 percent of manufactured products, from airplanes to zippers.[1] The industry provides widespread economic benefits,[2] but has long been associated with severe pollution problems. Historically, the primary source of air pollution from foundries was the melting process and its associated particulate emissions (fly ash, soot, metallic dust, and other forms).[3] However, by the early 1960s those living in the vicinity of foundries began to notice, and complain about, "burnt rubber" chemical fumes. The cause was a change in the technology of casting and the introduction of newly developed synthetic resins into the process.[4]

Benzene, formaldehyde, naphthalene, and phenol are some of the carcinogens and other Hazardous Air Pollutants (HAPs) that are often present in these foundry fumes.[5] HAPs emissions from foundries were among those that the 1990 Clean Air Act regime was intended to control. But by the end of 2002 this task remained unfulfilled. In the meantime, as has been the case since the 1960s, foundry fumes—defined as "odors"—are for the most part subject to public nuisance regulation via local and state agencies.

While the chapter's focus is on a single industry, there is no implication that metal casting should be singled out from the many other industries emitting odorous and hazardous pollutants. Refineries, pulp mills, and chemical manufacturers are among the many industries that would have been equally appropriate candidates for study; however, comparative cases needed to be analyzed within a single industrial category. The importance of intra-industry comparison stems from the similarity of the pollution problems attending each industry, of technological options for pollution abatement, and of juxtaposition of firms and neighborhoods.

The default assumption of the "odor" regime is that the fumes are not a nuisance and do not require intervention. While the presumption is rebuttable, the burden of proof falls on communities to demonstrate its inadequacy in a particular setting. Consistent with the "perpetual mobilization" regimes described in chapter 6, however, such proof is not demanded once, but generally needs constantly to be reestablished for abatement efforts to be maintained. In principle, the law provides absolute guarantees against odor nuisances. But in reality, the response, following the long-standing tradition in the common law is, in many instances, to raise the evidentiary burdens required of communities as to the existence of such a nuisance. In the meantime, opportunities for developing and implementing feasible pollution reductions are not pursued.

FOUNDRIES: PROCESS, POLLUTION, AND CONTROL TECHNOLOGY

The production of casting typically takes three steps. First, electric induction furnaces or coke-fired cupolas melt scrap metal or pig iron. Second, the molten metal is poured into molds that give the cast its external shape, with cores placed inside the molds creating internal cavities. Molds and cores are usually made of sand that has been bonded and shaped to the desired specifications. Third, casts are cooled and removed from the molds.

Foundry air-pollution control was among the topics addressed in 1966 during the Third National Conference on Air Pollution. At that meeting, the Chief of the City of Detroit and Wayne County Air Pollution Control Agencies presented a paper focusing on emissions from the largely uncontrolled cupolas on which the vast majority of grey-iron foundries relied to melt their scrap metal at the time.[6] But under the category of "other foundry problems worthy of note" the same paper reported that "[r]ecent technological advances in core making and certain molding operations . . . cause the generation of odorous and sometimes acrid fumes which can cause local nuisance conditions. Effective, practical, and financially acceptable control systems have not been developed to solve this problem."[7]

The introduction of synthetic resins, was the technological advance to which the paper referred. Prior to the creation of these resins, foundries relied largely on various plant-based bonding agents, including linseed oil and cereal-based materials, to bind the molds and cores. Chemical binders contributed greatly to the strength of molds and the ability of foundries to produce ever more sophisticated castings, and they are credited with making high-volume casting production facilities possible. Offsetting these very real advantages was the fact that with the shift in the binders, foundries imposed a new, and to many of their neighbors, far more troubling, air pollution burden on their locale.[8]

The fumes were a pollution problem without easy solutions. To protect workers, casting was generally conducted outside or in highly ventilated areas to help diffuse the fumes emitted. Control demanded the hooding of the molding operation to channel fumes toward devices for treating them; these included incineration or adsorption in carbon beds, both of which were expensive propositions. The alternative of material substitution existed, but it faced the challenge of producing castings of equal quality or with the same speed.

These technological challenges to abatement encouraged the industry to avoid action on the problem, a goal that was well served by its definition as an "odor" rather than as localized pollution. The following quotation from a 1967 foundry industry manual is indicative both of growing concerns regarding air toxics from foundries and the industry's attempt to adhere to particulate-focused definitions of its pollution problems:

> The major air pollution problem for most foundries arises from their metal casting processes. Although there are instances when stack emissions contain toxic materials . . . the fact remains that many of the air pollutants from foundries are of a nuisance nature, consisting of innocuous oxides and silicates in the form of relatively coarse cinders and dust. . . . Most complaints come from irate housewives whose clothesline laundry becomes soiled, from owners of cars parked on nearby lots, or from other property owners who find the settled dust a nuisance. Fortunately, this type of pollution is the most easily corrected.[9]

The visibility of the particulate problem tended to attract attention, and its relative ease of control encouraged mitigation efforts. By the early 1970s, under pressure from air pollution agencies, foundries began to control particulates through hoods connected to baghouses, electrostatic precipitators, and / or wet scrubbers.[10] Since these technologies were not directed at the control of molding fumes—which remained largely uncontrolled—odor-related complaints continued to mount. By 1973 the industry, at least for a short while, appeared ready to tackle the problem. In August 1973, a leading foundry trade journal titled *Modern Casting* devoted an entire issue to what it termed the industry's "odor" problem. "Few industries can match the metalcasting process in its ability to generate a super profusion of aromas," acknowledged the issue's opening editorial. The article went on to describe foundries as "a virtual 'smellorama' of SO_2, CL_2, HCl, $MgCL_2$, phenols, napthalenes, styrenes, formaldehydes, glycerines and other hydrocarbons."[11]

Most importantly, the editorial emphasized that there existed viable (albeit costly) control mechanisms for this problem. The journal identified three primary means for reducing organic emissions from the molding process already available at the time: incineration, chemical absorption, and carbon adsorption, a technology that shortly before appeared to have had significant pollution reduction success in a large Chrysler foundry in Detroit.[12] But, the editorial emphasized, technological controls of this type "are really only temporary, stop-gap expensive solutions." The long-term remedy lay in replacing "the sources of the odor with processes that use inorganic chemicals instead of organic." The editorial optimistically pointed out that promising efforts to develop alternative inorganic binders were already underway, even if, in the meantime, "EPA-approved clean air sounds more expensive than ever before!"[13]

These statements, along with *Modern Casting*'s decision to devote an entire issue to available foundry odor-control solutions, would appear to indicate that the industry anticipated far-reaching EPA regulation of odorous fumes. As the editorial indicates, this was seen as a strong incentive for the development of alternative resins. Since the expected pressure from the EPA failed to materialize, regulatory impetus for the development of such environmentally safer resins was never generated.

Continuing concern over foundry emissions was evident in the 1979 National Research Council (NRC) report undertaken following the 1977 CAA's odor directive to the EPA, discussed in the previous chapter. The NRC report attributed odor problems associated with the molding process to phenol, hexamethylene tetramine, and free formaldehyde vapors. The report suggested that these emissions could be controlled by hooding the molding operations and the subsequent treatment of the fumes via incineration, catalytic combustion, or wet scrubbing.[14] But the focus there, as in the rest of the NRC, report, was on the relevant pollutants as "odorants" rather than HAPs.

Throughout the 1980s, evidence of significant risk to foundry workers as a result of occupational exposure to the fumes began to accumulate.[15] By 1984 the EPA, in a departure from the prevailing "odor" constructions of the impact of the fumes, commissioned a study on organic emissions from ferrous metallurgical industries. The study estimated that annual organic emissions for typical iron foundries ranged between 13.5 and 17.2 tons / year. Recognizing that the installation of expensive organic emission-control devices may have a severe economic impact on foundries due to their typically small size, the study pointed to a number of modifications in foundry operating practices that could yield significant pollution reductions short of installing costly control technology. These included increasing the cooling time for molds in order to reduce emissions from the shakeout process and the conversion from chemically bonded sand molds to inorganically and physically bonded molds, a solution envisioned a decade earlier in the *Modern Castings* editorial.[16]

Subsequent to the inclusion of foundries within the industrial categories targeted for HAPs control under the 1990 CAA, the EPA undertook an extensive survey of the entire foundry industry regarding pollution control practices. Under the 1990 CAA, the EPA was required to subject industrial facilities whose HAPs emissions qualify them as a "major source" to Maximum Achievable Control Technology (MACT) standards. A major emitter of HAPs is defined as one emitting more than ten tons of a particular HAP or twenty-five tons of a mix of HAPs per year. For existing sources, the statute requires that standards shall not be less stringent than "the average emission limitation achieved by the best performing 12 percent of the existing sources for which the Administrator had emissions information."[17] This mandate required the EPA to engage in two separate information gathering tasks: first, to identify the control technologies put in place by the best performing facilities (as defined in the statute), and second, to identify facilities whose HAPs emissions qualify them as major sources under the act. In an effort to answer both questions, the EPA undertook an extensive survey of individual foundries' HAPs emissions, emission control production facilities, production capacity, emission control devices in place, and other pollution prevention programs.[18]

Since up to this point "foundry odors" were the almost exclusive domain of local and state-enforced nuisance law, the EPA survey offers a rare opportunity to observe the aggregate pattern of mitigation efforts that the nuisance law regime produced across one industry. The results show unequivocally that the regime, with extremely few exceptions, yielded next to no pollution controls directed at the HAPs of concern: of the 816 foundries surveyed, only 1.8 percent reported use of air-pollution control devices directed at reducing organic emissions from the molding process.[19] These divided between incinerators (1.6 percent of foundries) and carbon adsorption units (0.2 percent of foundries).[20] The latter group includes only two foundries, Pacific Steel Casting in Berkeley, California, and ME-West in Tempe, Arizona, both of which are among the four foundries selected for study in this chapter.

The inclusion of these two foundries in this study derived from the exceptional financial investment that both of these firms ultimately made in controlling organic molding emissions compared to their competitors across the country.[21] A third foundry selected for study, Wells Manufacturing / Castwell Products of Skokie, Illinois, avoided implementing similarly comprehensive controls after the Illinois Supreme Court ruled that the Illinois Environmental Protection Agency had failed to meet pertinent evidentiary burdens for mandating such controls. In an environment in which non-control of casting fumes is far and away the norm (as evident by the EPA survey), studies of these three exceptional cases can illuminate the factors that account for their deviation from the overall pattern within the industry, and—by implication—why so little control of foundry fumes has taken place elsewhere. The chapter begins, however, with the ubiquitous case of no abatement represented by a single case study (New Haven Foundry, Michigan) documenting citizens' failure to win pollution relief under public nuisance odor regimes.[22]

NEW HAVEN, MICHIGAN

Situated approximately thirty miles northeast of Detroit, the village of New Haven started as a train stop built in 1859 on the Detroit Grand Trunk run between Port Huron and Detroit. In 1867 a small foundry was established east of the railroad tracks, and in 1869 the village was incorporated.[23] Despite its initially promising beginning, New Haven evidently did not feel much like celebrating its centennial in 1969. Unlike the surrounding communities, the village had failed to thrive. A large and profitable foundry dominated its center, but few other businesses sought sites in the town. A once bustling Main Street stood dilapidated and largely deserted. Asked why things turned out the way they did, the village clerk, a woman who had first arrived as a young teacher in the 1920s, explained, "[u]ntil the air pollution thing is whipped, how can we expect people to remain in our community or hope to attract new families?"[24] The owner of a local clothing store wrote to the state governor that year,

> The poor people that live in the foundry vicinity have no chance for a clear breath of air. . . . During the past years, several times the village council would write up a strong proposal for equipment to be installed by the foundry owner to stop air pollution. This proposal would be presented to the foundry owner Mr. Somner [Lamkins], with a lot of motivation from the council president and each time it would get hushed up. No prevention or stopping air pollution was ever done.[25]

In 1926 Sumner Lamkins (the foundry owner mentioned above), an industrialist from the neighboring city of Mount Clemens, bought and drastically enlarged what had been up until then a small, local foundry. Lamkins soon began bringing busloads of African-American men from the South to serve as workers. The work he offered was grueling and dangerous, but the pay was decent, and, especially during the 1930s, alternative employment options were few. Lamkins housed his workers in a special district immediately adjacent to the foundry. He prohibited them from entering other areas of New Haven, and was said to have paid local officials to enforce his segregationist policies.[26] Situated right next to the completely uncontrolled plant, the workers' living quarters bore the brunt of the foundry's pollution, which often included falling debris and pieces of burning ash. Those injured or sickened by work in the foundry remained in New Haven, no longer employable and without any alternative means of support. In time, disease, pollution, poverty, and racial barriers transformed the foundry's immediate surroundings into an "impoverished ghetto."[27] Urban renewal programs demolished the ghetto and relocated its residents during the early 1970s. Nevertheless, close to a third of New Haven households fell below the poverty line throughout the 1980s.[28]

Veteran residents still remember a time when Main Street bustled with business and social activity, but gradually the restaurant, pubs, meat market, clothing store, and hotel closed in the decades following World War II. Only a handful of businesses and many boarded-up storefronts remained by 1994.[29] Upwind of the foundry, the shady, attractive streets that had characterized the village earlier in the century can still be seen, along with a small public library built by the collective efforts of local residents. The town's emblem today, defying Lamkin's legacy, features an image of clasping white and black hands.

Local Mobilization

On November 16, 1953, in response to a petition from local residents earlier that year, the New Haven Village Council unanimously adopted an ordinance prohibiting smoke, fly ash, and odors from any source.[30] The ordinance was never enforced, and subsequent appeals throughout the 1950s and 1960s by the Village Council to the foundry met with a similar lack of response. In August 1970, sometime after opening a new social service program in New Haven, its staff wrote to the newly established State Air Pollution Control Section: "You have never seen pollution until you've seen the pollution from the New Haven Foundry."[31] Around that time, local residents began to write to the Michigan governor and other officials. In one such letter—written on a piece of torn notebook paper and signed "concerned citizen of New Haven"—one resident implored "Dust and dirt has been coming out of the [disgusting] factory for years. The citizens of New Haven have been trying to do something for years with no avail. . . . Do we have to breath[e] all that dust and dirt or can you all do something about it."[32]

As with other foundries of the period, smoke and soot, rather than fumes, were the main pollution concerns in New Haven during the 1950s and 1960s. However, this changed around 1970 when New Haven residents began to notice fumes suggestive of burnt rubber. In 1973, a village administrator contacted the Michigan Department of Public Health with a request for ambient monitoring because of concerns regarding the " 'noxious gases' that the New Haven Foundry has been spewing out."[33] The following year a local citizen wrote to the Air Pollution Division of the Michigan Department of Natural Resources (DNR):

I was outside and had to come in because I could not stand the fumes coming from the foundry. The air was full of a sharp, pungent odor which irritated my nose, throat and eyes. . . . Keeping in mind that I live over ¼ of a mile from the foundry, I must believe the people living next to the foundry suffer greatly. I can be sure of this, because I worked on a broken water line last fall along side the foundry. It was almost unbearable! However, the people who live there and their children had to bear it. I might add that there are a lot of small children that live in the trailer city where I was working.[34]

A letter from another citizen, two years later, speaks of growing worry and frustration:

Terrible air pollution. The smell is so bad it has been making us physically sick!! Also, my pet has been vomiting when the foundry smoke and soot is blowing right at the house. The soot gets all over everything, but worst of all the air we are breathing is not at all good for anyone, and if the government and air control centers care so damn much here is one place they should have been taking action against long ago.[35]

Ten village residents, some of whom were former foundry employees, filed a class action suit for injunctive relief and damages against New Haven Foundry in 1972. They complained that the fumes, odors, gases, and dust from the foundry impaired their health and interfered with their use and enjoyment of their property.[36] The plaintiffs asked for a permanent injunction that would enjoin the defendant from activities causing the nuisance, along with damages in favor of the plaintiffs and "all other persons similarly situated" in the amount of two million dollars.[37] By the time the first pretrial conference was held in June 1974, the list of plaintiffs had grown to forty. Attorneys for the plaintiffs submitted pretrial statements in January 1975. In these statements, they asked for $1,250,000 for a trust fund on behalf of the class and members not yet involved, and $500,000 for upgrading the business area and creating an industrial buffer zone to the benefit of the village of New Haven.[38]

The case languished during the next four years as the judge and plaintiffs' attorneys squabbled over the size of the relevant class and notice requirements.[39] The case was finally dismissed in 1979, after the plaintiffs' attorneys failed to produce an expert report required by the judge, but which they claimed they could not afford.[40] Abandoning the class action strategy, twenty-one of the original plaintiffs later that year filed a second suit asking for an injunction and one million dollars in damages and compensation for "discomfort from smells, odors and soots, harm to property and clothing, medical problems caused by pollutants and a reduction in the quality of social and recreational activities."[41] Shortly thereafter the case ended in a settlement that provided some manner of financial compensation to the plaintiffs but no pollution relief. As the following section describes, those in New Haven who sought administrative, rather than judicial, remedies against the fumes fared no better.

Regulatory Responses

The state of Michigan passed an Air Pollution Control Act in 1965. In 1967 the state initiated its first program for the control of particulate emissions from foundries.[42] Accordingly, the first of the New Haven Foundry's two cupola melting-ovens received a wet scrubber in 1970, the second in 1972.[43] These reduced, but failed to eliminate, particulate emissions from the foundry because the equipment repeatedly malfunctioned and because parts of the melting and pouring process remained uncontrolled. For the next two-and-a-half decades, the New Haven Foundry was found to be in violation of pertinent visible emissions standards on numerous occasions and faced intermittent pressure to correct the problem from both the Michigan Department of Natural Resources and the U.S. EPA.

The most typical and nearly the sole response to the fumes was a sporadic investigation of complaints. The New Haven Foundry fell within the purview of the Michigan Department of Natural Resources (DNR)—reorganized and renamed the Michigan Department of Environmental Quality (DEQ) in 1995—whose authority to intervene in odor disputes of this nature derived from rule 336.1901 of the Michigan Air Pollution Control Commission. Under this rule, all permitted industrial equipment is subject to the requirement that its operation "shall not result in the emission of an air contaminant which causes injurious effects to human health or safety, animal life, plant life of significant value, or property, or which causes unreasonable interference with the comfortable enjoyment of life or property." To the extent that New Haven Foundry's fumes were found to constitute such an "unreasonable interference," the Michigan DNR had the authority to require that they be controlled.

In deciding when pollution amounts to such an "unreasonable interference," the state agency has traditionally relied on the reports of inspectors sent to investigate air quality conditions near sources whose emissions have been the object of citizen complaints. To determine whether a particular odor amounts to a nuisance violation, inspectors are instructed to consider the concentration, duration, and frequency of the odor but are given no formal guidelines or standards.[44] Over the decades, the DNR's inspectors repeatedly investigated air quality complaints in New Haven but these investigations did not result in a finding of air pollution amounting to an "unreasonable interference" in violation of the nuisance rule.

The first inspector's report on file with the DNR regarding odors from New Haven Foundry dates to the fall of 1973 and speaks of "[b]luish haze and odor hanging at ground level."[45] In a letter sent to a New Haven Village administrator in December of the same year, a DNR inspector wrote,

> On November 16, 1973, we investigated the New Haven Foundry relative to excessive emissions from the plant as reported by you. . . . That same day you expressed concern over the fact that these fumes may be toxic. I discussed this with engineers from our office who have had contact with this company before, and they assured me that these emissions would not be of a toxic nature.[46]

For the next two decades inspectors intermittently returned to the village to investigate continuing odor complaints. The following three reports were written in response to visits conducted in 1976, 1987, and 1991. The first explained, "Downtown was full of haze that nearly took my breath away a couple of time[s]."[47] The second report confirmed the first, stating,

> This plant does smell at times more than others. There was nothing different done that day. I drove by the plant more than on one occasion and I did smell odor downwind of the plant. At the time when I was at the site last to evaluate for this complaint the odor was slight but detectable. I would not call it a 901 violation at this time but more observations will be conducted.[48]

The third report added, "There was some foundry odor detected downwind from the company. This is an odor associated with all foundry operations. The odor was not strong enough that day. But it could be a problem some other days."[49] Despite these reports, on no such occasion were odors from New Haven Foundry found to amount indeed to a nuisance violation.

By contrast, the DNR was much more responsive where visible emissions were concerned. Particulates are among the pollutants subject to National Ambient Air Quality Standards (NAAQS) under the CAA, and during the 1970s the DNR placed an air-pollution monitoring station in the village that documented repeated violations of secondary NAAQS for total suspended particulates. With this monitoring, the New Haven Foundry made it onto the EPA's list of significant violators. Following a major upgrading of its scrubbers, New Haven Foundry was removed from the EPA's list but was found in 1993 to be again in violation of the pertinent particulates standard.[50]

In a pattern persisting across two-and-a-half decades, New Haven residents' complaints against invisible fumes and odors met with, at best, more rigorous enforcement of visible emission rules. Initially, the DNR inspectors may have been ignorant about the processes responsible for the odors, and they may have honestly assumed that better particulate controls would resolve the problem.[51] But well beyond the point of any lingering doubt as to the source of, or possible solutions for, the odors in question, the DNR and the federal EPA continued to respond to local complaints by taking action on particulates, but ignoring the fumes motivating the complaints.

Thus, after a severe soot fallout incident in the winter of 1985 galvanized antipollution protest in New Haven, a petition signed by 300 village residents began with "a request that enforcement action be taken to prevent the New Haven Foundry from emitting obnoxious odors."[52] In a meeting held in the aftermath of the incident, village officials told representatives of the foundry that the "black snow" was only "the frosting on the cake after numerous complaints all summer of the odors."[53] Yet all the DNR required the foundry to do following this protest was to adjust and upgrade the scrubbers used to control particulate emissions.

Likewise, a plan for inspection and control of the foundry's smoke was the only response offered by the U.S. EPA Region 5 administrator to a local citizen whose complaint focused on odors. As the administrator explained, the agency intended to inspect the company in the near future to evaluate its compliance with visible emissions regulations and "any other federally enforceable air pollution regulations." These words appear to have been chosen carefully. No mention was made of the fact that the fumes, which had long been of primary concern in New Haven, fell outside the scope of such "federally enforceable regulations," due to the EPA's 1980 odor decision."[54] Furthermore, the letter offered no suggestions as to what alternative recourse was open to the citizen with regard to pollution that was not "federally enforceable," most likely because the EPA administrator knew well that there was little the citizen could do besides adding another complaint to those that had accumulated for the previous two decades in the files of the Michigan DNR.

New Haven, Michigan, epitomizes the kind of locale where odors might not be perceived "as a problem" under "community sensibilities and preferences."[55] There is little in the above to support that image or its attendant assumption of consent to pollution exposure. The people of New Haven voiced their protest, in myriad ways, against the fumes that diminished their town, but to no avail.

BERKELEY, CALIFORNIA

Half a continent away in California, Berkeley residents mobilized against a similar foundry pollution problem from the mid-1970s onward. Home to the University of California's flagship campus, Berkeley is better known for academics than for manufacturing industry. But the city has long included an industrial base, mostly located at its western edge, where the Pacific Steel Casting (PSC) foundry has operated since 1934. The company expanded significantly in 1975 and again in 1980, opening two additional plants next door to its first facility. As no agency conditioned their permits on deployment of fume mitigation technology, the new plants did not install any pollution devices to control fumes.

Although PSC is located in an area zoned for heavy industry, and its immediate neighbors have included an ink manufacturer, a cement company, and a tire repair shop, the surrounding area has long interspersed industrial land uses with older homes. As a result, homes are found only a few blocks away from the plant. Half a mile further away lie a number of residential neighborhoods, including a large, University of California housing complex for students with families. Fumes from PSC's three uncontrolled plants could be easily detected at least a mile away during the early 1980s.

PSC and Odor Regulation in the Bay Area Air Quality Management District (BAAQMD)

Two of PSC's three facilities in West Berkeley were built during the 1970s, after the problems associated with the use of synthetic foundry resins were well recognized. Even so, and despite the close proximity to residential and commercial locales, the air pollution agency in charge required no fume controls when it approved the plans. This is a direct outgrowth of the reactive odor-nuisance regime; the default arrangements entailed no controls, unless the surrounding local community could prove that it's "annoyed."

In 1974 when the Berkeley Board of Adjustments approved PSC's request to construct a second plant, it invoked the regional agency's reputation for close regulation of "[h]eavy industry of this type."[56] The same argument was invoked in 1979, when PSC's application for a permit to construct plant number three lay before the Board of Adjustments. The company wrote that "[a]ll areas of the facility generating dust and fumes will be provided with the latest and most modern dust collection system and will be in full compliance with requirements of the Bay Area Air Pollution Control District."[57] Although this statement alluded to both dust and fumes, PSC made no mention of the fact that the Bay Area Air Quality Management District's (BAAQMD) regulations pertained only to the control of particulates, thereby leaving control of any fumes to post hoc regulation and only if deemed a public nuisance.

Complaints against PSC-generated odors began to stream into the BAAQMD soon after plant number two opened in 1975, but the agency had taken no action (beyond investigation) by the time PSC's request for approval of plant number three reached the table. While aware that fumes from PSC's existing two plants were a source of prior and ongoing concern, the Secretary of the Berkeley Board of Adjustments nevertheless recommended granting the permit. He explained, "[a] tour through plant 2 was *nearly* convincing that this kind of use does not have the potential to cause detriment as in earlier years, especially given the control by BAAPCD [emphasis added]."[58] Nearly convinced or not, the board granted the permit and PSC's plant number three, like the other two, began operating in 1980 without any fume controls.

The BAAQMD, the regional air-pollution control district for the San Francisco Bay Area, is one of the larger and professionally expert air pollution agencies in the country. In keeping with this reputation the agency devotes systematic and extensive attention to odor regulation. The BAAQMD operates a toll-free odor complaint line, logging thousands of complaints each year against a large number of industrial sources.[59] The agency's policy is to investigate each and every such complaint for the purpose of evaluating whether the pollution amounts to a public nuisance—an "injury, detriment, nuisance, or annoyance to any considerable number of persons or to the public" in the language of section 41700 of the California Health and Safety Code.[60]

BAAQMD rules impose very specific evidentiary criteria as a condition for finding a public nuisance violation, most often through what is colloquially known as the "rule of five." Under this procedure, industrial emissions are considered a public nuisance when complaints from five separate households downwind are confirmed by district inspectors within a twenty-four-hour period.[61] A complaint is confirmed when a BAAQMD inspector can, simultaneously with the citizen who filed the complaint, smell the odor in question and trace it to a particular industrial source. This formalized set of rules leave inspectors relatively little discretion in the handling of complaints.

Satisfying the conditions outlined by the "rule of five" is a greater challenge than might appear at first glance. The difficulty derives both from what it takes to confirm five complaints during the time period in question and, more importantly, what is required to translate any such nuisance findings into pollution reduction measures. Response time varies with the availability of inspectors, and complaint investigation can take place an hour or more after a complaint is first registered, by which time the wind direction may have shifted or the relevant industrial process stopped. Consequently, complaint verification depends on the confluence of the following factors: the continuation of the relevant industrial process, stable meteorology, the presence of the complainant at his / her home, and the inspector's ability to trace the odor to the alleged industrial source.

Not surprisingly, most complaints are never confirmed. Yet only when five such confirmations occur within twenty-four hours would the BAAQMD find an odor nuisance violation.[62]

When unidentified burnt-plastic smells in the environment began to trouble neighbors of Pacific Steel Castings during the late 1970s, it was up to them to discover, often after fruitless complaints to the fire and police departments, that the BAAQMD was the proper organization to address their complaints. Once they learned this, they began to register complaints, and the task of complaint confirmation got underway. Whereas most complainants, at least initially, did not know where the burnt-plastic fumes originated, there ought to have been little mystery involved for the BAAQMD's staff, given the widely recognized propensity of foundries to cause pollution problems of this nature. Such knowledge, however, was immaterial to the BAAQMD's complaint confirmation procedures, which required inspectors to trace each and every complaint to its source and to issue a public nuisance violation notice only when five such confirmations occurred in the course of one day. Furthermore, BAAQMD policies during that time required four such violation notices to be issued before the offending source could be called to the office for a conference to begin discussing potential pollution control.

The resulting regulatory process conditioned any prospect for intervention on complainants' willingness to persevere in negotiating a regulatory obstacle course, as a 1983 article in a local newspaper described:

> You've gotten the number of the air district, the air stinks during the day, you call the district, an inspector comes out, it still stinks by the time the inspector gets there, the inspector can smell it and you think you know where it's coming from! . . . [however] unless there are five confirmed complaints within 24 hours, the district inspector can't issue the company a notice of violation for polluting the air (another district guideline). That means that you and four of your neighbors must all call the district when the air stinks during the day, and an inspector has to respond to each of your calls, and smell the smell at each of your doors, and each time identify the source of the odor as the same outfit before the polluter gets one ticket.[63]

By 1980 growing frustration with the BAAQMD's policies led approximately thirty local citizens to organize against the pollution under the name "Neighbors for Clean Air" (Neighbors). Over the next decade the group (whose composition changed and whose numbers fluctuated over time) filed, and encouraged others to file, thousands of air pollution complaints. They contacted dozens of officials, politicians, and journalists and came to testify, over and over, in public hearings. They brought lawsuits, and otherwise engaged in pollution protest activities in which hundreds of people took part at various stages of the long dispute. They were motivated, first and foremost, by the concern that pollutants posed a serious long-term threat to their health.

It was due to the organizational efforts of Neighbors for Clean Air that PSC received its first nuisance violation notice, in November 1981. Up to that point, five separate complaints had never been confirmed on a single day, notwithstanding repeated complaints submitted to the agency, beginning soon after PSC's second plant opened in 1975. Between April 1981 and March 1982, over one hundred complaints were confirmed by the BAAQMD, but about seventy additional complaints were not. On March 4, 1982, the BAAQMD held its first office conference with PSC.[64] This conference coincided with the appointment of a new inspector who, soon after assuming her position in November 1982, discovered that the BAAQMD had never granted an operating license to plant number two, which had opened in 1975. Plant number three similarly lacked a valid permit, since it was operating at the time on a "start-up" basis. In view of the by-then undeniable odor problems created by the plants, that inspector and her supervisor recommended against granting operating permits to the new plants, thereby forcing the company to choose between shutting down or abating the odors. The company countered that "no one else in the industry controls the odor and no known method for control exists," and it further claimed that a denial of permit for plant three would bankrupt PSC.[65] The BAAQMD granted the permits (without requiring controls) but brought a public nuisance accusation in March 1982 before the district's independent hearing board.[66]

Under California law, all air-pollution control districts must include a quasi-adjudicative hearing board with authority to issue two kinds of abatement orders following a finding of violation of state law or district regulation. In most cases, notices of violation result in conditional orders of abatement that set a schedule and a specific list of control measures that the pollution source is required to undertake. Firms comply with such orders by completing these measures, whether or not the relevant pollution problem is resolved or even mitigated in the process. The second type of abatement order is an unconditional order that imposes a requirement to abate the pollution as such, rather than to install a particular means of control. Unconditional orders are generally reserved for cases where the board believes that a firm has been acting in less than good faith, and are rarely employed. The hearing board decisions are subject to appeal in superior court.

Following the filing of the accusation, the BAAQMD held a series of meetings on the PSC matter during the spring, summer, and fall of 1983. The hearings served two purposes: to allow the hearing board to determine whether the odors amounted to a nuisance violation under section 41700; and to formulate an abatement order, once a finding of public nuisance had been made. In its 1982 hearings, the board heard extensive, forceful, and, at times, emotional testimony from local residents who reported smelling the odor for years before identifying its source. Many complained of headaches, nausea, and other symptoms, but their worries about the long-term safety of living and raising children in their neighborhood dominated the testimony. Also evident was growing frustration with the BAAQMD's policies and the pace of its response.[67] Persuaded that the BAAQMD staff would not adequately represent their interests before the hearing board, the Neighbors retained their own attorney in May 1982, and the board granted their application for intervention in the proceeding.[68] In August 1982, the board made a formal finding of a public nuisance violation by PSC and issued a conditional order of abatement that required the company to study a number of specified control measures and then to present a plan for controlling its odors.

In expectation of such a ruling, PSC had hired the services of an environmental consulting firm to help identify the source of the odors and to propose control solutions shortly after the March 1982 accusation. The consulting firm identified the shell molding process as the primary culprit, a diagnosis with which the district staff concurred and which confirmed what was generally known about the primary sources of odor in foundry manufacturing processes. On the basis of this assessment, PSC asked a manufacturer of wet scrubbers for the steel industry to submit a proposal for controlling the shell molding line. However, PSC later backed away from this diagnosis and solution in part "[b]ecause the scrubber installation on the shell molding line involved very substantial expenditures on the part of the company." Instead, relying on advice from a different consultant, PSC argued that the biggest source of odor complaints was a specific baghouse (a control device for particulate air pollutants) rather than the molding line, and it contended that raising the stack connected to that baghouse would "render emissions from that source undetectable."[69]

The district air pollution staff went along with this proposal, in part because it doubted (correctly) that scrubbers would prove sufficient to eliminate odors from the shell molding process.[70] The Neighbors disputed the second consultant's diagnosis of the problem and strongly opposed the proposed solution. Their skepticism was shared by the district's hearing board, which issued an unconditional order of abatement on February 11, 1983, coming into effect after the installation of the stack. Should the stack solution succeed, the company would be in compliance with the terms of the order. If, on the other hand, it were to fail, PSC would be subjected to high fines and potential shutdown orders. The unconditional order was the hearing board's ultimate weapon, and its use attested to the board's growing impatience not only with PSC but also with the district staff's passivity. The stack was built in March 1983 but, as the board and the Neighbors had predicted, it did not reduce the odors. In the weeks following the installation of the stack, the BAAQMD received forty-six complaints against PSC and confirmed eight.[71]

The timing of these events could not have been worse for PSC. The early 1980s brought a severe economic downturn to the foundry industry nationwide, and PSC was especially hard hit because of its drastic expansion during the 1970s. PSC laid off approximately 150 workers between 1981 and 1983, and its remaining employees went on a two-month strike at the end of March 1983 in response to the company's demands for cuts in wages and benefits.[72] Against this background but without explicit reference to PSC's financial troubles, the BAAQMD staff strongly opposed enforcing the unconditional order. It expressed concern about the possibility of protracted litigation and repeatedly argued for another negotiated solution. When PSC appealed the hearing board's unconditional order in Superior Court, the BAAQMD legal staff refused to defend the hearing board, which had to retain its own legal representation.

The court remanded the unconditional order back to the hearing board in May 1983. Following further hearings, and at the request of all parties, the board issued in August 1983 another conditional order for abatement that relied on a negotiated plan for the installation of dry scrubbers. As expected by the BAAQMD staff, the scrubbers failed to resolve the problem, and the district received and confirmed a large number of complaints throughout September. The hearing board held five separate hearings on the matter during the fall of 1983, where fifty area residents detailed, once again, the odors' physical and emotional impact on their lives.[73]

When months of negotiations between the company, the Neighbors, and the district failed to yield agreement upon a control plan, the hearing board issued a second unconditional abatement order in December 1983. In a sharply worded document perhaps more critical of the district staff than of PSC, the board wrote,

> Although it is indisputable that the elimination of this nuisance never would have been easy, it could have and should have been accomplished long ago. . . . The Hearing Board has been told repeatedly in this case that a solution is "finally" at hand, only later to be told that the experts were mistaken, the data were incomplete, and the problem is different from what the Hearing Board previously was told. . . . The burden of this uncertainty has been borne by the citizen neighbors of Respondent during all of this time. . . . The Company will now bear the burden of the continuing uncertainty it has created. It also will bear the risk of failure. . . . It is time for the company to comply with the law or to bear the consequences of continuing to violate the law. Enough is enough.[74]

In March 1985 the district filed a complaint for injunction in the Alameda County Superior Court. Soon thereafter, PSC, the Neighbors, and the BAAQMD agreed to a settlement, the central feature of which was the installation of a carbon adsorption system, a state-of-the-art technology, in two baghouses in plant number two. The plan, however, left plants number one and three without any fume controls, and did not provide for the hooding and channeling of fugitive emissions escaping from plant number two's large and open doors. Consequently, the plan left uncontrolled a significant proportion of PSC's molding fumes. A Superior Court judge signed the consent order on March 12, 1985, and the carbon adsorption unit began operating by the end of that year. The number of air quality complaints significantly declined soon thereafter, although the extent to which this resulted from improved air quality or a lull in local organizational efforts is unclear. Whether or not the problem had indeed been alleviated, after five years of intensive mobilization, the Neighbors were tired, financially overextended, and desperate to believe their efforts had borne fruit.

By 1987, however, the BAAQMD was once again receiving a growing number of odor complaints regarding PSC. Many were traced to emissions from plant number one, whose fumes had been left uncontrolled under the 1985 settlement. The year between November 1987 and November 1988 saw the filing of two hundred complaints against PSC, of which fifty were confirmed. On no single day, however, were five complaints confirmed, and the BAAQMD took no action, in accordance with its long-standing "rule of five." When outraged citizens brought the matter before the district's hearing board in February 1989, the BAAQMD's attorney justified the district's inaction, stating, "Now we are in a gray area. We don't have a public nuisance, but we are very close to a public nuisance situation. If the community is effectively mobilized, as they were in the past, we know we will have a public nuisance next year."[75] A public nuisance within the BAAQMD, as this statement makes clear, was not determined on the basis of the objective level of the pollution, but was rather a direct function of community mobilization.

Effective mobilization had in fact begun, this time with many of the complaints coming from the University of California's Albany Village family housing complex. Village residents had filed some complaints with the BAAQMD in the early 1980s, but the transience of its population and its isolation from other impacted residential neighborhoods meant that village residents remained unaware of both the dispute's long history and the Neighbors' role in it until the February 1989 hearing brought the two groups together. When village residents began mobilizing against PSC's odors in late 1988, their efforts were greatly aided by the neighborhoods' high population density, efficient communication channels, and underlying sense of community. Because of their complaints and renewed activity by the Neighbors and others, the "rule of five" requirement was satisfied on twenty-four separate occasions in 1989 and on eighteen days in 1990.[76] Between the end of 1987 and the end of 1989, the district's Inspection Section received approximately 500 complaints against PSC and confirmed approximately 200.[77]

In March 1989, a regrouped Neighbors for Clean Air filed suit for injunctive relief against PSC in Alameda County Superior Court. Two weeks later it was joined by the BAAQMD. In June 1989, the BAAQMD, the Neighbors, PSC, and the local glass molders union (which intervened on behalf of the company) reached another settlement. The settlement focused on the installation of a second carbon adsorption unit in plant number one. In addition, emissions from the shell mold area in plant number two were to be routed to the existing carbon adsorption unit. The work was completed in April 1991 at a cost of approximately $1.8 million, according to PSC.[78]

A decade after completing the odor control measures required by its second consent decree, PSC's website proudly hailed the deployment of the very pollution mitigation technology that it had resisted for so long. The website explains,

> Our environmental consciousness—which includes an investment in the United States' second largest carbon adsorption unit—lets us work in an area famous for its technology, its skilled workforce, its top caliber engineering talent and its highly developed ocean and land transportation. . . . Strong environmental and safety performance is essential for long term viability in our industry. Our leadership lets us serve our customers today at the high levels of social responsibility that will eventually be required of all U.S. steel component suppliers.[79]

Notwithstanding the extensive investment that PSC ultimately made in controlling its fumes, it's important to note that one of PSC's three plants, plant number three, was not controlled even under the second consent decree (beyond an adjustment to that plant's ventilation system). Consequently, as the BAAQMD recognized from the start, the controls imposed were only partial in that fumes from one of the three facilities were not controlled.[80] While community mobilization largely subsided after 1992, the Pacific Steel controversy resurfaced in the summer of 1999 and 2000. The BAAQMD held hearings in Berkeley where residents, once again, expressed concern over noxious odors and their health impact.[81]

TEMPE, ARIZONA

Tempe, Arizona, like Berkeley, is home to a large university, and this town of about 160,000 residents has many high-tech firms and a moderate-sized foundry, ME-West, formerly known as Capitol Castings. When

Capitol Castings was established in 1952, it was surrounded by cotton fields, but this changed in the early 1970s, when a residential subdivision along with schools, commercial property, and Kiwanis Park, Tempe's largest recreational area, were developed near the plant. Up until the mid-1990s, most of the casting in the plant was conducted outdoors, with the uncontrolled emissions going directly into the atmosphere. During the 1970s, in rough parallel to the situation in Berkeley and New Haven, complaints against the fumes began to stream in to the air pollution agency in charge, the Maricopa County Air Pollution Control Division (MCAPCD).[82]

Similarly to California's Health and Safety Code, Arizona state law prohibits unreasonable interference "with the comfortable enjoyment of life or property of a substantial part of the community."[83] As in California, the burden of proof as to the presence of such an interference lies with the community. However, the MCAPCD, in contrast to the BAAQMD, directed relatively little attention (at least up to the mid-1990s) to the investigation of odor complaints or the management of odor disputes. Complaints filed during the 1970s and 80s against Capitol Castings' fumes met with little if any regulatory response, and over the years, most of those complaining about the company's "burnt-plastic" smells gave up.

An important exception was the almost five-year, solitary campaign against Capitol Castings' emissions waged by a faculty member at Arizona State University, who had become aware of the fumes shortly after moving into the neighborhood in 1987. His persistent complaints to the MCAPCD, similar to the situation in New Haven, prompted greater regulatory scrutiny of Capitol Castings' visible emissions and resulted in two notices of violations regarding excessive smoke, although no action was ever taken against the odors. Next, the citizen contacted a number of local and state officials, including Arizona Senator Dennis DeConcini, to whom he relayed his concerns regarding the fumes' potential health effects and predicted that "nothing will be done, unless pressure is brought upon Maricopa County Air Pollution officials or if help is offered from other sources."[84] Senator DeConcini's office referred the letter to the U.S. EPA administrator for Region 9, who asked the MCAPCD to investigate the matter.[85] The MCAPCD subsequently found Capitol Castings to be a source of significant particulate emissions and possibly in violation of Maricopa County restrictions on the emission of volatile organic compounds (VOCs).[86] Capitol Castings responded by moving some core oven processes to another facility in Chandler, Arizona, but this did little to alleviate odorous fumes from the molding process.

Correspondence between Senator DeConcini's office and the EPA regarding Capitol Castings continued for the next two years. Prompted by the EPA, the MCAPCD monitored particulate emissions in the vicinity of the plant between March 1990 and March 1991 and found elevated levels of total suspended particulates (TSPs). In the opinion of the MCAPCD, the monitoring results could not prove conclusively, however, that the TSPs emissions came from Capitol Castings, rather than from a nearby freeway or other sources in the area. Nevertheless, the MCAPCD departed from its usual practice and refused to extend Capitol Castings' permit automatically after its 1991 expiration. Instead, the district asked the company to document its compliance with applicable restrictions on particulate and VOCs emissions. Negotiations over the terms of the permit and what would constitute an accurate estimate of the plant's emissions languished for almost two years, during which time the company, like many others overseen by the MCAPCD, continued to operate under an expired permit.[87] Only when local mobilization began in earnest during the winter of 1993 did the MCAPCD take action.

Until 1993, complaints against Capitol Castings came from scattered individuals who knew little of each other's efforts. This changed during a Parent Teachers Organization (PTO) meeting at a local elementary school, when one mother mentioned her concern over the fumes she had repeatedly noticed on the school grounds and sometimes in the classrooms. Other parents indicated that they, too, harbored similar worries, and someone mentioned the ongoing efforts of the citizen who had been corresponding with Senator DeConcini's office for the previous four years. A PTO representative got in touch with that individual, and soon a local grassroots group called Clean Air Now (CAN) coalesced. The group contacted the media, distributed flyers, advertised in the local paper, and consulted various experts at Arizona State University. A number of newspaper articles and TV news stories followed, and in March 1993, CAN held a public meeting attended by about 100 residents. Many spoke of years of concern about emissions that they associated with headaches and nausea. Others mentioned respiratory ailments and fears about latent carcinogenic effects. The principal of the school asked whether Capitol Castings' emissions were responsible for the fact that 25 percent of her students suffered from asthma and allergies.[88]

Capitol Castings reacted to the controversy with surprise. In newspaper interviews given in March 1993, the plant's senior engineer stated, "[W]e don't have the foggiest idea what the odor is,"[89] and "[w]e don't think the odors come from this facility. We've investigated the facility on a number of occasions. We don't know what it's coming from."[90] The MCAPCD responded by reviving the long stalled permit negotiations. Just prior to CAN's public meeting on March 31, 1993, Capitol Castings was asked to apply for an operating permit containing restrictions necessary to achieve compliance with VOCs and other standards. When Capitol Castings declined to do so, the MCAPCD finally denied it the permit and issued an order of abatement that Capitol appealed to the division's hearing board.[91]

The matter came before the MCAPCD hearing board on June 4, 1993. At issue was Capitol Castings' alleged violation of standards regulating particulates and VOCs, two categories of pollutants subject to control under the federal Clean Air Act. While the odor controversy had brought Capitol Castings to the attention of the EPA and seemed to be behind the company's permit difficulties with the MCAPCD, it was not directly relevant to the appeal. Nevertheless, CAN succeeded in turning the hearing into a forum for airing and publicizing its concerns. It presented a petition signed by 266 of Capitol Castings' neighbors and scores of angry letters detailing symptoms and concerns associated with the fumes. A woman who spent countless hours during the previous months on the campaign explained her motivation:

> I would describe the smell to be like burning electrical wires. Only minutes after inhaling these fumes I experienced headaches and lightheadedness with the natural reflex of not wanting to breathe in. . . . Upon experiencing my ill effects to the fumes, I was extremely fearful for the health of my infant daughter who always accompanied us. I wondered what pain her new and fragile lungs and body were experiencing. Now I, like others, do not use our park, walk in our neighborhood, open my windows in the afternoon or evening hours, have picnics or family events in our backyard, allow my child to participate in sports after school . . . just to avoid being exposed to these noxious fumes.[92]

Capitol Castings countered with an organized campaign of its own. It presented many letters in which its employees expressed their gratitude to and dependence upon the company. One such letter read,

> I can not begin to tell you what my career and my job at Capitol Castings means to me and my wife. As you know, today's economy is not what it used to be and jobs are not easy to come by. Three years ago I began the nightmare of job searching . . . then I was hired at Capitol Castings in 1992. In September of 1992 I got married. Together the three of us have a good life together and only dream of more.[93]

A sales administration supervisor in the company described the following predicament, "We produce wear-resistant steel castings for the mining industry. Our market is very sensitive to price and our competition is fierce."[94] Additional letters and presentations were offered by union representatives, business associates, suppliers of the company, and the Arizona Association of Industries.

The Hearing Board granted Capitol Castings a one-year conditional permit on June 21, 1993. Capitol was required to test and quantify its particulate and VOC emissions and was instructed to submit a report to the division regarding any odor control measures it intended to take. In March 1994, the hearing board convened again, and Capitol Castings relayed the conclusion of a report written by its consultant (who had worked closely with PSC since 1984). His key finding was that "the odors don't pose a health risk," but he added that an alteration in the binders used had already significantly decreased odors. Capitol Castings nonetheless conceded that it continued to receive odor complaints, and the company presented a plan to reduce odors by using fans to diffuse the air better.[95]

Once again, CAN members told the hearing board about their health fears and the symptoms they suffered. They also expressed increasing frustration with the MCAPCD's refusal to regulate odors and its inability to address the health issues at stake. Regarding the very definition of the pollution problem as one of "odors," one man stated,

> Since odor has been mentioned, please understand that I don't believe that the issue here is odor. Anyone will tell you that any odor you smell is produced by the substituent molecular content of whatever it is that brings it your way. . . . So, it is not a question of bad smell. It is a question of what is almost patently obvious which is a nauseous substance coming into the neighborhood in vapor form. So you can quit talking about odor for my point because that is not an issue at all. It is the contents of the vapor itself.[96]

Another CAN member asked, "We have been told in between the lines that the County is not going to deal with the smell problem, that is not part of their problem. How much truth is there?" To this question the MCAPCD representative responded,

> What I have said is that we cannot do anything about the odor problem right now. We can't tell them stop making odors. . . . We can't go out and smell an odor and tell Capitol Castings to stop doing what they are doing. Particularly since they have thousands of pounds of molds giving off odors.[97]

As to the question of toxicological risk the same official stated, somewhat obscurely,

> If we say these emission levels are acceptable, we are talking about acceptable within our regulations. We don't have something that says that this is the health base level or this is how much concentration is considered helpful or not. It is a numerical emission limitation for some kind of work practice standard.

An attorney for the MCAPCD concurred, adding that "right now there is no numerical limit which can be enforced for many hazardous air pollutants."[98]

By that time CAN was running out of momentum. Two of CAN's most active members were leaving the neighborhood, the media had lost interest in the story, and few local citizens attended the poorly publicized March 1994 meeting. A woman who had shouldered much of the organizational work during the previous year wrote soon thereafter, "Due to my own stupidity and lack of time I stopped logging all the time I've spent and all the people whom I've talked to on this issue. I'm just about at the end of my rope."[99] Yet just as it appeared that community mobilization, and with it any prospect of regulation, was about to disappear, Capitol Castings was purchased by ME International, a Minnesota-based company with plants in Duluth, Minnesota, and in Mexico. The new owners renamed the foundry ME-West and embarked on a $14 million modernization plan in the Tempe facility, including a major investment in air pollution control. Following ME International's purchase, the molding process was enclosed and its fumes funneled to a large carbon adsorption unit. These and other measures aimed at reducing VOCs emissions from the plant were undertaken voluntarily, since the MCAPCD had never determined that Capitol Castings' odors violated any law.

A number of factors seem to account for ME-West's cooperative approach and extensive investment in response to the problem. Unlike smaller companies, ME International could better afford the costs of pollution control. As the facility was undergoing a major upgrading, the timing for implementing pollution control measures was right, especially if the company considered the EPA likely to require better control of HAPs emissions by foundries in the near future. Additionally, ME International appears to have been motivated by a sense of social obligation and a commitment to do whatever was technically possible and economically feasible to control its fumes. In March 1995 Tim Wieland, the President of ME International, said of the long-brewing controversy, "What we're trying to do is tell people that we're working hard to address their concerns and make those problems disappear."[100] The statement, to the surprise of many in the area, proved sincere. But little in this case would suggest that this outcome was a product of efforts of the MCAPCD or the governing nuisance regime.

SKOKIE, ILLINOIS

Like Capitol Castings, Wells Manufacturing (currently Castwell) was surrounded by farmland when it was first built in 1947. But the cornfields soon gave way to residential subdivisions, and Wells found itself on the seam between the industrial section of Skokie and new suburban communities, most notably the village of Morton Grove, half a mile to the east. Across the street from the foundry now sits a large high school, built during the 1950s on land purchased in part from the company. Complaints regarding the foundry's smoke and fumes began shortly after Niles West High School opened its doors in 1958.

Between 1958 and 1964, representatives of the company and the school met several times with regard to the fly ash, smoke, and odor emitted by the foundry, which at that time completely lacked controls. Wells accordingly announced in 1964 a decision to replace its coke-powered, iron-melting cupolas with electric furnaces.[101] The first of two large, new arc furnaces was installed in 1967 and the second in 1969. But the cupolas continued to operate until July 1970, when the Cook County Circuit Court ordered them sealed. The enforcement action that hastened the cupolas' demise was triggered less by concern over particulate emissions from the melting process than by growing pressure for the control of odorous fumes from the molding process.

An October 1969 letter to the *Chicago Tribune* Action Express included the following complaint: "Can anything be done to stop the pollution pouring from the smoke stacks of Wells Manufacturing Co. . . . The smell is terrible and the slightest breeze sends it washing over the athletic fields of the nearby high school."[102] The newspaper referred the letter to the Cook County Air Pollution Control Bureau, which responded that Wells, was "in the process of installing control equipment" and that "[t]he problem should be corrected by the Fall of 1970."[103] The control step referred to by the agency was the switch from cupolas to arc furnaces, a measure that had little bearing on the "smell" or fumes motivating the letter to the *Chicago Tribune*.

When complaints persisted despite the cupolas' shutdown, the Cook County Air Pollution Control Bureau began pressuring Wells to investigate the odor and to suggest alternatives for its control.[104] By May 1971, Wells had identified phenolic binders from core-baking operations as the primary source of odors and outlined four alternative control approaches: (1) finding a substitute for the phenolic binder, (2) oxidation by washing the fumes with a permanganate scrubber, (3) thermal incineration, and (4) bacterial degradation of the phenol. The Environmental Control Bureau rejected the binder substitution approach because "there was no way of knowing how long the development of a new binder will take," the scrubber proposal because it lacked "concrete data to assure its success," and bacterial degradation (which it considered potentially promising), for lack of sufficient data. Instead bureau staff concluded that thermal incineration, the most costly and direct solution to the problem, ought to be the control technology of choice.[105] In search of a more optimistic diagnosis, Wells Manufacturing hired a consulting firm, which decided that extremely fine, micron-size particulates transmitted the odors into the atmosphere, and which recommended installing three baghouses to capture these particulates. After the baghouses installed in 1972 failed to bring improvement, local residents successfully elicited intervention by the newly created Illinois Environmental Protection Agency (IEPA).

The IEPA, and the Environmental Protection Act that it was to enforce, came into being in 1970 at the height of the environmental era. A central goal of this legislative reform was to create an aggressive and autonomous regulatory body capable of achieving a degree of insulation from the courts. Accordingly, the act established the Pollution Control Board and granted it authority to issue abatement orders (including shutdowns) and to impose civil penalties, including fines. More fundamentally, the drafters of the initial bill sought to depart from the preexisting common law regime by focusing on available technology, rather than the scope of proven injury, as the foremost determinant of regulatory interventions. The bill's original draft pursued this goal by prohibiting all air pollution resulting in interference with life or property under section 9 (a) of the law, leaving it up to facilities held responsible for creating such pollution to show that, because there existed no feasible means of control, "abatement would cause unreasonable hardship."[106] An amendment during the legislative process added the word "unreasonable" to describe the level of pollution justifying abatement in a move that—following the traditional nuisance formula—placed the initial burden of proof on the enforcing agency (section 9 (a) of the 1970 Illinois Environmental Act). Section 9 (b) of that act defines an air pollution violation as "the presence in the atmosphere of one or more contaminants in sufficient quantities of such characteristics and duration as to be injurious to human, plant, or animal life, to health or to property, or to unreasonably interfere with the enjoyment of life or property." An assessment of unreasonableness of emissions from a particular firm under section 9 (b), section 33 (c) of the act requires the Pollution Control Board to consider the following four factors: (1) the character or degree of injury or interference, (2) the social and economic value of the pollution source, (3) the suitability of the pollution source to the area and the chronology ("priority") of location, and (4) the technical practicability and economic reasonableness of reducing emissions. A series of odor enforcement cases ensued, in which the newly created IEPA (backed by the Illinois Pollution Control Board) and the Illinois Appellate courts divided over the meaning of unreasonable pollution under section 9 (a) and the evidentiary burdens implied.

In a 1971 opinion, the Illinois Pollution Control Board (a quasi-adjudicative body parallel to the BAAQMD's hearing board) stated, "It is the position of this Board that air contaminant emissions are 'unreasonable' within the meaning of the Act when there is proof that there is an interference with life and property and that economically reasonable technology is available to control the contaminant emissions."[107] The reviewing Illinois courts soon disagreed, arguing that the section 33 (c) criteria required that beyond the feasibility of technological solutions, the IEPA base pollution enforcement on the degree of injury and the nature of the locale.[108] On two separate occasions IEPA's attempts to subject Wells's fumes to what the agency viewed as economically reasonable pollution controls failed before the Illinois Supreme Court, on these traditional common law grounds.

In 1973 the IEPA charged Wells with creating air pollution in violation of section 33 (c). In 1974, through ten days of hearings before the control board, the IEPA set out to establish that emissions from Wells Manufacturing constituted an unreasonable interference under the statute. The bulk of the evidence pertained to the "character or degree of injury" as specified in section 33 (c) (i). Twenty-two local citizens, including the principal, teachers, and coaches from the high school as well as housewives, a police officer, and a Morton Grove Village Trustee, testified about the impact of Wells's fumes, including burning sensations in the eyes and throat, dizziness, and nausea. The Morton Grove Board of Trustees asked the board to issue an injunction against the phenolic odor problems that had troubled the community since 1966 and mentioned the particular concerns of local physicians as to the pollution's impact on patients with severe pulmonary problems.[109]

In an attempt to establish the technical practicability and economic reasonableness of controlling the emissions, the IEPA offered testimony regarding the feasibility of four alternative control approaches: ozonation, adsorption in activated carbon, absorption, and incineration. Without discussing any of these methods, Wells offered four arguments in response. The first conceded that Wells, like all foundries, emitted odors but denied that they were more intense than those of any other foundry. Second, Wells suggested that local phenolic odors might well come from another company in the area that had been a target of citizen odor complaints in the past. Next, the company offered the results of odor tests conducted by its consultants as proof that changing the chemical composition of its binders had already reduced odors significantly in the area. Finally, it contended that no feasible means of eliminating the problem existed. The Pollution Control Board found Wells guilty of releasing offensive odors and of failure to possess a permit. It fined the company $9,000 and ordered it to submit to an abatement plan, a performance bond, and periodic progress reports.

Wells appealed to the First District Appellate Court, and in an opinion issued in April 1977, the court overturned the Pollution Control Board's order for having been insufficiently attentive to three of the four section 33 (c) statutory criteria previously outlined.[110] With respect to the "character and degree of injury," the First District Court categorized the injury attributed to the odor as a "mild discomfort" and, in contrast to the IEPA, accepted the testimony of the Wells consultant who contended that the odor had been cut between 60 and 90 percent once Wells changed the makeup of its resin in 1971. Regarding the suitability of the area and priority of location (another Section 33 (c) criterion), the court noted,

> [I]t is clear both the residents of the area and the Niles West High School were well aware of the nature of the area when they moved in. . . . It is not responsible for the residents or the school to complain about Wells when they had, or should have had, after a cursory examination of the area, full knowledge of the fact that they were moving next to a heavily industrialized district. Finally, and most importantly, with regard to the practicability of technological controls the First District Court faulted the IEPA for producing three "experts," who in fact are three competing salesmen who had failed to sell their devices to Wells.[111]

In this respect, the court concluded "[w]e find this 'expert' testimony to be self-serving attempts by these salesmen in order to make a sale. It is clear from the record there is no working model anywhere in existence to completely control the odor from the foundry."[112]

The Illinois Supreme Court affirmed the First District Court's judgment. It defined the board's task under the statute as one of balancing "the costs and benefits of abatement in an effort to distinguish 'the trifling inconvenience, petty annoyance or minor discomfort' from 'a substantial interference with the enjoyment of life.' "[113] The burden of proof as to the unreasonableness of the pollution belonged to the control board, which had not met the burden in this case, said the Illinois Supreme Court as it concurred with the First District Court's review of the evidence.

After a short lull in local activism following this defeat, Wells's pollution again became the object of organized protest by 1984, when S.T.O.P. (Suburbs Turn Off Pollution) formed. In an effort to help the IEPA make the case that the odor had persisted well beyond the change of binders, and that it posed more than a "mild discomfort," S.T.O.P. held a rally at the local high school. It collected 524 signatures for a petition that called upon the IEPA "to analyze the content of the air as a result of this odor to determine its toxicity and any potential health hazard to establish and enforce standards or limits for any airborne toxic chemicals being released into the environment in which we live, work or have children attending school."[114] Later that month S.T.O.P wrote to the IEPA,

> To the best of our knowledge, no one has ever been able to determine what is being released from the stacks and what potential health hazards are in question. Maybe people are not becoming fatally ill immediately but again no one has ever been able to determine the long term affects of this air pollution. . . . If you study the I.E.P.A. complaint forms pertinent to this case we are sure

you will find just how greatly people are affected, not only with physical symptoms of illness, but just as important great emotional anxiety as well as tremendous stress.[115]

The IEPA again attempted to force Wells to reduce its odorous emissions. In February 1985, it denied Wells's application to renew its permit for its shell-pouring and molding process, due to expire in April 1986, on the grounds that uncontrolled fumes from that process were a primary source of odors. The IEPA made reference to "verified citizen complaints" and the possibility of a violation of section 9 (a) of the Environmental Protection Act, but added that its decision would be reevaluated following Wells's submission of information pertaining to the plant's operations, stack tests, and monitoring.[116] In lieu of seeking such a reevaluation, Wells appealed directly to the Pollution Control Board, invoking two main arguments: first, as a procedural matter, any additional information necessary for evaluation of the permit ought to have been requested before, rather than after the agency's decision to deny the permit. Second, and more fundamentally, Wells once again disputed the allegation that the shell molding process generated odors in violation of section 9 (a) of the Illinois Environmental Protection Act.

Under section 1040 (a) (1) of the Illinois Environmental Protection Act, the burden of proof in a permit-denial appeal falls upon the petitioner. The IEPA consequently hoped that a shift from pollution enforcement to permit denial would allow it to avoid the evidentiary problems that had doomed its earlier efforts to force Wells to control its odors. In its brief to the Pollution Control Board, the agency pointed to 250 signed citizen complaints as proof of the existence of an objectionable odor and noted,

These injuries to human health as well as the interference with the use and enjoyment of property have caused area citizens to attend meetings, write complaints and resulted in a large attendance at the hearings in the case at bar. Such actions would not occur were there no odor problem sufficient for the area citizens to fear for their health and safety.

Having thus shown the existence of a significant likelihood of air pollution violation in the area, the agency further contended, "[I]t is Wells' burden to prove that the shell molding and pouring process, the subject of the permit renewal application, alone or in combination with other sources is not the source of the odor emissions in question."[117]

The Pollution Control Board held hearings in July and September 1986. Citizen testimony regarding the impact of Wells's fumes on the neighborhood was repeated. Much of it focused on growing local anxiety as to the fumes' potential toxicity and the perception that rates of cancer and other diseases in the area were higher than normal. One resident testified during the 1986 hearings, "My main comment is in my area (there are) six cases of cancer. My wife and I lost a 19 year old son to leukemia. . . . I mean something has got to be done because we are losing lives over it." More cautiously, another man stated,

> We don't know what we are breathing. We don't know what the long-term effects of what we are breathing is doing to us. I am very, very concerned about the fact that twenty years down the road, Mr. Wells comes up and says well, gee, I didn't know that this was doing this to your bodies. I am real sorry. . . . This is what really concerns me.[118]

The Pollution Control Board affirmed the agency's denial of the permit renewal application in March 1987.[119] Referring to the earlier litigation in the case, the board stated in its decision,

> The First District Appellate Court characterized the effect of the odor on citizen complainants as "mild discomfort." . . . However, the record in the case at bar indicates much more persuasively that Wells' emissions may cause unreasonable interference with the enjoyment of life and property and hence, air pollution. . . . Interference of the sort alleged in this case goes far beyond "trifling inconveniences, petty annoyance, or minor discomforts." We view the interference alleged by the citizen complainants as more approximately reaching the level of pervasive intrusion, affecting nearly every aspect of the lives of those living or working in close proximity to the Wells facility.[120]

Wells appealed to the First District Appellate Court, and in 1990 the court once again sided with the company and remanded the board's decision for further consideration. The chief reason given was the procedural argument that the IEPA had not allowed Wells the chance to present evidence that it was not a polluter before denying its renewal application, and that a postdenial reevaluation could not rectify this omission.[121]

Following its second defeat in the courts, the IEPA ultimately settled on a list of incremental process changes, the bulk of which concerned particulates, rather than odors. "The Wells Manufacturing Company welcomes the recent cooperation shown by the Illinois EPA" began a March 1990 letter from the company to the IEPA Division of Air Pollution Control. The letter outlined a list of pollution control measures that the company was prepared to undertake as a condition of its permit, primarily the upgrading and expansion of wet scrubbers (which were directed primarily at the capture of particulates). In addition, the company outlined a number of actions intended to reduce organic emissions, most importantly the use of precoated sands in its shell core- and mold-making operations, a move that eliminated the fumes previously emitted in the process of chemically coating the sand. In addition, Wells committed to continue experimenting with the use of alternative "low odor" materials in various parts of its manufacturing process.[122] Although these were nontrivial incremental pollution reduction steps, they nowhere approximated the level of controls that the IEPA envisioned when it began its Sisyphean effort—almost two decades before—to implement a technology-based pollution control regime with respect to Wells and other sources of odorous fumes in Illinois.

EVIDENTIARY BURDENS AND PERPETUAL MOBILIZATION

Roughly contemporaneous, the four preceding foundry disputes unfolded in complete isolation across the country. In each locale the odor was discovered and investigated, and the feasibility of its control evaluated, as if the problem were being encountered for the very first time and as if it were unique to the foundry and community in question. Initially perplexed citizens filed complaints, agencies dispatched inspectors, and foundries hired consultants in a waltz that looks almost absurd when viewed in the aggregate. Instead of drawing on existing knowledge of the problem and sharing technical expertise, each dispute unfolded as if in a vacuum while the relevant agencies investigated, documented, and evaluated the odors, sometimes for decades on end. What explains this almost ritualistic mode of investigation, given its often substantial consumption of administrative resources and its tendency to provoke public antagonism?

A partial answer comes from the agencies' need to support administrative determination of a nuisance violation with evidence sufficient to satisfy the standards of reviewing courts. The last word regarding the validity of fines, or the enforceability of orders of abatement belongs to judges, and as the Illinois courts' response to the Wells dispute amply shows, the courts' deference to administrative decisions cannot be assumed. But agencies seemed to be going beyond that which was necessary to build an evidentiary record. With the important exception of the IEPA, the agencies acted themselves in an umpire-like fashion, preempting the courts in defining away pollution injuries. Like common law courts over the past century, they appeared to have no independent air-pollution control mission. Instead, perpetual administrative investigation served as a de facto mechanism for concluding, as the common law courts have long done, that the vast majority of cases failed to meet the evidentiary burden of establishing the existence of a nuisance. This can be seen most readily in the cases of the Michigan Department of Natural Resources and the Maricopa County Air Pollution Control Division, two agencies that during the period under investigation never found the relevant foundry fumes to constitute an illegal nuisance. Perhaps less visibly, the substitution of investigation for regulation also characterized the Bay Area Air Quality Management District to a significant degree.

Unlike the first two agencies, the BAAQMD demonstrated significantly more rigor and commitment in its approach to complaint investigation, and it repeatedly found Pacific Steel's odors to be in violation of California nuisance law. However, closer examination of the agency's reliance on the "rule of five" for issuing nuisance citations raises doubts about its actual level of commitment to regulating odors. Much of the problem derives from defining a nuisance incident in terms of a discrete twenty-four-hour period, rather than as a chronic problem within a particular locale.

For its part, the BAAQMD explains the rationale behind the "twenty-four hour" rule as follows:

> We do not believe that we could reasonably expect a court to award civil penalties for any given violation of Health and Safety Code Section 41700 unless the District Staff were able to confirm and prove that *on the day in question* the offending odor affected such a "considerable number of persons."[123]

This "day in question" approach finds little support, however, in either the language of the relevant California statute or the doctrinal tradition of nuisance law where, notwithstanding a general reluctance to intervene in response to noxious fumes, judges rarely framed pertinent evidentiary requirements with reference to temporally compartmentalized pollution episodes.

Confidence in the judicial review explanation for the evidentiary obstacles is further undermined by the fact that, with extremely few exceptions, odor nuisance citations by the BAAQMD terminate in negotiated settlements rather than litigation. If the cases rarely proceed to court, why is the BAAQMD so willing to incur and endure the extensive financial and public relations costs associated with its "rule of five"? On one of the few occasions that a BAAQMD nuisance violation did reach the court, the strategy backfired. Far from withstanding judicial review, the "rule of five" paradoxically contributed indirectly to the BAAQMD's defeat.

The case pertained to a notice of violation issued against PSC in 1990 based on odor complaints mobilized through the use of a "phone tree." Mobilized citizens used the phone tree to coordinate the timing of complaints in order to increase the likelihood that inspectors would confirm five or more complaints in the course of one investigation. When one member of the phone tree noticed the smell, he or she would alert others on the list who, after verifying that the odor could be detected at their own homes, also filed complaints with the BAAQMD. PSC disputed the authenticity of any phone-tree-generated complaints, arguing that only spontaneous complaints could establish the requisite communal discon-

tent. The case was adjudicated in Berkeley / Albany Municipal Court before Judge Norris Goodwin, who was brought in from outside the county
especially for this case. Concurring with the company that the phone tree
invalidated the complaints, Judge Goodwin dismissed the violation notice
(and implicitly all others like it), stating,

> The complaint process has been skewed by the arborial complainants. In order
> to validate the constitutionality of the statute authorizing these penalties, one
> must have confidence in the spontaneity and self-generation of the complaints
> themselves. If it is not spontaneous and self-generating and of a nature in and
> of itself to impel the "victim" to complain, it is probably not a nuisance. A true
> "nuisance" must be presumed to be so offensive as to be recognizable as such
> by ordinary reasonable people in substantially large portions of the community.

More fundamentally, the judge appeared to suggest that no matter how
generated, complaints from area residents could not successfully establish
PSC's legal liability under the relevant public nuisance provision. Echoing
a long line of common law decisions that equate residence in polluted
locales with consent to its conditions, Judge Goodwin noted,

> In this regard the nature of the surrounding area must be considered, for what
> is a nuisance in one area may not be a nuisance in another. . . . People who
> move into an industrial area must adjust their sensibilities to the realities of
> commerce. They live there cheaper than elsewhere because of the area's short-
> comings, and should not expect the refinements of the lakeside country club. It
> is clear that from the nature of the area in which the defendant's business is
> located, that the odors which it occasionally emits are not such as to constitute
> a public nuisance in that area.[124]

The BAAQMD chose not to appeal, perhaps for pragmatic reasons.
By that time PSC was in the midst of implementing its pollution control
program under the consent decree, and these particular violation notices
were of marginal importance to the resolution of the case. Nevertheless,
because Judge Goodwin's opinion cast doubt on the validity of all organized efforts to establish nuisance violations under "the rule of five," the
agency's decision to let the opinion stand underscores a more fundamental quandary. Appealing the decision would have forced the BAAQMD
to mount two central arguments. First, the agency would need to acknowledge that, to negotiate successfully the "rule of five," citizens all
but had to resort to mobilization of the type that took place in Berkeley,
and thus their organizational efforts ought not to detract from the perceived authenticity of their complaints. Second, BAAQMD would have
to challenge Judge Goodwin's assumption that nuisance standards ought
to vary with the character of various communities and locations.

An agency concession that a "phone tree" might well be necessary for successful negotiation of the "rule of five" would have been difficult to reconcile, however, with the District's long-standing insistence that the rule offered a reasonable and workable evidentiary policy. Furthermore, the BAAQMD's odor enforcement policies implicitly shared the view that nuisance thresholds indeed ought to vary with community characteristics. Shortly after Judge Goodwin handed down his decision, one of the BAAQMD's advisory subcommittees discussed a proposal that the agency take into account the odor potential of a proposed facility when reviewing its permit application. The agency's Director of Enforcement replied that considering a facility's odor impact during the permitting process would be inappropriate because the threshold of odor tolerance varies across communities, and odor abatement cases therefore "warrant site-specific solutions on a case by case basis."[125] It was, his argument implied, preferable to build the facility without odorous fume controls, and then to wait and see whether the odors prove objectionable to the community in question.

This argument resembled that used by the EPA a decade earlier, when it decided not to make odors an object of federal control. As the agency explained, the particular ability of nuisance law to tailor interventions to the sensibilities of each community and locale made it a better method of regulation. However, when it comes to the differences in outcome of the above four foundry disputes, variations in local community norms and efforts appear to have little explanatory power. Norms did not vary, in that none of the communities found the fumes unproblematic. Although the neighbors of ME West and Pacific Steel would hardly have won their carbon adsorption units without their active and sophisticated organizational efforts, neither would their efforts alone probably have sufficed without the intervention of additional circumstances specific to each of the two cases: ME-West's acquisition of Capitol Castings in the Tempe instance, and the intervention of the BAAQMD Hearing Board in the Berkeley dispute.

Capitol Castings' plan for the odor, before ownership of the plant shifted to ME-West, was to install fans to increase diffusion of the uncontrolled fumes. At that juncture, nothing indicated that the MCAPCD was about to require any additional means of odor control, and community organizational efforts seemed to be on the decline. The facility's major upgrade following the arrival of ME-West, coupled with that firm's cooperative attitude, however, created an opening for a voluntary implementation of pollution controls that would otherwise most likely not have taken place.

More than a decade of complaints, letters, press releases, testimony, litigation, and myriad other modes of community action against PSC's odors likewise would have produced few results had the BAAQMD's independent hearing board not intervened. Acting against the explicit wishes of the BAAQMD staff, the board twice issued unconditional orders against PSC in an effort to shift the cost of failed pollution control approaches from the Neighbors to the company. At the same time, the board's sympathetic response to citizens' concerns and its open criticism of the BAAQMD's "rule of five" and other odor-related policies played a crucial role in sustaining local mobilization efforts. In 1989, shortly before concluding his hearing board service, Kenneth Manaster publicly stated at an odor-related hearing,

> There is a very large number of aspects of the District's approach to odor nuisance cases . . . which I simply cannot understand . . . why members of the public dealing with the agency, with respect to odor nuisance complaints, end up so frequently feeling that they, the members of the public, somehow were at fault in failing to figure out how to get the message through to the agency. . . . [T]here's an awful lot of what appears to me to be a serious lack of responsiveness and aggressiveness on the part of the District staff in these odor nuisance cases. I find it extremely frustrating, extremely disappointing, for an agency that in so many other respects is expert and aggressive.[126]

With respect to forms of pollution other than odors, the BAAQMD has indeed shown significantly greater resolve. The agency's primary regulatory mission is to bring the Bay Area into compliance with governing regulatory requirements under the CAA, and it has displayed much greater willingness to take on polluters and demand controls in implementing this mission. As the above accounts relate, comprehensive controls for particulates from the relevant foundries were eventually instituted not only under the BAAQMD but also under the Michigan DNR and the MCAPCD. When it came to odors, however, all three agencies seemed to lose their regulatory will. Instead, under default assumptions of community tolerance for localized pollution, they imposed practically insurmountable evidentiary burdens on the citizens involved. In similar fashion to the earlier smoke inspection bureaus, they demanded perpetual community mobilization as a condition for abatement, and used the common law's evidentiary burdens to mask their own policies of nonintervention.

In pursuing a technology-based regulatory orientation, the IEPA adopted a regulatory model rooted in nineteenth-century German pollution regulation and the British Alkali Act. The model is one that across the history of air pollution regulation has been offered against the prevailing common law view that "reasonable" regulation, by definition, means a pollution remedy tailored to proven legal injury defined in reference to the characteristics and "sensibilities" of particular locales. In Illinois, as elsewhere in the United States, these assumptions, through their influence across the legislative, administrative, and judicial branches, have stymied those who sought to implement technology-based regulatory reforms.

A 1989 article in the journal *Foundry Management and Technology* stated that "[f]oundries use sand binders that are hazardous, foul smelling, or expensive to dispose of because not many nonhazardous binders are available."[127] At the same time the article highlighted the availability of a number of effective, nonhazardous, foundry bonding-materials based on clays, plant oils, starches, animal proteins, sodium silicates, and epoxies, and concluded that "[u]ltimately we need to change the way we think about chemical binders. The environmental regulations are giving us added impetus to search for safe alternative systems." Not coincidentally, the author of that article was the president of a research and development consulting group that specialized in the development of nonhazardous binders. For his company and others like it, a federal push for the control of foundry fumes, under the soon to be enacted 1990 Clean Air Act Amendments, must have been welcome news. In the summer of 1973, the foundry industry had already recognized that a viable solution to its significant pollution problems would depend on the development of promising non-toxic alternatives for bonding foundry molds. Improved commercial prospects for environmentally safer binders subsequent to the 1990 CAA gave rise to increased entrepreneurial activity in this area.[128] Yet rather than directing its efforts toward bringing about this goal, the governing regulatory regime—across scores of foundry-adjacent communities in the United States—directed its resources toward the investigation of citizen "odor complaints."

CHAPTER NINE

Conclusion

THE BENEFITS of industrialization, from its inception, have been accompanied by the problem of troublesome air emissions. Though names for the phenomenon have changed over the centuries—"noxious vapors," "smoke," "fumes," "odors," or "air pollution"—the dilemma posed by the conjoined benefits and harms of industrialization has remained. Almost as old as the emission problem itself are two alternative families of public response: one reactive, and one proactive. Neither approach avoids imposing and distributing sacrifice on people affected by pollution, since neither regulatory method has been able to eliminate all of pollution's harms while allowing industrial production to continue. Yet the differing approaches have had far-reaching implications for both the level of sacrifice that pollution imposes and the distribution of the pollution burden.

The reactive approach, focusing on the ultimate end of protection from pollution's harms, promises a total remedy, if not through elimination, then through full monetary compensation. The proactive approach, focusing on the means of abatement, offers pollution reduction through substituting materials (such as clean coal) or the imposition of end-of-pipe controls (such as "smoke consumption devices"). But it promises nothing greater than incremental relief based on the feasibility of mitigation. The core logics of the two regimes diverge, as do the institutional processes used to implement them. Whereas the reactive regime ultimately relies on courts to determine the legitimate extent of intervention, the proactive approach places considerably more discretion in the hands of administrators. Though the regimes are conceptually distinct, hybrid interventions have developed, as when courts have taken on administrative tasks through BAT injunctions.

This book has traced the historical roots of these regimes to their national systems' respective conceptions of the scope of regulatory authority under the police power. The civil law foundation, associated with states of the European continent, supports the proactive pollution regime; and English common law—later transplanted to North America—forms the core logic of its reactive counterpart. This historical difference has continued to shape air pollution regulation in Europe and the United States, with the clearest indicator of the divergence between the two approaches being the difference in the prevalence of technology standards in the alternative regimes. At a more fundamental level, the regimes are distinguished by their core legitimating idea: whereas the American regulatory paradigm aspires to scientific determination of the level of pollution mitigation required, policy on the European continent—notably in Germany—relies on the precautionary principle both as a foundational idea and as legitimating rhetoric.

Air pollution policy constitutes one instance of a broader pattern of divergence between American and European social policy responses to industrialization. Research into the roots of these differences has focused on the continuing impact of nineteenth-century structures and ideas on both sides of the Atlantic.[1] In keeping with this research tradition, this book looks to the origins and evolution of the contemporary American air pollution regime to explain its distinctive characteristics. Preindustrial absolutist nuisance doctrine—geared toward the separation of incompatible land uses rather than incremental mitigation of environmental emissions—set the stage for the common law's subsequent response to industrial pollution. Hallmarks of this response included the regime's orientation toward land-use separation rather than deployment of available technology, and an attendant exclusion (under the "trifling inconvenience" doctrine) of scientifically uncertain harms from the realm of remediable legal injury.

This book has argued that the continued reliance on science as the primary mode of legitimation for the U.S. environmental regime is a current-day outcome of this common law tradition. This stands in contrast to European regulation, which bases interventions not in evidentiary demands for scientific proof of harm, but in governmental expertise and in the requirement that industrial operators undertake feasible measures of mitigation.

It is important to note that significant variations exist among the various European states, with England and Germany frequently representing opposing views. For example, within the framework of the European Union, the United Kingdom resisted Germany's push for technology-based regulation in response to acid rain and other environmental problems. Within this debate, the British invoked the need for greater scientific evidence, a sentiment occasionally shared even by some British environmental interests.[2] In, England a hybrid common law statutory regime existed since the nineteenth century. Compared to U.S. policy, the British Alkali Act introduced a significantly greater emphasis on the implementation of feasible technological reductions of noxious vapors, under the rubric of "Best Practicable Means" (BPM). Yet, even this technology-based approach differed significantly from the German *Stand der Technik*. In making judgment on BPM, the Alkali Inspectorate considered local conditions and the assimilative capacity of the particular environment, this stands in contrast to the German insistence on uniform application across firms.[3]

In tracing the evolution of American air pollution policy since the Civil War, the book highlights the impact of common-law-derived notions of reasonable versus arbitrary governmental intervention on patterns of air pollution regulation (and nonregulation). These ideas have affected both the definition of pertinent problems and the pursuit of solutions. The ongoing significance of these notions of regulatory rationality—and regulatory democracy—to contemporary American policy debates reveals the common law sensibilities of governance in the United States. The defining characteristic of this "common law state" is a distrust of administration and a consequent insistence on judicial oversight to check its potential for abuse. Requirements for oversight of a tight nexus between means and ends grow directly from this fundamental distrust. Regulatory actions that cannot meet this test are suspect and are held to be arbitrary and unreasonable by virtue of their apparent origin in independent agendas of the state.

Paradoxically, the two features of the Clean Air Act broadly viewed as key elements of its radical transformation away from the earlier regime—its absolutism and its view of the courts as antidote to regulatory capture—instead constitute evidence of the law's continuity with the common law tradition. An act that implemented an incremental technology-based regime—in lieu of promising to eradicate all (scientifically proven) air pollution harm—would have been a much greater departure from the established patterns of the common law. Likewise, in opting to give a central oversight role to federal courts, the law fits neatly within a long-standing effort to impose judicial constraints on administration in the United States. This project had suffered a temporary setback when the New Deal created more autonomous and insulated agencies. However, beginning in the 1950s, the European-modeled agencies of the New Deal were subject to ever growing criticisms regarding their alleged complacency, insularity, and even capture by the economic interests that they were supposed to regulate. By the late 1960s, as Richard Harris and Sidney Milkis describe, the New Left's suspicion of "the establishment" and an attendant emphasis on "participatory democracy" gave rise to what they term "the public lobby regime."[4] As a corrective to the perceived deficiencies of the New Deal model, the New Left activists pushing this regime "attempted to advance their aims and protect their achievements through judicial mechanisms, thus thrusting the federal courts into a new and more positive role in the policy process."[5] The emphasis on judicial review was novel only relative to the New Deal, however. American lawyers concerned about the dangers of bureaucratic autonomy have long prescribed judicial oversight to check the inevitable excesses of administrative government. Actors with otherwise opposing political interests in the United States could nonetheless agree that administrative government should not be trusted, but that courts should.

Throughout the history recounted here there were some who stood to win and some to lose from the adoption of one regulatory approach or the other, and there is little doubt that their power and resources mattered to the outcome of legislation and policy-making. American distrust of administration and notions of regulatory reasonableness did not operate in a vacuum, detached from the economic interests at stake. Thus ideas and institutions are viewed here not as proximate causes of observed phenomena, but as the framework that structured political battles "and in so doing influence[d] their outcome."[6] The failure of the United States to respond more than tepidly to air pollution for so long can be explained in large measure through the economic interests that benefited from the common law's noninterventionist stance. Nevertheless, against those who were served by the timid regime of nuisance law, there always stood strong and countervailing economic, political, and financial interests who would have profited from a technology-based approach to pollution control. These interests included not only the extensive business and real estate investments damaged by pollution, but also those who produced the control technology or the raw materials for which pollution prevention standards might have created substantial new markets. For example, it is difficult to explain through sheer economic and political power alone why bituminous coal survived for so long against a coalition of producers of anthracite coal, gas, and electrical powers, or why makers of various smoke consumption devices were undermined by governmental inaction, or why smoke was allowed to diminish vast financial interests.

Nor is it evident that reactive, nonuniform standards always leave pollution sources themselves more favorably positioned than would a technology-based regime. Whereas technology standards generally apply uniformly across industrial sectors, nuisance law and even risk-based standards tend to target a few facilities while sparing others. This can spell financial ruin for those firms that are burdened with extensive pollution control investments that most of their competitors were able to avoid.[7] But in addition, the adversarial process can exact significant costs in legal expenses, community goodwill, and long-term regulatory uncertainty even for firms that successfully defend against nuisance complaints. These considerations were among those that prompted the British alkali industry during the 1860s to support a statutory requirement for an across-the-board reduction of hydrochloric acid emissions through already available means of control.

Thus rather than attributing American opposition to harm-independent interventions to economic efficiency or sheer political power alone, this book highlights the influence of common-law-driven conceptions of regulatory legitimacy on the ways economic and political actors define and pursue their interests. Opponents of harm-independent regulatory interventions have been able to tap into broadly shared understandings of civil-law-modeled rules as inconsonant with core principles of American democracy. The common thread running from nineteenth-century constitutional battles on the scope of the police power, through New Deal–era administrative law debates, to the contemporary "command and control" label for technology-based standards, is the choice between two alternative conceptions of the rule of law.

The U.S. choice to stick with core common law principles can be seen not only in the risk-based provisions of the CAA, but perhaps more importantly in the de facto reign of nuisance-based structures that continue to serve as the primary recourse for those affected by localized pollution. In many cases, local pollution sources operate without fume controls, despite their proximity to residential areas and the feasibility of mitigation. This outcome stems directly from a regulatory system built on the principle that sources—even newly constructed sources free from the added burden of retrofitting—will remain uncontrolled until and unless surrounding communities mobilize to demonstrate their annoyance from the fumes. Legal reference to these emissions as "odors" confers a benign, and even dismissive, meaning on fumes that citizens suspect may be toxic, a suspicion that derives some support from the absence of rigorous federal or state regulation of air pollutants already acknowledged to be hazardous. Making the case for regulatory abatement of "odors" is, for the vast majority of those who embark on this course, a Sisyphean task.

This book seeks not only to explain the origins of the risk and nuisance regime but also to demonstrate the deficiency of the judicialized approach that it has engendered in the United States. As a consequence of this judicialized regulatory regime for air pollution (both under common law and the CAA), resources that might otherwise have been directed toward pollution abatement were diverted to legal contestation and the quixotic pursuit of scientific certainty regarding safe thresholds, a certainty elusive at best and fictitious at worst. This has left underutilized alternative mitigation technologies—from smoke consumption devices to safer resins—and systematically underregulated localized pollution concentrations.

As the book has demonstrated, ignoring localized pollution is endemic to the risk / nuisance regime. Studies of the distribution of environmental burdens have largely focused on the siting decisions of polluting or otherwise hazardous firms and public facilities.[8] Environmental justice critiques of discriminatory siting practices have been met with counterarguments about market-driven household relocations underlying observed demographic-environmental patterns.[9] The question as framed by this debate implicitly accepts the common law's view that land-use separation is the appropriate response to localized pollution. As the nineteenth-century history discussed here demonstrates, large-scale urbanization renders land-use separation only a partial answer to the harms of localized pollution, making mitigation a necessary component of air-pollution control policy. This study has considered the kinds of regimes that are most capable of ensuring such reduction. While technology-based standards cannot eliminate localized air pollution completely, they are capable of bringing incremental improvements by imposing a technology-based pollution mitigation floor.[10]

Beyond their distributional implications, risk and nuisance regimes end up diverting attention and resources from pollution mitigation by pitting camps against each other in an adversarial legal environment. Two features of this regime discourage compromise solutions and stunt opportunities for cooperation. The first is the absolutist—if chimerical—nature of the regime's promise. As John Dwyer has argued,

> Environmental groups take the legislation's promise of a risk-free environment at face value and tend to refuse to compromise the "rights" inherent in such promises. Industry fears that regulators will implement the statute literally and, consequently, vigorously opposes the regulatory process at every stage. By making promises that cannot be kept, and by leaving no middle ground for accommodation, the legislature makes it more difficult to reach a political compromise.[11]

The second element discouraging cooperation is the regime's requirement that interventions be closely tailored to harms—that is, to avoid both over- and underregulation. Since local conditions are presumed to vary relevantly in geography and in environmental preferences of the population, this principle ends up requiring some firms to employ pollution controls that their competitors can avoid, placing the targeted firms at a competitive disadvantage. In principle, if such a regime succeeded in imposing mitigation costs predictably on industrial production in densely populated regions, it might successfully encourage an effective land-use separation solution by providing incentives for location in low-impact areas. The reality is one of unpredictable retrofitting demands based on local capacities for sustained mobilization that hit firms only after they have made massive and unmovable capital investments in buildings and production facilities. Since only the exceptional few losing firms end up having to deploy mitigation technologies, those firms who are the focus of such actions feel unfairly targeted and cornered into a dispute with their surrounding communities.

Studies of environmental regulation in Germany, France, Sweden, and England demonstrate the possibility of a more consensual regulatory process; these countries exhibit regulatory decisions reached largely through negotiation and a near-absence of litigation. By comparison, U.S. agencies that regulate chemicals labor under the ever-present prospect of judicial review.[12] This outcome is a product of numerous factors including national cultures, but the decision between either technology or risk standards is among the most significant policy choices that determines whether the chemical regulatory process will be an adversarial or consensual one.

In a study comparing the adversarial course of American regulation of vinyl chloride (VC) to its more consensualist history in Germany, France, and Japan, Joseph Badaracco argues that while institutional arrangements do not determine levels of cooperation or conflict, they "load the dice" in favor of one or the other. He further finds that cooperation is "probably much better suited to questions of means than to questions of ends." Unlike in the United States, representatives of the relevant industrial interests in Europe and Japan "all agreed from the beginning on the goal of cutting VC levels dramatically. Given this objective, they concentrated on what were essentially technical questions of implementation."[13]

Robert Kagan has identified "formal legal contestation and legal activism" or "adversarial legalism" as hallmarks of a distinctly American policy-making and implementation process. While acknowledging that "American lawyers, litigation, and courts serve as powerful checks against official corruption and arbitrariness, as protectors of essential individual rights, and as deterrents to corporate heedlessness," Kagan also concludes that "adversarial legalism is a markedly inefficient, complex, costly, punitive, and unpredictable method of governance and dispute resolution."[14] The drawbacks of court-governed regulatory processes of air pollution control have been the overarching theme of this book. Yet the recipe for correcting these deficiencies is far from obvious, not least because of the dissonance between the logic of trust in government, upon which more cooperative, less legalistic regulatory processes depend, and deeply embedded, reactive conceptions of the American state.

Mirjan Damaška has argued that, in their respective orientations toward either ends or means, legal processes reveal underlying reactive or proactive conceptions of the authority of the state. "The task of the reactive state," he writes, "is limited to providing a supporting framework within which its citizens pursue their chosen goals . . . it protects order, and it provides a forum for the resolution of those disputes that cannot be settled by citizens themselves." In contrast, the proactive state "strives toward a comprehensive theory of the good life and tries to use it as a basis for a conceptually all encompassing program of material and moral betterment of its citizens."[15] Whereas in the activist state the "controlling image of law is that of the state decree," the reactive state is "first and foremost an adjudicative body." While in practice neither purely reactive nor purely proactive states exist, on the continuum along which real states divide, common and civil law societies fall at opposite ends. The specter of totalitarianism at the extreme end of the proactive spectrum consequently casts a long shadow over proposals for even incremental shifts away from reactive governmental structures.

Short of a totalitarian threat, there remain important reasons for concern about moves toward increased reliance on administrative expertise and discretion. Comparative studies of European chemical regulation show not only less litigation but also less public participation than in the United States. Negotiated solutions, under European regimes, are reached largely without input or supervision by public interest groups.[16] This has been an important source of criticism not only by American writers but also by some in Germany.[17] Although European Community directives have brought greater access than before, Germany does not match the United States in the openness of governmental processes.[18]

Yet the assumption that risk-based regulatory processes are inherently amenable to public participation seems unwarranted. The often fictitious nature of "safe threshold" determinations can constitute a "science charade" that renders regulatory processes opaque for the purposes of meaningful public input.[19] Furthermore, the participation that these processes do engender is often less an indication of vibrant democratic engagement than a reflection of the suspicion that "no one is minding the store"; without a clear and implementable mission on the part of government, absence through nonparticipation amounts to consent to the outcomes of an adversarial process in which one's opponents are virtually certain to pursue their interests single-mindedly.

Nonetheless, moves to increase the autonomy of administrative agencies, and to insulate regulatory processes from interest group and judicial oversight, limit opportunities for public participation by definition, and for this reason are not to be taken lightly. Ultimately, the loss of public oversight might be a cost worth bearing in *this* policy domain. This is not a universal argument for insulating bureaucratic decision-making from the watchdog function that courts and publics can play. In areas such as preventing government abuse and protecting individual and minority rights, such oversight is a necessary check on the potential for governmental excess. But the rights model for control of pollution has proven itself neither under the common law nor under its statutory risk-based progeny. The impossibility both of providing complete protection from pollution's harms and of precisely tailoring interventions ultimately mean that air pollution decision-making is best pegged to feasibility and thus to the administrative realm.

Critiques of moves toward increased administrative discretion are likely to come from multiple directions. Those who worry primarily about excessive pollution control will tend to prefer judicially overseen cost-benefit testing of individual regulations. Others concerned by the insufficiency of regulation will be loathe to abandon policy statements guaranteeing absolute protection from pollution's harms; even if unimplementable, they can set a desirably high bar, under this view. Both sides are correct insofar as enhanced administrative autonomy and a greater reliance on technical expertise are not likely—and are not even designed—to lead to regulation that perfectly fits its targeted harm.

Yet the search for such perfect regulation has been futile all along. "The impossible mission of pursuing perfection," argues former EPA Administrator William Ruckelshaus, has led to a "devolution of all important environmental decisions to the courts."[20] He contrasts the U.S. approach with the more consensual practice of environmental regulation in the Netherlands, a model he deems worthy of emulation. While acknowledging the challenges of transplanting European-styled environmental regulation to the United States, he warns that "somehow we have to get past this situation where EPA is out there in the boat and everyone else is on the shore jeering as the ship struggles to stay afloat. Somehow, we have to use whatever civic consciousness and sense of community we have left to bring all the interests into the same boat."[21]

Trust in the capacity of government to do what is best makes little sense without an accompanying belief in the existence of a common good—at least in a limited number of realms—that governments properly exist to serve. If the state exists merely to arbitrate between competing claims, it is incumbent upon citizens to advance their interest with rigor if they hope for a political response. In the reactive state, fighting the good fight is the rule of the game because where no independent regulatory mission exists, the avoidance of conflict can only mean consent. The very freedom from such a mission and the coercion that collective visions of this nature are prone to impose is the great appeal of the common law state. As David Schoenbrod writes, "What to me, makes the common law so attractive in comparison to the administrative state is that the administrative state is 'idealistic' in a phony, intellectualized sort of way. . . . Such ideals seek to 'improve' or to 'reform' society through the coercive power of the state in contrast to the common law, which seeks to vindicate the values of society."[22]

The common law can be seen as avoiding coercion, however, only if we accept that legally or scientifically uncertain harms are not harms by definition. The fiction of avoidance of coercion is based further on the idea that what constitutes proof for this purpose can be determined objectively and thus kept separate from conceptions of the rule of law and from policy or distributive concerns. But the history of air-pollution nuisance regulation shows that, far from avoiding coercion, the common law managed to define it away. This process conveyed a dual message to those to whom it denied air quality relief: for their legal and or political failure they had only themselves to blame; and someday they may well yet prevail, if only they marshal better evidence, mobilize more effectively, and complain more vigorously. Thus failure need never be final, and future victory—if and when it arrives—will produce perfect and complete relief.

Holding out no such absolute promises, technology-based standards offer instead immediate, and most likely partial pollution-reduction measures, leaving citizens with the implicit knowledge that for the foreseeable future, this is all they have reason and right to expect. At the same time, these standards impose a duty upon pollution sources to bring their emissions to the lowest practicable level whether or not harm can be scientifically proven. Inherent to both sides of this demand is a notion of a larger collective good on whose behalf both individual citizens and industrial actors can be expected to make sacrifices.

The powerful logic of the common law state lies in the belief that a slippery slope separates sovereign governmental pursuit of the common good from despotism. This view has always distinguished the tenor of American regulatory politics from that of Europe, where administrative authority has long derived directly, unapologetically, and, many in America would add, dangerously from state sovereignty. As the history of Europe amply illustrates, a fine line has at times separated pursuit of the common good from despotism. Trust in government can indeed be misplaced, and for some states the need to protect against totalitarian threats ought to be of paramount concern. In the United States, however, the tendency has been to err in the opposite direction. In the absence of a collective vision in whose name government may act forthrightly, a web of evidentiary burdens, fictions, and problem definitions serve to disguise the pollution sacrifices that social existence inevitably requires. More importantly, the process has exacted not only inevitable sacrifices, but also preventable social costs because in committing to narrowly tailored, strictly remedial interventions, it failed to deploy incremental and feasible means of mitigation.

Developing the collective vision and the degree of trust necessary to sustain precautionary regulatory regimes cannot happen by decree or take place overnight. "Have the other side go first," would be the likeliest response of both industrial and environmental interest groups if asked to yield on the absolutist promises of the common law state. An important first step in fostering the climate necessary for such change would be for us to acknowledge the democratic legitimacy of technology-based standards by freeing them of the insidious authoritarian connotations inherent in the label "command and control."

Notes

INTRODUCTION

1. 42 USC 7409 (b) (1994). See discussion in Cass R. Sunstein, *Risk and Reason*: Safety, Law, and the Environment (Cambridge: Cambridge University Press, 2002), 230–34.

2. As chapter 1 will show, both the federal Clean Air Act and the German air pollution regime rely primarily on performance rather than on prescriptive technology standards.

3. Michael Faure and Marieke Ruegg, "Environmental Standard Setting through General Principles of Environmental Law," in *Environmental Standards in the European Union in an Interdisciplinary Framework*, ed. Michael Faure, John Vervaele, and Albert Weale (Antwerpen: Maklu, 1994). See also Organisation for Economic Co-Operation and Development, "Hazardous Air Pollutants," paper presented at the London Workshop, 1995.

4. See Bruce Albert Ackerman and Richard B. Stewart, "Reforming Environmental Law," *Stanford Law Review* 37 (1985): 1333, 1334; Allen V. Kneese and Charles L. Schultze, *Pollution, Prices, and Public Policy* (Washington, D.C.: Brookings Institution, 1975), 69–84; A. Myrick Freeman III, "Air and Water Pollution Policy," in *Current Issues in U.S. Environmental Policy*, ed. Paul R. Portney (Baltimore: Johns Hopkins University Press, 1978), 49–58; Stephen G. Breyer, *Regulation and Its Reform* (Cambridge: Harvard University Press, 1982), 271–84; Richard B. Stewart, "Controlling Environmental Risks Through Economic Incentives," *Colum. J. of Envtl. L.* 13 (1988:153); Cass R. Sunstein, "Administrative Substance," *Duke L. J.* 1991 (1991): 607, 627–42.

5. See Richard B. Stewart, "Madison's Nightmare," *U. Chi. L. Rev.* 57 (1990): 335, 340; Richard H. Pildes and Cass R. Sunstein, "Reinventing the Regulatory State," *U. Chi. L. Rev.* 62 (1995):1.

6. In its originally military context "command and control" denotes hierarchical exercise of authority "over assigned forces in the exercise of a mission" (*Dictionary of Military Terms* [New York: H.W. Wilson, 1986], 54).

7. A prime example of the reliance of contemporary takings jurisprudence on nuisance law is found in Justice Scalia's opinion in *Lucas v. South Carolina Coastal Council*, where he wrote in reference to the state's authority to prohibit construction on beachfront property without having to pay compensation under the Fifth Amendment's takings clause: "To win its case, South Carolina, . . . as it would be required to do if it sought to restrain Lucas in a common-law action for public nuisance, must identify background principles of nuisance and property law that prohibit the uses he now intends in the circumstances in which the property is presently found. Only on this showing can the State fairly claim that, in proscribing all such beneficial uses, the Beachfront Management Act is taking nothing" (*Lucas v. South Carolina Coastal Council*, 112 S. Ct. 2886, 2901).

8. Since 1995, the Supreme Court has struck down at least six federal statutes in part on the basis of deficiencies in the written congressional record associated with their enactment. In this, the court extended the logic of the administrative "hard look" doctrine to the realm of legislation in a manner evocative of the reasoning of the *Lochner* court. See William W. Buzbee and Robert A. Schapiro, "Legislative Record Review", *Stan. L. Rev.* 54 (2001): 87, 109–19.

CHAPTER ONE
REGULATING AIR POLLUTION: RISK- AND TECHNOLOGY-BASED PARADIGMS

1. Ronald Brickman, Sheila Jasanoff, and Thomas Ilgen, *Controlling Chemicals: The Politics of Regulation in Europe and the United States* (Ithaca: Cornell University Press, 1985).
2. For comparative analyses of chemical regulation in Europe and the United States, see, e.g., ibid.; David Vogel, *National Styles of Regulation: Environmental Policy in Great Britain and the United States* (Ithaca: Cornell University Press, 1986); Steven Kelman, *Regulating America, Regulating Sweden: A Comparative Study of Occupational Safety and Health Policy* (Cambridge: MIT Press, 1981); Joseph L. Badaracco, *Loading the Dice: A Five-Country Study of Vinyl Chloride Regulation* (Boston: Harvard Business School Press, 1985); Robert A. Kagan and Lee Axelrad, *Regulatory Encounters: Multinational Corporations and American Adversarial Legalism* (Berkeley: University of California Press, 2000); Robert A. Kagan, *Adversarial Legalism: The American Way of Law* (Cambridge: Harvard University Press, 2001).
3. "Annual Message to the Congress on the State of the Union," Jan. 22, 1970. Reprinted in *Public Papers of the President: Richard M. Nixon* 8, 13 (1970). Cited in Cass R. Sunstein, *After the Rights Revolution: Reconceiving the Regulatory State* (Cambridge: Harvard University Press, 1990), 29, n. 25.
4. Sunstein, *After the Rights Revolution*, 12–13.
5. 116 *Congressional Record* 42, 381. As the bill's accompanying report further explained, "all Americans" in this context meant that even those sensitive to very low concentrations of pollutants by reason of age or disease would find full protection under the law. Senate Comm. on Public Works, 93rd Cong. 2d Sess., *A Legislative History of the Clean Air Amendments of 1970* (1974), 410.
6. David Schoenbrod, "Goals Statutes or Rules Statutes: The Case of the Clean Air Act" *UCLA L. Rev.* 30 (1983): 740, 746.
7. Sonja Boehmer-Christiansen, "The Precautionary Principle in Germany-Enabling Government," in *Interpreting the Precautionary Principle*, ed. Timothy O'Riordan and James Cameron (London: Cameron & May, 1994), 46.
8. Carsten Stark, "Germany: Rule by Virtue of Knowledge," in *Democracy at Work: A Comparative Sociology of Environmental Regulation in the United Kingdom, France, Germany, and the United States*, ed. Richard Münch et al. (Westport: Praeger, 2001), 116.
9. Lennart Lundqvist provides an illuminating comparative account of American and Swedish clean air legislation during the 1970s that suggests strong parallels with the German example. His study contrasts America's "obsession with

radical goals and a seeming neglect for the availability of means" with Sweden's "obsession with means and resources rather than goals. Instead of going for what they *wanted* to do, the policymakers went for what they *could* do" [emphasis in the original]. See Lennart Lundqvist, *The Hare and the Tortoise: Clean Air Policies in the United States and Sweden* (Ann Arbor: University of Michigan Press, 1980), 185.

10. Heinrich Pehle, "Germany: Domestic Obstacles to an International Forerunner," in *European Environmental Policy: The Pioneers*, ed. Mikael Skou Andersen and Duncan Liefferink (New York: St. Martin's, 1997), 160.

11. Albert Weale, "*Vorsprung durch Technik?* The Politics of German Environmental Regulation," in *The Politics of German Environmental Regulation*, ed. Kenneth Dyson (Aldershot: Dartmouth, 1992), 161–62.

12. The German act invokes the "precautionary principle" to take "preventive action against the development and occurrence of harmful environmental effects." See Boehmer-Christiansen, "The Precautionary Principle," 45–46.

13. Sunstein, *Risk and Reason*, 102. See also Indure M. Goklany, *The Precautionary Principle: A Critical Appraisal of Environmental Risk Assessment* (Washington, D.C.: Cato Institute, 2001).

14. Sunstein, *Risk and Reason*, 102–2.

15. Albert Weale, Geoffrey Pridham, Michelle Cini, Dimitrios Konstadakopulos, Martin Porter, and Brendan Flynn, *Environmental Governance in Europe: An Ever Closer Ecological Union?* (Oxford: Oxford University Press, 2000), 67.

16. Id., 67.

17. K. von Moltke, *The "Vorsorgeprinzip" in West German Environmental Policy* (London: Royal Commission on Environmental Pollution, HMSO, 1988).

18. BMI (Federal Interior Ministry) 1984, 53, cited in Boehmer-Christiansen, "Precautionary Principle."

19. Boehmer-Christiansen, "Precautionary Principle."

20. For a discussion of the problems of uncertainty in the regulation of chemicals, see Wendy E. Wagner, "The Science Charade in Toxic Risk Regulation," *Colum. L. Rev.* 95 (1995): 1613. See also Carl F. Cranor, *Regulating Toxic Substances: A Philosophy of Science and the Law* (New York: Oxford University Press, 1993).

21. David M. O'Brien, *What Process is Due? Courts and Science-Policy Disputes* (New York: Russell Sage Foundation, 1987), 30.

22. Sometimes disciplinary traditions or methodological approaches produce such disagreements, but they can also result from a preference for more or less conservative risk estimates inherent in a particular methodology. The line separating "purely" scientific divisions from policy disputes may not always be clear, even to the scientists who work on behalf of environmental, industrial, or government interests and who are arrayed on opposite sides of these debates. See Stephen G. Breyer, *Breaking the Vicious Circle: Toward Effective Risk Regulation* (Cambridge: Harvard University Press, 1993).

23. Joseph M. Feller, "Non-Threshold Pollutants and Air Quality Standards," *Envtl. L.* 24 (1994): 821, 838.

24. Cited in R. Shep Melnick. *Regulation and the Courts: The Case of the Clean Air Act* (Washington, D.C.: Brookings Institution, 1983), 239.

25. Clean Air Act Amendments of 1977, H. Rept. 95–294, p. III; cited in ibid., 243.

26. Arnold W. Reitze, Jr., "Overview and Critique: A Century of Air Pollution Control Law: What's Worked; What's Failed; What Might Work," *Envtl. L.* 21 (1991): 1549, 1585.

27. Congress first addressed air pollution in 1955 in a law that authorized an annual expenditure of five million dollars for five years for federal research and assistance to the states on air quality issues. The law emphatically stressed, however, that the control of air pollution at its source remained the responsibility of individual states and not the federal government. See Act of July 14, 1955, 69 Stat 322.

28. Pub. L. No.90–148, Nov. 21, 1967.

29. Lester Goldner, "Air Pollution Control in the Metropolitan Boston Area: A Case Study in Public-Policy Formation," in *The Economics of Air Pollution*, ed. Harold Wolozin (New York: W. W. Norton, 1966), 30–31.

30. The historical impact of community characteristics on common law adjudication of air pollution disputes is discussed in chapters 3 and 5.

31. Statement of Senator Young, *Legislative History*, 418. Cited in Frank B. Cross, "Section 111 (d) of the Clean Air Act: A New Approach to the Control of Airborne Carcinogens," *B. C. Envtl. Aff. L. Rev.* 13 (1986): 215, 232, n. 110.

32. CAA § 109(b)(1), 42 U.S.C. 7409(b)(1) (1994).

33. 42 U.S.C. § 7412(a)(1) (1982).

34. 42 U.S.C. § 7412(b)(1)(B) (1982).

35. 40 *Federal Register* at 59,534 (1975). Cited in Cross, "Section 111 (d)," 222, n. 40.

36. CAA § 111 (a)(1), 42 U.S.C. § 7411 (a)(4).

37. Statement of Senator Young, *Legislative History*, 418. Cited in Cross, "Section 111 (d)," 232, n. 113.

38. Cross, " Section 111 (d)," 234.

39. See Arnold W. Reitze, Jr., *Air Pollution Control Law: Compliance and Enforcement* (Washington, D.C.: Environmental Law Institute, 2001), 17.

40. U.S. Environmental Protection Agency, *Environmental Investments, The Cost of a Clean Environment: Report of the Administrator of the Environmental Protection Agency to the Congress of the United States* (Washington, D.C.: U.S. EPA, Policy, Planning, and Evaluation, 1990).

41. *Latest Findings on National Air Quality: 2000 Status and Trends* (Research Triangle Park, N.C.: U.S. EPA, Office of Air Quality Planning and Standards, 2001).

42. In June 2001, 98 million people lived in "nonattainment" regions, where emissions had exceeded air quality standards for several consecutive years. See U.S. EPA, *Summary Population Exposure Report*, June 8, 2001, http://www.epa. gov/airs/nonattn.html (last visited 7/10/2002). As of May 2002, 96 million people were living in regions classified as being in "serious," "severe," or "extreme" nonattainment of federal air quality standards for ozone. See U. S. EPA, *Ozone Nonattainment Area Summary*, http://www.epa.gov/oar/oaqps/greenbk/onsum.html (last visited 7/10/2002).

43. Feller, "Non-Threshold Pollutants," 868.

44. See *American Petroleum Inst. v. Costle*, 665 F.2d 1176, 1185 (D.C. Cir. 1981), which ruled that cost should not be considered in setting standards for ozone. *Lead Indus. Ass'n v. EPA* (647 F.2d 1130, 1148–56 [D.C. Cir. 1979]) held cost to be irrelevant in promulgation of NAAQS for lead.

45. Feller, "Non-Threshold Pollutants," 868.

46. Evidence regarding the PM-10 threshold is somewhat less conclusive than that for ozone. For a discussion of the scientific evidence behind the EPA's decision to revise the PM-10 and ozone standards, see Cass R. Sunstein, "Is the Clean Air Act Unconstitutional?," *Mich. L. Rev.* 98 (1999): 303, 324–30.

47. See *J. W. Hampton, Jr. & Co. v. United States*, 276 U.S. 394, 409 (1928). The court argued that delegation of legislative power is constitutional "if Congress shall lay down by legislative act an intelligible principle to which the person or body authorized to [legislate] is directed to conform."

48. *American Trucking Associations, Inc. v. EPA*, 175 F. 3D 1027, 1037 (1999).

49. *Whitman v. American Trucking Associations*, 531 U.S. 457 (2001).

50. Ibid., 467.

51. Communities for a Better Environment (CBE) was the organization that brought the complaint. In its complaint, CBE pointed to the fact that these pollution credits were primarily purchased by four oil companies that used them in lieu of installing vapor recovery equipment at their oil tanker loading terminals. The CBE complaint argued that this trade resulted in the creation of hot spots of concentrated air toxics in the poor residential neighborhood adjacent to the credit-purchasing refineries. CBE's complaint halted the car scrapping program, and exposed within the EPA an underlying tension between two central current EPA policy commitments: the development of market-based alternatives to direct regulation, on the one hand, and the amelioration of disproportionate environmental burdens in poor and minority locales, on the other. See Richard Toshiyuki Drury et al., "Pollution Trading and Environmental Injustice: Los Angeles' Failed Experiment in Air Quality Policy," *Duke Envt'l L. & Pol'y F.* 9 (1999): 231, 283–85. Regarding the reform of emissions trading programs to correct for any localized impacts, see Jonathan Remy Nash and Richard L. Revesz, "Markets and Geography: Designing Marketable Permit Schemes to Control Local and Regional Pollutants," *Ecology L. Q.* 28 (2001): 569.

52. For an early challenge to such an offset program, see *Citizens Against the Refinery's Effects, Inc. v. Environmental Protection Agency*, 643 F. 2d 183, 187 (1981). For an early discussion of the distributional impact of permit markets, see "Note: A Remedy for the Victims of Pollution Permit Markets," *Yale L. J.* 92 (1983): 1022.

53. Richard Lazarus describes the Clean Air Act's focus on "general ambient air quality concerns" rather than particular "toxic hot spots" in Richard Lazarus, "Pursuing 'Environmental Justice': The Distributional Effects of Environmental Protection," *Nw. U. L. Rev.* 87 (1992): 787, 814.

54. The pollutants listed were arsenic, asbestos, benzene, beryllium, mercury, radionuclides, and vinyl chloride. For a discussion of the EPA's failure to promulgate air toxics standards, see Frank B. Cross, *Environmentally Induced Cancer*

and the Law: Risks, Regulation, and Victim Compensation (New York: Quorum, 1989), 104–7.

55. Arnold W. Reitze and Randy Lowell, "Control of Hazardous Air Pollution," *B. C. Envtl. Aff. L. Rev.* 28 (2001): 229, 238.

56. In 1981 testimony before a congressional committee, Walter C. Barber, then Director of the EPA's Office of Quality Planning and Standards, noted, "(T)he Agency has been reluctant to list chemicals without some assurance that adverse effects could actually occur and can be prevented by control strategies." See *Clean Air Act (Part 2): Hearings before the Subcomm. On Health and Environment of the House Comm. On Energy and Commerce*, 97th Cong., 1st Sess. 737 (1981).

57. "Health Risk and Economic Impact Assessments of Suspected Carcinogens: Interim Procedures and Guidelines," *Federal Register* 41, no. 21 (1976): 402.

58. John P. Dwyer, "The Pathology of Symbolic Legislation," *Ecology L.Q.* 17 (1990): 233, 257.

59. *EDF v. Train*, No. 76–2045 (D.C. Cir. *Settled and dismissed* June 24, 1977). Cited and discussed in Dwyer, "The Pathology of Symbolic Legislation," 253, n. 87.

60. *Natural Resources Defense Council v. EPA*, 824 F. 2d 1146, 1163 (1987).

61. Ibid., 1152.

62. Ibid., 1153.

63. Feller, "Non-Threshold Pollutants," 838.

64. Cross, "Section 111 (d)," 228.

65. Reitze and Lowell, "Control of Hazardous Air Pollution," 245.

66. Pre-1990 CAA §172, 42 U.S.C. § 7502.

67. Best Available Control Technology (BACT) applied to attainment areas; lowest achievable emissions rate (LAER) applied to nonattainment areas. See 42 U.S.C § 7479 (3), 7501 (3).

68. See, Christina C. Caplan, "The Failure of Current Legal and Regulatory Mechanisms to Control Interstate Ozone Transport: The Need for New National Legislation," *Ecology L.Q.* 28 (2001): 169.

69. Concern over localized air toxics mounted after the 1984 Bhopal, India, disaster in which thousands were killed or seriously injured by an accidental release of methyl isocyanate from a pesticide plant. The 1986 Toxics Release Inventory Act spurred data collection that highlighted concerns about the risks facing residences near particular industrial sources. See Gary C. Bryner, *Blue Skies, Green Politics: The Clean Air Act of 1990 and Its Implementation*, 2nd ed. (Washington, D.C.: CQ Press, 1995).

70. CAA, 42 USC § 7412 (1990).

71. The EPA estimates that, when fully implemented, these standards will reduce toxic emission by 1.5 million tons per year, almost fifteen times the reductions achieved prior to 1990. See U.S. Environmental Protection Agency, *Taking Toxics Out of the Air: Progress in Setting "Maximum Achievable Control Technology" Standards Under the Clean Air Act* (Research Triangle Park, N.C.: Office of Air Quality Planning and Standards, 2000), 6.

72. Gertrude Lübbe-Wolff, "Efficient Environmental Legislation—On Different Philosophies of Pollution Control in Europe," *J. of Envtl. L.* 13 (2001). 79, 85.

73. Schoenbrod, "Goals Statutes or Rules Statutes," 748.

74. John D. Graham, "The Failure of Agency-Forcing: The Regulation of Airborne Carcinogens under Section 112 of the Clean Air Act," *Duke L. J.* 1995 (1985): 100.

75. Bruce A. Ackerman and William T. Hassler, *Clean Coal/Dirty Air or How the Clean Air Act Became a Multibillion-Dollar Bail-Out for High-Sulfur Coal Producers and What Should be Done about It* (New Haven: Yale University Press, 1981), 7.

76. The intricacies of current doctrine on the proper judicial stance toward administrative decision-making are beyond the scope of this book. In general, Supreme Court decisions are split between those advocating close scrutiny and those calling for deference. The scrutiny-based "hard look doctrine" achieved its clearest Supreme Court articulation in *Motor Vehicle Manufacturers Association of the United States v. State Farm Mutual Automobile Insurance Co.* (463 U.S. 29 [1983]). In that decision, the court imposed a requirement for comprehensive administrative explanation for rule making under the Administrative Procedure Act's notice and comment procedures. By contrast, the court provided a particularly strong endorsement of the principle of deference to agency decisions in *Chevron U.S.A., Inc. v. Natural Resources Defense Council, Inc.* (467 U.S. 837 [1984]). In *Chevron* the Court held that following a finding of ambiguity in the statutory mandate governing an agency, courts must defer to the implementing agency's reasonable interpretation of the statute. The *Chevron* doctrine is restricted to agency decisions on statutory interpretation, rather than those that execute policy under the statute, such as the setting of specific pollution standards under the CAA. For the argument that the Supreme Court in practice did not subsequently exercise the deference required under *Chevron*, see Theodore L. Garrett, "Judicial Review After Chevron: The Courts Reassert Their Role," *Nat. Resources & Env't.* 10 (1995): 59. For a study arguing that lower federal courts exercised greater deference in the wake of *Chevron*, see Peter H. Schuck and E. Donald Elliott, "To the Chevron Station: An Empirical Study of Federal Administrative Law," *Duke L. Rev.* 1990 (1990): 984.

77. Melnick, *Regulation and the Courts*, 29.

78. By 1973, D.C. Circuit review had led the EPA to drop its secondary standard for sulfur dioxide, but encouraged it to regulate lead in gasoline. See discussion in ibid., 240–41.

79. William H. Rodgers, "A Hard Look at Vermont Yankee: Environmental Law Under Close Scrutiny," *Georgetown L. J.* 67 (1979): 699, 706.

80. Melnick, *Regulation and the Courts*.

81. Ibid., 255–61. Wendy Wagner has referred to the resulting regulatory process as a "science charade"; see Wagner, "The Science Charade in Toxic Risk Regulation."

82. Melnick, *Regulation and the Courts*, 257.

83. "Tragic choices," in Guido Calabresi and Philip Bobbitt's formulation, entail great suffering or death, yet remain inevitable under existing conditions of scarcity. As they write, "In such conflicts, at such junctures, societies confront the tragic choice. They must attempt to make allocations in ways that preserve the

moral foundations of social collaboration. If this is successfully done, the tragic choice is transformed into an allocation which does not appear to implicate moral contradictions." See Guido Calabresi and Philip Bobbitt, *Tragic Choices*, 1st ed. (New York: W. W. Norton, 1978), 18.

84. Ackerman and Stewart, "Reforming Environmental Law," 1334. See also Bruce A. Ackerman, *The Uncertain Search for Environmental Quality* (New York: Free Press, 1974), 328–30; Kneese and Schultze, *Pollution, Prices, and Public Policy*, 49–58; Breyer, *Regulation and Its Reform;* Stewart, "Controlling Environmental Risks." For a critique emphasizing the potential of technology standards to leave excessive levels of residual risk uncontrolled, see Troyen A. Brennan, "Environmental Torts," *Vand. L. Rev.* 46 (1993): 1, 35.

85. James Krier and Edmund Ursin explain the obstacle posed by a technology-based approach to the implementation of incentive-based alternatives: "The technological fix had become a persistent fixation; there was little consideration given to whether other means of control might help accomplish improvements impossible or too costly to realize through technical devices alone-most importantly pricing mechanisms." See James E. Krier and Edmund Ursin, *Pollution and Policy: A Case Essay on California and Federal Experience with Motor Vehicle Air Pollution, 1940–1975* (Berkeley: University of California Press, 1977), 283. For a different perspective on this issue, see Daniel H. Cole and Peter Z. Grossman, "When is Command-and-Control Efficient? Institutions, Technology, and the Comparative Efficiency of Alternative Regulatory Regimes for Environmental Protection," *Wis. L. Rev.* 1999 (1999): 887, 889–91. See also Lisa Heinzerling, "Selling Pollution, Forcing Democracy," *Stan. Envtl. L. J.* 14 (1995): 300, 310.

86. The following are examples of works contending that BAT standards impede pollution control innovation: D. Bruce La Pierre, "Technology-Forcing and Federal Environmental Protection Statutes," *Iowa L. Rev.* 62 (1976–77): 771. Stephen Breyer, "Analyzing Regulatory Failure: Mismatches, Less Restrictive Alternatives, and Reform," *Harv. L. Rev.* 92 (1979): 547, 595; Krier and Ursin, *Pollution and Policy*, 24–27; Ackerman and Stewart, "Reforming Environmental Law," 1335; Kneese and Schultze, *Pollution, Prices, and Public Policy*, 59–60.

87. See Nicholas Ashford, Christine Ayers, and Robert F. Stone, "Using Regulation to Change the Market for Innovation," *Harv. Envtl. L. Rev.* 9 (1985): 419; Nicholas A. Ashford, "An Innovation-Based Strategy for the Environment," in *Worst Things First? The Debate over Risk-Based National Environmental Priorities*, ed. Adam M. Finke and Dominic Golding (Washington, D.C.: Resources for the Future, 1994).

88. See Howard Latin, "Ideal Versus Real Regulatory Efficiency: Implementation of Uniform Standards and 'Fine-Tuning' Regulatory Reforms," *Stan. L. Rev.* 37 (1985): 1267; Howard Latin, "Regulatory Failure, Administrative Incentives, and the New Clean Air Act," *Envtl. L.* 21 (1991): 1647; Sidney A. Shapiro and Thomas O. McGarity, "Not So Paradoxical: The Rationale for Technology-Based Regulation," *Duke L. J.* 1991 (1991): 729; Oliver A. Houck, "BAT Birds and B-A-T: The Convergent Evolution of Environmental Law," *Miss. L. J.* 63 (1994): 403; David M. Driesen, "Is Emissions Trading an Economic Incentive Program? Replacing the Command and Control/Economic Incentive Dichotomy," *Washington & Lee L. Rev.* 55, (1998): 289; Rena I. Steinzor, "Reinventing Environmental

Regulation: The Dangerous Journey from Command to Self-Control," *Harv. Envtl. L. Rev.* 22 (1998): 103; Wendy E. Wagner, "Innovations in Environmental Policy: The Triumph of Technology-Based Standards," *Univ. of Ill. L. Rev.* 2000 (2000): 83.

89. Latin, "Ideal Versus Real," 1332.
90. Ibid., 1329.

Chapter Two
"Command and Control": Means, Ends, and Democratic Regulation

1. Following are four of the many available examples from relevant scholarship where the term "command and control" is used as a synonym for technology standards: "Under technology-based command-and-control regulation, the government instructs each resource user on exactly how to operate its activities—for example, what pollution-control technology it should install or even how much it should operate a business. Command-and-control 'performance standards' require resource users to achieve a given, uniform level of environmental performance but allow them some flexibility in choosing the specific technology to achieve that performance" (Richard B. Stewart, "Models for Environmental Regulation: Central Planning versus Market-Based Approaches," *B. C. Envtl. Aff. L. Rev.* 19 [1992]: 547, 548). "A pervasive source of regulatory inefficiency in the United States is the use of rigid, highly bureaucratized 'command-and-control' regulation, which dictates, at the national level, control strategies for hundreds, thousands, or millions of companies and individuals in an exceptionally diverse nation. Command-and-control regulation is a dominant part of American government in such areas as environmental protection and occupational safety and health regulation. In the environmental context, command-and-control approaches usually take the form of regulatory requirements of the 'best available technology' ('BAT')" (Pildes and Sunstein, "Reinventing the Regulatory State," 97). "That preference for cost-efficiency has led to sustained criticism of so-called 'command and control' environmental regulation, under which (i) all regulated firms must meet uniform, technology-based pollution control standards, and (ii) regulators often specify not only the firm's pollution control goal, but the means of achieving it as well" (David B. Spence and Lekha Gopalakrishnan, "Bargaining Theory and Regulatory Reform," *Vand. L. Rev.* 53 [2000]: 599, 605). And the final example here is from Edward P. Weber, *Pluralism by the Rules: Conflict and Cooperation in Environmental Regulation* (Washington, D.C.: Georgetown University Press, 1998, 6–7): "In its most formal sense, command and control is premised on a strict hierarchical authority relationship between regulators (principals) and the regulated community (agents). The federal government uses its authority to 'command' compliance with mandated policy goals and to fill in the details of regulatory programs using a top-down notice-and-comment rulemaking process. States and the private sector—both agents, or subordinates—must then comply with the rules as written. The behavior of agents during program implementation is then 'controlled' by limiting their discretion regarding the means by which goals are to be achieved and by enforcement actions based largely on punitive sanctions.

In practice, this means a regulatory system designed to capture all polluter variance within national uniform rules and to manage both the substance and the process of compliance decision-making. Regulators adopt a detailed, source-specific, industry-by-industry strategy of control over virtually every aspect of implementation. They identify and prescribe uniform end-of-pipe pollution control standards, best available control technologies (BACT) that industry must use to achieve pollution reductions, and detailed decision processes that guide industry step-by-step towards compliance."

2. See Stewart, "Madison's Nightmare," 340.

3. *Lochner v. New York*, 198 U.S. 45 (1905). The historical backdrop to this decision is the subject of chapter 4.

4. *Industrial Union v. American Petroleum Institute*, 448 U.S. 607, 653 (1980).

5. Richard B. Stewart, "Antidotes for the 'American Disease,' " *Ecology L. Q.* 20 (1993): 85.

6. Stewart, "Controlling Environmental Risks," 154.

7. See Stewart, "Madison's Nightmare," 341–42.

8. In this connection, Theodore Lowi cites two federal health and safety statutes, the Occupational Health and Safety Act (OSHA) and the Consumer Safety Commission Act (CPSC). As he explains, in failing to articulate any substantive legal goal, "(T)he OSHA legislation took as its purpose 'to assure so far as is possible every working man and woman in the nation safe and healthful working conditions and to preserve human resources.' The CPSC Act is, if possible, even more vague and universal, in that it ordains the commission to reduce unreasonable risk of injury from use of household products but does not identify a single risk, does not suggest what might be a reasonable undertaking of that risk, and definitely does not suggest how to make such risks reasonable" (Theodore J. Lowi, *The End of Liberalism: Ideology, Policy, and the Crisis of Public Authority*, 1st ed. [New York: Norton, 1969], 117).

9. Ralph Nader and John C. Esposito, *Vanishing Air: The Ralph Nader Study Group Report on Air Pollution* (New York: Grossman, 1970), 264.

10. Pildes and Sunstein, "Reinventing the Regulatory State," 100.

11. Ibid., 100–101.

12. Ibid., 100.

13. Cass R. Sunstein, "*Lochner*'s Legacy," *Colum. L. Rev.* 87 (1987): 873. See also his "Neutrality in Constitutional Law (With Special Reference to Pornography, Abortion, and Surrogacy)," *Colum. L. Rev.* 92 (1992): 1.

14. Sunstein, "*Lochner*'s Legacy," 874.

15. *Lochner v. New York*, 52.

16. Daniel T. Rodgers, *Atlantic Crossings: Social Politics in a Progressive Age* (Cambridge: Harvard University Press, Belknap Press, 1998), 235–36.

17. *Lochner v. New York*, 58.

18. Sunstein, "*Lochner*'s Legacy," 877.

19. *Lochner v. New York*, 58. The majority concluded that baking was less dangerous than the average occupation because of a section on medical statistics that Lochner's counsel appended to their brief. On the other hand, Justice Harlan referred in his dissent to the state's conflicting medical evidence that showed baking to be an extremely unhealthy occupation (69). He and Justice Holmes differed

from the majority insofar as they understood the state to benefit from a strong presumption in its favor, thereby tipping the balance in favor of the legislation unless, in Justice Holmes's language, no "reasonable man might think it a proper measure on the score of health" (76).

20. Ibid., 68.

21. Cross, *Environmentally Induced Cancer*, 99.

22. Charles Noble, *Liberalism at Work: The Rise and Fall of OSHA* (Philadelphia: Temple University Press, 1986); Eula Bingham, "The New Look at OSHA: Vital Changes," *Labor L.J.* 29 (1978): 487.

23. John D. Graham, Laura C. Green, and Marc J. Roberts, *In Search of Safety: Chemicals and Cancer Risk* (Cambridge: Harvard University Press, 1988), 84.

24. Occupational Safety and Health Act, 29 U.S.C. 655(b)(5) (1988).

25. Cross, *Environmentally Induced Cancer*, 100.

26. That the inhalation of benzene vapors could contribute to cancer and other serious diseases, most notably aplastic anemia, was by that time a matter of general scientific agreement. Evidence for this came, however, from instances of occupational exposure to high or unknown levels of benzene and thus left the degree of toxicological risk posed by low concentrations unanswered. Subsequent epidemiological and animal-based studies designed to assess the health risk associated with exposure to low levels of the chemical yielded inconclusive results. Ibid., 113.

27. Ibid., 86.

28. *Industrial Union v. American Petroleum Institute*, 628–29, 700.

29. Ibid., 641–42.

30. Ibid., 639.

31. Ibid., 653, 55–56.

32. Sunstein, *After the Rights Revolution*, 196.

33. Ibid.

34. Ibid.

35. Ibid., 86.

36. *Lochner v. New York*, 58–59.

37. *Industrial Union v. American Petroleum Institute*, 642.

38. In a famous 1908 article Roscoe Pound decried judges' use of the "derogation" principle as an instrument of courts determined to "impede or thwart social legislation demanded by the industrial conditions of today" (Roscoe Pound, "Common Law and Legislation," *Harvard L. Rev.* 21 (1908): 383, 385. See *Norfolk Redev. & Housing Auth. v. Chesapeake & Potomac Tel. Co.*, 464 U.S. 30,35 (1983) for a relatively recent Supreme Court decision referring to the derogation canon as "well established."

39. *Industrial Union v. American Petroleum Institute*, 638.

40. Ibid., 645.

41. Ibid., 689.

42. Ibid., 724.

43. Martin Shapiro, "The Supreme Court's 'Return' to Economic Regulation," *Studies in American Political Development* 1 (1986): 139, 140.

44. Ibid., 140–41.

CHAPTER THREE
REGULATING "NOXIOUS VAPOURS": FROM *ALDRED'S CASE* TO THE ALKALI ACT

1. *Chemical News* 6 (1862): 202. Cited in Roy M. MacLeod, "The Alkali Acts Administration, 1863–84: The Emergence of the Civil Scientist," *Victorian Studies* 9 (1965): 85, 87.

2. For a discussion of the transformation of English towns with the arrival of the steam engine and the industrial concentrations spawned in its wake, see John P. S. McLaren, "Nuisance Law and the Industrial Revolution—Some Lessons from Social History," *Oxford J. of Legal Studies* 3 (1983): 155, 162–63.

3. *Aldred v. Benton*, 9 Co Rep. 57 (1610). Cited in J. H. Baker and S.F.C. Milsom, *Sources of English Legal History: Private Law to 1750* (London: Butterworth, 1986), 599. Aldred's complaint against Benton additionally concerned a tall pile of wood that Benton had constructed, which, Aldred claimed, "stopped the windows and lights" of his house.

4. Ibid., 600.

5. *William Aldred's Case*, 77 Eng. Rep. 816, 817 (1611).

6. Ibid., 821.

7. Royal courts expanded their jurisdiction over these disputes by making the writ of "trespass on the case" readily available to large categories of nuisance litigants. See William A. McRae, "The Development of Nuisance in the Early Common Law," *U. Fla. L. Rev.* 1 (1948): 27. Prior to this writ's development, the "Assize of Nuisance" had been the only form of action available for bringing suits related to indirect interferences with property rights. The Assize of Nuisance was, however, applied only to the protection of a freehold estate against wrong by another freeholder, and was not available for "leaseholders, copyholders, guardians, and holders of rights of commons" (Daniel R. Coquillette, "Mosses from an Old Manse: Another Look at Some Historic Property Cases about the Environment," *Cornell L. Rev.* 64 [1979]: 761). "Action on the case" initially developed as an alternative for litigants who could not find remedy in available common law writs (such as the Assize of Nuisance), but by the turn of the seventeenth century, litigants could choose between the writs (J. H. Baker, *An Introduction to English Legal History*, 3rd ed. [London: Butterworth, 1990], 482). On the probable relationship between the increased population density in British cities such as London and the emergence of a more restrictive nuisance law regime, see Coquillette, "Historic Property Cases," 779.

8. Joel Franklin Brenner points to the 1850s and 1860s as the time when English nuisance law was both "invaded by a standard of care" and "applied differently to factories than to private individuals." Subsequently, "under the guise of semantic continuity," nuisance doctrine fundamentally shifted course. See Joel Franklin Brenner, "Nuisance Law and the Industrial Revolution," *J. Legal Stud.* 3 (1974): 403, 408–9. In reference to the evolution of nuisance doctrine in antebellum America, Morton Horwitz similarly argues that while "the law of nuisances for the longest time appeared on its face to maintain the pristine purity of a preindustrial mentality," it had, in fact, been quite radically transformed in a direction more supportive of economic development. See Morton J. Horwitz, *The Transfor-*

mation of American Law, 1780–1860 (Cambridge: Harvard University Press, 1977), 74. Horwitz highlights a number of liability-narrowing doctrinal mechanisms, including a shift from absolute to negligence-based standards of liability for defendants who were statutorily authorized enterprises, such as railroads, and the imposition of a higher bar on private lawsuits against nuisances inflicted on the public at large (99–101).

9. Paul M. Kurtz, "Nineteenth Century Anti-Entrepreneurial Nuisance Injunctions—Avoiding the Chancellor," *Wm. & Mary L. Rev.* 17 (1976): 621, 663, 67.

10. See e.g., Gary T. Schwartz, "Tort Law and the Economy in Nineteenth-Century America: A Reinterpretation," *Yale L. J.* 90 (1981): 1717, 1722; Michael S. McBride, "Critical Legal History and Private Actions Against Public Nuisances, 1800–1865," *Colum. J. L. & Soc. Probs.* 22 (1989).

11. Brenner, Horwitz, and Kurtz see the relevant doctrinal transformation as instrumental responses to changing economic and political constraints. In contrast, Robert Bone highlights the role of diverse conceptions of property, operating separately from economic interests, on the evolution of nuisance doctrine. He faults strictly materialistic explanations of late nineteenth-century nuisance doctrines for attending only to legal outcomes, while dismissing the language and justifications that courts offered in support. See Robert Bone, "Normative Theory and Legal Doctrine in American Nuisance Law: 1850 to 1920," *S. Cal. L. Rev.* 59 (1986): 1101, 1108.

12. William Blackstone, *Commentaries on the Laws of England* (Chicago: University of Chicago Press, 1979), 216.

13. For discussion of the distinction between *injuria* (legal injury) and *damnum* (material damage) and its role in the evolution of early nuisance doctrine, see Coquillette, "Historic Property Cases," 768–71.

14. Henry Campbell Black and Joseph R. Nolan, *Black's Law Dictionary: Definitions of the Terms and Phrases of American and English Jurisprudence, Ancient and Modern*, 6th ed. (St. Paul, Minn.: West, 1990), 393.

15. *William Aldred's Case*, 820–21.

16. Ibid., 821.

17. Brenner, "Nuisance Law and the Industrial Revolution," 403.

18. Baker, *An Introduction to English Legal History*, 455.

19. Blackstone, *Commentaries on the Laws of England*, 217–18.

20. *William Aldred's Case*, 821.

21. *Aldred v. Benton*, 9 Co Rep. 57 (1610). Cited in Baker and Milsom, *English Legal History*, 600.

22. An understanding of the *sic utere* rule declared in *Aldred's Case* as the establishment of a new doctrine is consistent with Coke's proclivity, noted elsewhere, to introduce new legal rules through reference to an "ancient maxim." As Samuel Edmund Thorne wrote, "As a rule of thumb it is well to remember that sentences beginning 'For it is an ancient maxim of the common law', followed by one of Coke's spurious Latin maxims, which he could manufacture to fit any occasion and provide with an air of authentic antiquity, are apt to introduce a new departure" (Samuel Edmund Thorne, *Sir Edward Coke, 1552–1952* [London: Bernard Quaritch, 1957], 7). *Coke's Reports* were only in part intended to provide historical record of the cases that they discussed. He also conceived of his reports

as "instructional law books built around actual cases." In reading his reports, it is consequently often difficult to distinguish Coke's own views on what ought to be the correct doctrine from his account of the actual historical case. See Baker, *An Introduction to English Legal History*, 210.

23. Edmund Newell, "Atmospheric Pollution and the British Copper Industry," *Technology & Culture* 38 (1997): 655, 656–57.

24. L. F. Haber, *The Chemical Industry During the Nineteenth Century: A Study of the Economic Aspect of Applied Chemistry in Europe and North America* (Oxford: Clarendon, 1958), 13.

25. MacLeod, "Alkali Acts Administration," 87.

26. Newell, "Atmospheric Pollution," 674–75.

27. The primary drawback of the Gossage towers was that the liquid in which the chlorine was condensed was too diluted to allow profitable recovery of by-products. This reduced the incentive for producers to condense, and the release of the liquid into streams contributed to their heavy pollution. The development of processes using hydrochloric acid to produce bleaching powder later solved the water pollution problem. *See* Haber, *The Chemical Industry During the Nineteenth Century*, 23.

28. Newell, "Atmospheric Pollution," 675.

29. *Cambrian*, February 11 and 12, 1823. Cited in ibid. p. 675.

30. Ibid., 676.

31. MacLeod, "Alkali Acts Administration," 88.

32. McLaren, "Nuisance Law and the Industrial Revolution," 197.

33. Daniel C. Webb, *Observations and Remarks, during Four Excursions Made to Various Parts of Great Britain in the Years 1810 and 1811* (London, 1812), 353–54. Cited in Newell, "Atmospheric Pollution," 655, n. 22.

34. See Ronald Rees, "The Great Copper Trials," *History Today* 43 (1993): 38, 40, 41.

35. Newell, "Atmospheric Pollution," 671–72.

36. Ibid., 680.

37. Report of the Royal Commission on Children's Employment in Mines and Manufactories 17 (1842), p. 681. Cited in Newell, "Atmospheric Pollution," 680, n. 67.

38. Anthony S. Wohl, *Endangered Lives: Public Health in Victorian Britain* (London: J. M. Dent, 1983), 118.

39. Ibid., 121.

40. The Leblanc process (named after its French inventor, Nicholas Leblanc) captured soda from the decomposition of salt. It replaced earlier methods that had relied on kelp and barilla. Liverpool's soap industry and abundant coal and salt supplies drew Musparatt to the area, and, following his success, a number of other alkali manufacturers. See T. C. Barker and J. R. Harris, *A Merseyside Town in the Industrial Revolution: St. Helen's 1750–1900* (London: Frank Cass, 1959), 225–26.

41. *Liverpool Mercury*, 7 Dec. 1827. Letter from J. H., cited in Harris, *A Merseyside Town*, 226, n. 3.

42. The case was one of several brought against Musparatt between 1828 and 1838, when the Liverpool Corporation, which campaigned particularly actively

against noxious vapors, indicted at least nine alkali manufacturers in public nuisance proceedings. These celebrated trials attested to the depth of local feelings about the pollution. After the proceedings, two alkali works, including Musparatt's, decided to relocate outside Liverpool's boundaries. See Sarah Wilmot, "Pollution and Public Concern: The Response of the Chemical Industry in Britain to Emerging Environmental Issues, 1860–1901," in *The Chemical Industry in Europe, 1850–1914*, ed. Ernst Homburg, Anthony S. Travis, and Harm G. Schröter, (Dordrect: Kluwer, 1998), 123.

43. See Rees, "The Great Copper Trials," 40–41.

44. See Newell, "Atmospheric Pollution," 671.

45. *Hole v. Barlow*, 140 Eng. Rep. 1113, 1114 (1858).

46. Ibid.

47. Ibid., 1118.

48. *Bamford v. Turnley*, 122 Eng. Rep. 27, 27 (1862)

49. Ibid., 33.

50. Ibid.

51. Ibid., 32.

52. A.W.B. Simpson, *Leading Cases in the Common Law* (Oxford: Clarendon, 1995), 175.

53. *St. Helen's Smelting Co. v. Tipping*, 11 Eng. Rep. 1483, 1483 (1865).

54. Ibid., 1483–84.

55. Simpson, *Leading Cases in the Common Law*, 186.

56. *St. Helen's Smelting Co. v. Tipping*, 1484.

57. For a quite different perspective regarding the impact of the gases on St. Helen's inhabitants during that time see the 1862 account quoted earlier in the chapter (*Chemical News* 6 (1862): 202, cited in MacLeod, "Alkali Acts Administration," 87, n.3).

58. *St. Helen's Smelting Co. v. Tipping*, 1484.

59. *The Oxford English Dictionary*, 2nd ed. (Oxford: Oxford University Press, 1998).

60. Lord Westbury's exemption of pollution "discomfort" from compensation was not part of the holding because it did not directly apply to the question before the court. The earlier jury had not explicitly restricted Tipping's injuries to the discomforts that Lord Westbury's rule would exempt. Therefore that exemption was not the issue on appeal before the court, and any comments made with respect to it were, from a strictly legal perspective, dicta. For discussion of this aspect of the decision, see Simpson, *Leading Cases in the Common Law*, 189–90.

61. *St. Helen's Smelting Co. v. Tipping*, 1486.

62. Within days of the Lords' decision, Tipping filed an additional bill requiring the company to abate the pollution. Thus even for Tipping, damages did not adequately solve the problem. Tipping ultimately prevailed, and the company moved three miles away. See Simpson, *Leading Cases in the Common Law*, 191.

63. Jury instructions given by the lower court are described in *St. Helen's Smelting Co. v. Tipping*, 1484.

64. MacLeod, "Alkali Acts Administration," 88, n. 8.

65. Report of the Select Committee appointed to study Noxious Vapours (hereafter SCNV), PP, 1862 (486) xiv, 7, cited in MacLeod, "Alkali Acts Administration," 89, n.9.

66. SCNV, 6–8, cited in Simpson, *Leading Cases in the Common Law*, 185.

67. 26 & 27 Vict.c.124., cited in Simpson, *Leading Cases in the Common Law* 178.

68. In its forbearance from prescribing a particular control technology, the Alkali Act foreshadows modern day performance standards (as distinguished from technology standards). See MacLeod, "Alkali Acts Administration," 89.

69. Ibid., 90–92.

70. Ibid., 94. Smith, the chief of the Alkali Inspectorate, was anxious to expand the scope of the act and pushed for this in his annual reports. In his 1872 report he argues that "(t)he Alkali Act, which was excellent for a time and has done some good, is becoming less valuable daily." Ninth Report of Alkali Inspectorate, 1873, PP, 1874 (C. 815).xix, 35, cited in MacLeod, "Alkali Acts Administration," 96.

71. Cited in ibid., 97. MacLeod also discusses the 1874 Alkali legislation (96–97).

72. Report of the Royal Commission on Noxious Vapours (hereafter RNV) at 1, cited in MacLeod, "Alkali Acts Administration," 100.

73. Brenner, "Nuisance Law and the Industrial Revolution," 418.

74. See ibid., 418–19. Chapter 4 of this book further discusses the "pollution as disinfectant theory."

75. *See* RNV, 7, 26; Mins. Evid., Q. 2852–53, 13194. Cited in MacLeod, "Alkali Acts Administration," 102, n. 49.

76. The discussion of copper smoke abatement focused on the benefits and drawbacks of furnaces such as the Gerstenhofer furnace, a German invention that was said to result in up to 40 percent reduction of sulfur emissions. This was not a complete solution to the problem; furthermore, the furnace was not suited for smelting ores with a sulfur content of less than 20 percent. Nevertheless, three of the eleven Swansea companies and one Lancashire company introduced the new furnaces. In Lancashire in 1878, Newton Keates and Co. was condensing 1,300 to 1,400 tons of emissions per year. See Newell, "Atmospheric Pollution," 676–78.

77. The Alkali Act dealt exclusively with gases, or noxious vapors, leaving smoke outside its centralized, technology-based regime. The Public Health Act of 1875 had lumped smoke together with other sanitary nuisances, the abatement of which was left to local authorities. See Newell, "Atmospheric Pollution," 683–84.

78. Peter Reed, "Robert Angus Smith and the Alkali Inspectorate," in *The Chemical Industry in Europe, 1850–1914: Industrial Growth, Pollution, and Professionalization*, ed. Ernst Homburg, Anthony S. Travis, and Harm G. Schröter (Dordrect: Kluwer, 1998), 162.

79. See Vogel, *National Styles of Regulation*, 32. Unlike industrial gases, the regulation of smoke was made the object of a separate regulatory regime under the Public Health Act of 1875. See Eric Ashby and Mary Anderson, *The Politics of Clean Air* (Oxford: Clarendon, 1981), 83.

80. See Vogel, *National Styles of Regulation*, 232–33.

81. Report of the Royal Commission on Noxious Vapours, pp. xliv (1878), at 27. Cited in Wohl, *Endangered Lives*, 231.

CHAPTER FOUR
ON THE "POLICE STATE" AND THE "COMMON LAW STATE"

1. *Georgia v. Tennessee Copper Co.*, 206 U.S. 230 (1907).

2. See ibid., 238–39. The case and the type of injunction issued in the case are discussed at greater length in chapter 5 of this book.

3. *Georgia v. Tennessee Copper Co.* (1907). 240.

4. Ibid., 237.

5. Ibid., 238–39.

6. *Lochner v. New York*.

7. The following three review essays include extensive references to the growing body of work falling under the rubric of "*Lochner* Revisionism." Paul Kens, "*Lochner v. New York*: Rehabilitated and Revised, but Still Reviled," *J. Sup. Ct. His.* 1995 (1995): 31; Gary D. Rowe, "*Lochner* Revisionism Revisited," *L. & Soc. Inquiry* 24 (1999): 221; Barry Friedman, "The History of the Countermajoritarian Difficulty, Part Three: The Lesson of *Lochner*," *N.Y.U. L. Rev.* 76 (2001): 1383.

8. See discussion of the various strains within the "revisionist" scholarship in Friedman, "Countermajoritarian Difficulty," 1389–402.

9. Howard Gillman, *The Constitution Besieged: The Rise and Demise of "Lochner" Era Police Powers Jurisprudence* (Durham: Duke University Press, 1993), 20, 73, 7–8.

10. Robert C. Post, "Defending the Lifeworld: Substantive Due Process in the Taft Court Era," *B. U. L. Rev.* 78 (1998): 1489, 1529, 35.

11. Ibid., 1540.

12. See the discussions of *Lochner* in Sunstein, "*Lochner*'s Legacy"; Gillman, *Constitution Besieged*, ch. 2.

13. Stephen Skowronek, *Building a New American State: The Expansion of National Administrative Capacities, 1877–1920* (Cambridge: Cambridge University Press, 1982), 20–24. See also Harry N. Scheiber, "Economic Liberty and the Modern State," in *The State and Freedom of Contract*, ed. Scheiber (Stanford: Stanford University Press, 1998).

14. Skowronek, *Building a New American State*, 20.

15. William J. Novak, *The People's Welfare: Law and Regulation in Nineteenth-Century America* (Chapel Hill: University of North Carolina Press, 1996), 1.

16. Ibid., 7.

17. Ibid., 35.

18. Ibid., 36, 38.

19. Ibid., 38–39.

20. *Lochner v. New York*, 56.

21. William E. Forbath, *Law and the Shaping of the American Labor Movement* (Cambridge: Harvard University Press, 1991), 37.

22. Judith F. Stone, *The Search for Social Peace: Reform Legislation in France, 1890–1914* (Albany: State University of New York Press, 1985), 5–6.

23. Rodgers, *Atlantic Crossings*, 111.

24. Charles W. McCurdy, "The 'Liberty of Contract' Regime in American Law," in *The State and Freedom of Contract*, ed. Harry N. Scheiber (Stanford: Stanford University Press, 1998), 162–63.

25. Ibid., 163.

26. Franz-Ludwig Knermeyer, "*Polizei*," *Economy and Society* 9 (May 1980): 174, 76.

27. After falling into oblivion after the Roman Empire collapsed, Roman law (more specifically Justinian's *Corpus Juris Civilis* [A.D. 534] from which the term "civil law" derives) was rediscovered in twelfth-century Italy, giving rise to a larger Roman law renaissance across the continent. This phenomenon was especially pronounced in Germany, where Roman law offered a common legal vocabulary and procedure and thus served as a unifying legal framework for the several hundred Germanic political units existing at the time. See Harold Berman, "The Origins of Western Legal Science," *Harv. L. Rev.* 90 (1977): 894; M. Cappelletti, John Henry Merryman, and Joseph M. Perillo, *The Italian Legal System* (Stanford: Stanford University Press, 1967); Martin Shapiro, *Courts, a Comparative and Political Analysis* (Chicago: University of Chicago Press, 1981), 132.

28. Kenneth H. F. Dyson, *The State Tradition in Western Europe: A Study of an Idea and Institution* (Oxford: Oxford University Press, 1980), 113.

29. John Henry Merryman, *The Civil Law Tradition: An Introduction to the Legal Systems of Western Europe and Latin America*, 2nd ed. (Stanford: Stanford University Press, 1985), 26–33.

30. Alec Stone, *The Birth of Judicial Politics in France: The Constitutional Council in Comparative Perspective* (New York: Oxford University Press, 1992), 24.

31. Martin M. Shapiro, *Who Guards the Guardians? Judicial Control of Administration* (Athens: University of Georgia Press, 1988), 134.

32. Greg Eghigian, *Making Security Social: Disability, Insurance, and the Birth of the Social Entitlement State in Germany* (Ann Arbor: University of Michigan Press, 2000), 31–32; Gerhard Albert Ritter, *Social Welfare in Germany and Britain: Origins and Development* (Leamington Spa: Berg, 1986), 31.

33. Eghigian, *Social Entitlement State in Germany*, 59.

34. J. Tampke, "Bismark's Social Legislation: A Genuine Breakthrough?" in *The Emergence of the Welfare State in Britain and Germany*, ed. W. J. Mommsen (London: Croon Helm, 1981), 72.

35. Dyson, *State Tradition in Western Europe*, 118.

36. Ibid., 114.

37. J.G.A. Pocock, *The Ancient Constitution and the Feudal Law: A Study of English Historical Thought in the Seventeenth Century*, 2nd ed. (Cambridge: Cambridge University Press, 1987), 16.

38. Sir Edward Coke, Preface to Third Reports (T. F. vol. 2) ix, Cited in Pocock, *Ancient Constitution and the Feudal Law*, 38.

39. Coke's opinion in Bonham's case is the most famous articulation of the doctrine that "in many cases the common law will control acts of parliament . . . sometimes it will judge them completely void" (David Lieberman, *The Province of Legislation Determined: Legal Theory in Eighteenth-Century Britain* [Cambridge: Cambridge University Press, 1989], 53).

40. Alexander Hamilton, "Federalist No. 78," in *The Origins of the American Constitution: A Documentary History*, ed. Michael Kammen (New York: Penguin, 1986).

41. Eghigian, *Social Entitlement State in Germany*, 33–34.

42. Christopher L. Tomlins, *Law, Labor, and Ideology in the Early American Republic* (Cambridge: Cambridge University Press, 1993), 39.

43. Ibid., ch. 2.

44. Novak, *People's Welfare*, 1.

45. Edwin Chadwick, *Report on the Sanitary Condition of the Labouring Population of Great Britain*, ed. Michael W. Flynn (Edinburgh: University Press, 1965), 348.

46. Ibid., 348–49.

47. McLaren, "Nuisance Law and the Industrial Revolution," 209.

48. Janet Loengard, "The Assize of Nuisance: Origins of an Action at Common Law," *Cambridge L. J.* 37 (1978): 144, 159.

49. David R. Hodas, "Private Actions for Public Nuisance: Common Law Citizen Suits for Relief from Environmental Harm," *Ecology L.Q.* 16 (1989): 883, 884; William L. Prosser, *Handbook on the Law of Torts*, 4th ed. (St. Paul, Minn.: West, 1971), 1005.

50. *See* Baker, *An Introduction to English Legal History*, 493; Prosser, *Handbook*, 88.

51. Black and Nolan, *Black's Law Dictionary*, 1066.

52. Prosser, *Handbook*, 1000.

53. H. G. Wood, *A Practical Treatise on the Law of Nuisances in their Various Forms: Remedies Therefore at Law and in Equity* (Albany, N.Y.: John D. Parsons, Jr., 1875), 132.

54. John A. Humbach, "Evolving Thresholds of Nuisance and the Takings Clause," *Colum. J. Envtl. L.* 18 (1993): 1, 17–20; Jan G. Laitos, "Legal Institutions and Pollution: Some Intersections Between Law and History," *Nat. Resources J.* 15 (1975): 423, 434–36.

55. Novak, *People's Welfare*, 66–67.

56. New York Laws, 1867, ch. 790, as cited by Leonard Dupee White, *Introduction to the Study of Public Administration*, 4th ed. (New York: Macmillan, 1955), 482, n. 7.

57. *Commonwealth v. Alger*, 7 Cush. 53, 61–62 (1851).

58. *Slaughter-House Cases*, 83 U.S. 36, 62 (1872).

59. Writing against the backdrop of a constitutional crisis, in light of which constructive ambiguity in defining the police power no longer sufficed, Ernst Freund opened his 1904 treatise *The Police Power* with the explanation that "the term 'police' had never been clearly circumscribed. It means at the same time a power and a function of government, a system of rules, and an administrative organization and force." This vagueness, he concluded, gave rise to what he

termed an "unwarranted assumption" that "the idea of the police power must be equally undefined." The remainder of his thesis analyzed the "mass of decisions, in which the nature of the power has been discussed, and its application either conceded or denied" (Ernst Freund, *The Police Power, Public Policy and Constitutional Rights* [Chicago: Callaghan, 1904], 2–3).

60. *Commonwealth v. Cyrus Alger*, 82.

61. *See* Freund, *The Police Power, Public Policy and Constitutional Rights*, 546–47; Edward S. Corwin, "The Basic Doctrine of American Constitutional Law," in *Selected Essays on Constitutional Law* (Chicago: Foundation Press, 1938). Leonard Levy challenged conventional understandings of Justice Shaw's police power jurisprudence in a 1957 book. Rather than confining the police power to traditional nuisance categories, Shaw stood for the proposition that "because the common law of nuisances imperfectly protected public rights . . . the state was impelled to establish by specific legislation authoritative and precise rules for the benefit and obedience of all" (Leonard Williams Levy, *The Law of the Commonwealth and Chief Justice Shaw* [Cambridge: Harvard University Press, 1957], 250).

62. Walton H. Hamilton, "The Path of Due Process of Law," *Ethics* 47 (1938): 269.

63. Novak, *People's Welfare*, 230.

64. *Slaughter-House Cases*, 81.

65. Ibid., 87.

66. Ibid., 87, 119.

67. *Munn v. Illinois*, 94 U.S. 113, 142 (1876).

68. William Letwin, "Economic Due Process in the American Constitution and the Rule of Law," in *Liberty and the Rule of Law*, ed. Robert L. Cunningham (College Station: Texas A&M University Press, 1979), 40.

69. *Munn v. Illinois*, 126.

70. *Mugler v. Kansas*, 123 U.S. 623, 661 (1887).

71. *Lawton v. Steele*, 152 U.S. 133, 137 (1893).

72. Ibid.

73. *Lochner v. New York*, 63.

74. Ibid., 62.

75. Thomas Cooley, *Treatise on Constitutional Limitations*, 6th ed. (Boston: 1890); Thomas Cooley, "State Regulation of Corporate Profits," *N. Am. Rev.* 137 (1883): 205. *See* generally Sidney Fine, *Laissez Faire and the General-Welfare State: A Study of Conflict in American Thought, 1865–1901* (Ann Arbor: University of Michigan Press, 1956).

76. *U.S. v. Carolene Products*, 304 U.S. 144, 152 (1938).

77. Woodrow Wilson challenged the then prevailing dichotomy between politics and administration, arguing that "administration lies outside the proper sphere of politics" and is rather the domain of "instructed and fitted" governmental experts (Woodrow Wilson, "The Study of Administration," *Pol. Sci. Q.* 2 [1887]: 197).

78. *Field v. Clark*, 143 U.S. 649, 692 (1892). The case concerned a law authorizing the president to raise American tariffs in retaliation against foreign nations that had raised their own tariffs on agricultural products. Notwithstanding its

own declaration regarding the unconstitutionality of delegation, the court upheld the tariff authorization in question.

79. At the center of Roosevelt's economic program stood the National Industrial Recovery Act (NIRA) of 1933, a law that delegated to the president unprecedented power to restructure America's ailing economy. In two 1935 decisions the court invalidated core provisions of the act as unconstitutional delegations of legislative power. See *Panama Refining Co. v. Ryan*, 293 U.S. 388 (1935); *Schechter Poultry Corp. v. United States*, 295 U.S. 495 (1935). Whereas *Panama Refining* took on one relatively minor NIRA provision, *Schechter* cut to the heart of the president's authority under section 3 of the NIRA to establish "codes of fair competition" for a virtually unlimited number of industries and trades. Congress's failure to provide any statutory standards explaining what "fair competition" might mean in this regard amounted to unconstitutional delegation, the court concluded in *Schechter*, because "Congress is not permitted to abdicate or to transfer to others the essential functions with which it is . . . vested" (529–30).

80. After lying dormant for many decades, the nondelegation doctrine has in recent years found its way back into the writings of some legal scholars and the opinions of a few influential judges. In a concurring opinion in *Industrial Union v. American Petroleum Institute*, the OSHA benzene case, Justice Rehnquist turned to the long-forgotten nondelegation doctrine to argue that the OSHA act contained an unconstitutional delegation to the Secretary of Labor because it did not provide any indication as to where on the continuum of relative safety the secretary should set the relevant toxic materials standard. More recently, in a decision subsequently overturned by the Supreme Court, the U.S. Court of Appeals for the District of Columbia invalidated air quality standards that the EPA had issued, arguing that the agency's interpretation of its CAA mandate transcended the boundaries of constitutional delegation of legislative powers. *American Trucking Associations, Inc. v. EPA*. The Supreme Court disagreed with this interpretation and overturned the D.C. Circuit's opinion. *Whitman v. American Trucking Associations* (2001). For an extensive treatment of legal and policy considerations in favor of reviving the nondelegation doctrine, see David Schoenbrod, *Power Without Responsibility: How Congress Abuses the People Through Delegation* (New Haven, Conn.: Yale University Press, 1993).

81. Shapiro, *Who Guards the Guardians?*

82. A. V. Dicey, *Introduction to the Study of the Law of the Constitution*, 8th ed. (London: Macmillan, 1915), 189. The first edition appeared in 1885.

83. Ibid., 326.

84. Shapiro, *Who Guards the Guardians?* 37.

85. John Dickinson, *Administrative Justice and the Supremacy of Law in the United States* (Cambridge: Harvard University Press, 1927).

86. Report of the Special Committee on Administrative Law, 63 A.B.A. REP. 331, 346–51 (1938), cited in Morton J. Horwitz, *The Transformation of American Law, 1870–1960: The Crisis of Legal Orthodoxy* (New York: Oxford University Press, 1992), 219, n. 59.

87. *See* "Message from the President of the United States Returning without Approval the Bill (H.R. 6324) Entitled, 'An Act to Provide for the More Expedi-

tious Settlement of Disputes, and for other Purposes,' " H. Doc. No. 986, 76th Cong. 3d Sess., pp. 2–3.

88. 5 U.S.C. §§ 554, 556, 557, 706(2)(E), 3105 (1982).

89. See 5 U.S.C. 706(2)(A) (1994).

90. See generally Martin Shapiro, "APA: Past, Present, Future," *Va. L. Rev.* 72 (1986): 447, 453–54.

91. Herbert Kaufman, "The Federal Administration Procedure Act," *B. U. L. Rev.* 25 (1946): 479, 491.

92. Christopher G. Tiedeman, *A Treatise on the Limitations of the Police Power in the United States Considered from Both a Civil and Criminal Standpoint* (St. Louis, Mo.: F. H. Thomas Law Book Co., 1886), vi–viii. Cited in Fine, *Conflict in American Thought*, 152–53.

93. Fine, *Conflict in American Thought*, 152.

94. Peter Stein, *Civil Law in Post-Revolutionary America: The Character and Influence of the Roman Civil Law* (London: Hambledon, 1988).

95. Charles Pinckney, speech during South Carolina Convention Ratification Debates, May 14, 1788. http://www.constitution.org/rc/rat_sc-c.htm, last visited 7/22/02.

96. Charles M. Cook, *The American Codification Movement: A Study of Antebellum Legal Reform* (Westport, Conn.: Greenwood, 1981).

97. J. C. Carter, "The Proposed Codification of Our Common Law," 83–84 *Evening Post* (1884), p. 6; cited in Horwitz, *Transformation of American Law, 1870–1960*, 119, n. 77.

98. Carter, "Proposed Codification," 6–7; cited in Horwitz, *Transformation of American Law*, emphasis in the original.

99. Robert Gildea, *Barricades and Borders: Europe 1800–1914*, 2nd ed. (Oxford: Oxford University Press, 1996), 227.

100. President Hughes Responds for the Association, *A.B.A. J.* 10 (1924): 567, 569, cited in Post, "Defending the Lifeworld," 1538, n. 240.

CHAPTER FIVE
FROM *RICHARDS'S APPEAL* TO *BOOMER*: JUDICIAL RESPONSES
TO AIR POLLUTION, 1869–1970

1. Other authors have used different terms for what are here termed BAT injunctions. William Rodgers uses the term "State of the Art Decrees" (William H. Rodgers, *Environmental Law*, [St. Paul, Minn.: West, 1994], 68). Halper refers to "conditional injunctions" (Louise A. Halper, "Nuisance, Courts and Markets in the New York Court of Appeals, 1850–1915," *Alb. L. Rev.* 54 [1990]: 301).

2. *Boomer v. Atlantic Cement Co. Inc.*, 26 N.Y. 2d 219 (1970).

3. In finding Atlantic Cement liable for nuisance yet refusing to enjoin on grounds of economic balancing, *Boomer* explicitly departed from New York's prevailing nuisance doctrine. This absolutist doctrine traces back to *Whalen v. Union Bag & Paper Co.*, 208 N.Y. 1 (1913). The New York Court of Appeals had ordered a large pulp mill to halt the pollution of a small stream without regard for the economic balance between the expense of abating the pollution and the

plaintiff's injury because "if followed to its logical conclusion [balancing] would deprive the poor litigant of his little property by giving it to those already rich" (5). Whether the Court intended this to be a BAT or an absolute remedy injunction cannot be read with certainty. The decree gave the company one year to develop a solution, and subsequent compromises extended the deadline, but the company opted to leave New York for Georgia, where it could avoid any and all controls. See Rodgers, *Environmental Law*, 67.

4. *Boomer v. Atlantic Cement Co., Inc.*, 231.

5. For a discussion of the extensive legal academic analysis of *Boomer*, see Jeff L. Lewin, "*Boomer* and the American Law of Nuisance: Past, Present, and Future," *Alb. L. Rev.* 54 (1990): 189. For the argument that the case presented little novelty, see Halper, "Nuisance, Courts and Markets in the New York Court of Appeals, 1850–1915," 307–8; H. Marlow Green, "Common Law, Property Rights and the Environment: A Comparative Analysis of Historical Developments in the United States and England and a Model for the Future," *Cornell Int'l L.J.* 30 (1997): 541, 557.

6. *Boomer v. Atlantic Cement Co. Inc.*, 223.

7. *Richards's Appeal*, 57 Pa. 105 (1868).

8. Ibid., 108.

9. *Hole v. Barlow*. See my discussion in chapter 3.

10. Ibid., 112.

11. Ibid.

12. *Richards's Appeal*, 108.

13. Ibid., 109.

14. Ibid., 112–13.

15. Ibid., 113.

16. Ibid., 107.

17. *Huckenstine's Appeal*, 70 Pa. 102 (1872).

18. Ibid., 104.

19. Ibid., 107.

20. Ibid., 108.

21. Ibid., 107.

22. Ibid., 106–7.

23. *Appeal of the Pennsylvania Lead Company*, 96 Pa. 116 (1881).

24. Ibid., 125.

25. Ibid., 127.

26. *Evans v. Reading Chemical Fertilizing Co.*, 160 Pa. 209 (1894).

27. Ibid., 212.

28. Ibid.

29. Ibid.

30. Ibid., 223.

31. *See* Bone, "American Nuisance Law," 1150; Kurtz, "Nineteenth Century Anti-Entrepreneurial Nuisance Injunctions-Avoiding the Chancellor," 647.

32. *Versailles Borough v. McKeesport Coal & Coke Co.*, Pitts. L. J. 83 (1935): 379.

33. *Waschak v. Moffat*, 379 Pa. 441 (1954).

34. *Versailles Borough v. McKeesport Coal & Coke Co.*, 382.

35. Ibid., 383.
36. Ibid., 384.
37. Ibid., 385.
38. Ibid., 384.
39. *Waschak v. Moffat*, 443.
40. Ibid., 452.
41. Ibid., 464.
42. Ibid., 465.
43. Ibid., 468.
44. Ibid., 462.
45. Ibid., 469.
46. Ibid., 464.
47. W. A. Damon, "Legal Aspects of Atmospheric Pollution and Methods of Control Used in Great Britain," in *Air Pollution: Proceedings of the U.S. Technical Conference on Air Pollution*, ed. Louis C. McCabe (New York: McGraw-Hill, 1952), 755.
48. Ibid., 747, 55.
49. Technical Coordinating Committee T-4, "Coal Report," *J. of the Air Pollution Control Association* 6 (1956): 105.
50. See *Waschak v. Moffat*, 467.
51. *Sullivan v. Jones & Laughlin Steel Co.*, 208 Pa. 540, 550 (1904).
52. Ibid., 551.
53. Ibid.
54. See *Sullivan v. Jones & Laughlin Steel Co.*, 222 Pa. 72 (1908).
55. Ibid., 83.
56. Ibid., 92–93.
57. Ibid., 94.
58. *Georgia v. Tennessee Copper Co.* (1907).
59. See *Georgia v. Tennessee Copper Co.*, 237 U.S. 474 (1915). The decree was then modified by *Georgia v. Tennessee Copper Co.*, 240 U.S. 650 (1916).
60. *Georgia v. Tennessee Copper Co.* (1915) 477–78. The Special Masters had been a frequent feature of Elizabethan English Chancery courts. See Linda J. Silberman, "Masters and Magistrates Part II: The American Analogue," *N.Y.U. L. Rev* 50 (1975): 1297, 1321–22. American nineteenth-century courts initially relied on masters only for the performance of essentially clerical duties but gradually delegated to them authority to take evidence and to issue nonbinding recommendations to the courts. See W. D. Brazil, "Authority to Refer Discovery Tasks to Special Masters: Limitations on Existing Sources and the Need for a New Federal rule," in *Managing Complex Litigation: A Practical Guide to the Use of Special Masters*, ed. Wayne D. Brazil, Geoffrey C. Hazard, Jr., and Paul R. Rice (Chicago: American Bar Foundation, 1983), 337–64.
61. *Georgia v. Tennessee Copper Co.*, 302 U.S. 660, 660 (1938) granted a joint motion to dismiss. *Georgia v. Tennessee Copper Co.*, 304 U.S. 546, 546 (1938) vacated all orders and decrees previously entered.
62. *Madison v. Ducktown Sulphur, Copper & Iron Co.*, 113 Tenn. 331 (1904).
63. Ibid., 366.
64. Ibid.

65. Christine Rosen, "Differing Perceptions of the Value of Pollution Abatement Across Time and Place: Balancing Doctrine in Pollution Nuisance Law, 1840–1906," *Law and History Review* 11 (1993): 371.

66. *Georgia v. Tennessee Copper Co.* (1970), 240.

CHAPTER SIX
"INSPECTED SMOKE": THE PERPETUAL MOBILIZATION REGIME

This chapter opens with a line from F. L. Rose, "The Smoke Inspector," *Chicago Record-Herald*, Aug. 11, 1903. Cited in R. Dale Grinder, "The Battle for Clean Air: The Smoke Problem in Post–Civil War America," in *Pollution and Reform in American Cities, 1870–1930*, ed. Martin V. Melosi (Austin: University of Texas Press, 1980), 98.

1. *Report on Smoke Abatement and Electrification of Railway Terminals in Chicago* (Chicago: Chicago Association of Commerce, 1915), 28–30.

2. Ashby and Anderson, *The Politics of Clean Air*, chs. 8, 9.

3. Raymond C. Tucker, "The St. Louis Code and Its Operation," in *Air Pollution: Proceedings of the U.S. Technical Conference on Air Pollution*, ed. Louis C. McCabe (New York: McGraw-Hill, 1952), 726.

4. Grinder, "Battle for Clean Air," 84.

5. *Richards's Appeal.*

6. "Pittsburgh," *Atlantic Monthly* 21 (1868), p. 18. Cited in David Stradling, *Smokestacks and Progressives: Environmentalists, Engineers and Air Quality in America, 1881–1951* (Baltimore: Johns Hopkins University Press, 1999), 38.

7. Ibid., 34. See also Martin V. Melosi, "Environmental Crisis in the City: The Relationships Between Industrialization and Urban Pollution," in *Pollution and Reform in American Cities, 1870–1930*, ed. Martin V. Melosi (Austin: University of Texas Press, 1980).

8. Grinder, "Battle for Clean Air," 93.

9. Frank Uekoetter, "Divergent Responses to Identical Problems: Businessmen and the Smoke Nuisance in Germany and the United States, 1880–1917," *Business History Review* 73 (1999): 641, 647.

10. The key to the German success in abating the smoke was, according to the report, a pair of practices: German homes relied on close stoves burning coke or briquettes for heat, and industrial furnaces were not allowed to burn bituminous coal. Committee on Smoke and Noxious Vapours Abatement (Ministry of Health), "Final Report" (London: HMSO, 1921). Cited in Ashby and Anderson, *The Politics of Clean Air*, 93–94, n.9.

11. Uekoetter, "Divergent Responses," 654.

12. Committee on Smoke and Noxious Vapours Abatement (Ministry of Health), "Final Report." Cited in Ashby and Anderson, *The Politics of Clean Air*, 93–94, n.9.

13. Peter Brimblecombe, *The Big Smoke: A History of Air Pollution in London Since Medieval Times* (London: Methuen, 1987), 85–86.

14. "Smoke Abatement and Electrification," 27–28; Brimblecombe, *Big Smoke*, 9.

15. John Evelyn, "A Character of England" (1659), cited in Brimblecombe, *Big Smoke*, 47–48.

16. Brimblecombe, *Big Smoke*, 47–48.

17. "Smoke Abatement and Electrification," 28.

18. Ashby and Anderson, *The Politics of Clean Air*, 1; Brimblecombe, *Big Smoke*, 94–98.

19. HC Debs, 8 June 1819, col. 976, cited in Ashby and Anderson, *The Politics of Clean Air*, 2, n.2.

20. Ashby and Anderson, *The Politics of Clean Air*, 4.

21. Novak, *People's Welfare*, 66–67.

22. Ashby and Anderson, *The Politics of Clean Air*, 5. The bill allowed courts to award costs to nuisance prosecutors and to order alterations to furnaces following conviction for nuisance.

23. Ibid., 8.

24. Rodgers, *Atlantic Crossings*, 119.

25. Ibid., 115.

26. Parl. Pp. (HC) 1852–53 (829) VI. Cited in Ashby and Anderson, *The Politics of Clean Air*, 16, n. 55.

27. HC Cebs, 8 Aug. 1853, col 1495 ff. Cited in Ashby and Anderson, *The Politics of Clean Air*, 17, n.56.

28. Ibid., 6.

29. Brimblecombe, *Big Smoke*, 102.

30. Ashby and Anderson, *The Politics of Clean Air*, 18.

31. Ibid., 27, 32–33; Vogel, *National Styles of Regulation*, 79–81.

32. Lord Palmerston made reference to obstacles the coal industry was putting before antismoke legislation in an 1853 parliamentary debate on the matter. Ashby and Anderson, *The Politics of Clean Air*, 17.

33. Ibid., 42–43.

34. Ibid., 55.

35. What demographic data of this sort still could not answer, however, was how and why the smoky fog killed, or whether something other than the smog was to blame. Perhaps for this reason, Russell himself was careful in his book to base his call for legislative reforms not only on health but upon the smoke's myriad economic injuries as well.

36. Ashby and Anderson, *The Politics of Clean Air*, 58.

37. See Rodgers, *Atlantic Crossings*, 52.

38. *See* "Smoke Abatement and Electrification," 82.

39. Grinder, "Battle for Clean Air," 89.

40. "Smoke Prevention: Report of the Special Committee on Prevention of Smoke, Presented to Engineers' Club of St. Louis," *Journal of the Association of Engineering Societies* 11 (1892); cited in Stradling, *Smokestacks and Progressives*, 43–44.

41. Proceedings of the Engineers' Society of Western Pennsylvania 8 (1892): 31, 44–46. Cited in Stradling, *Smokestacks and Progressives*, 208, n. 4.

42. Ibid., 43.

43. Ibid., 47.

44. *Franklin Institute* 144 (1897): 31, cited in Stradling, *Smokestacks and Progressives*, 209–10, n. 27.

45. Ibid., 50.

46. Ibid., 50–51.

47. E. D. Simon and Marion Fitzgerald, *The Smokeless City* (London: Longmans Green, 1922), 15.

48. Osborn Monnett, "U.S. Department of the Interior Technical Paper No. 273" (1923), quoted in L. Vernon Briggs, *Smoke Abatement: What Has Been Done and Is Being Done Today to Abate this Nuisance* (Boston: Old Corner Bookstore, 1941), 138–39. See also Stradling, *Smokestacks and Progressives*, 45.

49. "Smoke Abatement and Electrification," 28.

50. Committee on Smoke and Noxious Vapours Abatement (Ministry of Health), "Final Report," 1.

51. "Smoke Abatement and Electrification," 82–83.

52. Ibid.

53. Committee on Smoke and Noxious Vapours Abatement (Ministry of Health), "Final Report," 15.

54. Tucker, "St. Louis Code," 726.

55. "Smoke Abatement and Electrification," 32–33; Harold W. Kennedy and Andrew O. Portor, "Air Pollution: Its Control and Abatement," *Vand. L. Rev.* 8 (1955): 854, 66.

56. *Commonwealth of Pa. v. Standard Ice Co.*, 59 Pgh. L.J. 101 (1911), cited in Ralph H. German, "Regulations of Smoke and Air Pollution in Pennsylvania," *U. Pitt. L. Rev.* 10 (1948): 494, 495, n. 12.

57. Ibid.

58. Novak, *People's Welfare*, 68–69.

59. *City of St. Louis v. Heitzeberg Packing & Provision Co.*, 141 Mo. 375 (1897). See also Eugene Mcquillin, "Abatement of Smoke Nuisance in Large Cities by Legislative Declaration that Discharge of Dense Smoke is a Nuisance Per Se," *Cent. L. J.* 60 (1905): 343; Stradling, *Smokestacks and Progressives*, 63–64.

60. Stradling, *Smokestacks and Progressives*, 64.

61. Grinder, "Battle for Clean Air," 97.

62. See Stradling, *Smokestacks and Progressives*, 66, n. 12; Mcquillin, "Abatement of Smoke," 345.

63. Mcquillin, "Abatement of Smoke," 345.

64. See Marvin D. McKinley et al., *Waste Management Study of Foundries Major Waste Streams: Phase II* (Champaign: Illinois Hazardous Waste Research Information Center, 1994), ch. 1.

65. Freund, *The Police Power, Public Policy and Constitutional Rights*, 61.

66. *Northwestern Laundry v. City of Des Moines*, 239 U.S. 486, 491–92 (1916).

67. Ibid., 495.

68. Stradling, *Smokestacks and Progressives*, 75.

69. Grinder, "Battle for Clean Air," 97.

70. Tucker, "St. Louis Code," 727.

71. Briggs, *Smoke Abatement*, 138–39.

72. Henry Obermeyer, *Stop That Smoke!* (New York: Harper, 1933), 225.

73. Simon and Fitzgerald, *The Smokeless City*, 2–3.

74. Ashby and Anderson, *The Politics of Clean Air*, chs. 3, 11.

75. Vogel, *National Styles of Regulation*, 87.

76. Importantly, Germany lacked a civic antismoke movement of the type that flourished in many British and American cities. Uekoetter, "Divergent Responses," 654–55.

77. Ibid., 652.

78. Ibid., 654. Public complaints were, in fact, an element of this system in that citizens would alert authorities to apparent violations of the conditions of licensing. Responsible officials would then inspect the firms for deployment and proper operation of the abatement technologies that were a condition of their original operating permit, in a process that demanded no further public involvement or mobilization (648).

79. Ibid.

80. "Smoke Abatement and Electrification," 18.

81. Ibid.

82. Stradling, *Smokestacks and Progressives*, 56, 64–65.

83. Lawrence Meir Friedman, *A History of American Law* (New York: Simon and Schuster, 1973), 187.

84. Ibid.

85. *See* Grinder, "Battle for Clean Air," 95–96.

86. *See* Stradling, *Smokestacks and Progressives*, 86–88.

87. Brimblecombe, *Big Smoke*, 103–05.

88. Uekoetter, "Divergent Responses," 670.

89. Attesting to the influence of coal-saving smoke abatement rationales on both sides of the Atlantic, a 1922 British book offered the following critique of those who assume that coal consumers' economic self-interest would suffice to abate the smoke: "There are books by keen reformers who, with boundless enthusiasm and a complete lack of technical knowledge, do not hesitate to explain to manufacturers and engineers that smoke from a factory chimney always means waste and inefficiency and always proves that the manager of the factory in question is no less a fool to incure such waste than a knave to inflict such damage on his neighbours. This is, of course, sheer nonsense. While it is true under normal conditions that anything more than quite light smoke from an ordinary boiler furnace is unnecessary and should be prevented, yet every competent person who has given any serious consideration to the problem knows perfectly well that there are special processes in which the prevention of smoke may prove an exceedingly difficult and costly matter for the manufacturer" (Simon and Fitzgerald, *The Smokeless City*, 2.)

90. Stradling, *Smokestacks and Progressives*, 156.

91. Stradling, *Smokestacks and Progressives*, 166–67.

92. Obermeyer, *Stop That Smoke!* 188.

93. Stradling, *Smokestacks and Progressives*, 169.

94. Ibid., 169.

95. Berton Roueché, *Eleven Blue Men* (Boston: Little, Brown, 1954), 196–97. Cited in Charles O. Jones, *Clean Air: The Policies and Politics of Pollution Control* (Pittsburgh: University of Pittsburgh Press, 1975), 26.

96. Jones, *Clean Air*, 27.

CHAPTER SEVEN
"ODORS," NUISANCE, AND THE CLEAN AIR ACT

1. Krier and Ursin, *Pollution and Policy*, 57.

2. Ibid., 59.

3. Ibid., 64.

4. Ibid., 66.

5. Ibid., 65.

6. Ibid.

7. Harold W. Kennedy, "The Legal Aspects of Air Pollution Control with Particular Reference to the County of Los Angeles," *S. Cal. L. Rev.* 27 (1954): 373.

8. Krier and Ursin, *Pollution and Policy*, 66.

9. Ibid., 68–69.

10. Ibid., 68.

11. Kennedy, *The History, Legal and Administrative Aspects of Air Pollution Control in Los Angeles County* (Los Angeles County Board of Supervisors, 1954), 14–15. Cited in Krier and Ursin, *Pollution and Policy*, 120.

12. California Assembly Committee on Air and Water Pollution, *Final Summary Report* (n.d., 1952), 9. Cited in Krier and Ursin, *Pollution and Policy*, 72, n.59.

13. Kennedy, "Legal Aspects," 375. Notwithstanding the shift in priorities recommended by the scientists' committee, the APCD's regulatory policies continued to focus on a host of industrial sources (through its permitting program) throughout the 1950s. See Robert L. Chass, "Extent to Which Available Control Techniques Have Been Utilized by Communities (1)—Los Angeles County," in *Proceedings: National Conference on Air Pollution* (Washington, D.C.: U.S. Government Printing Office, 1958), 353.

14. Louis C. McCabe, ed., *Air Pollution: Proceedings of the U.S. Technical Conference on Air Pollution* (New York: McGraw-Hill, 1952), 3.

15. Ibid.

16. Ibid.

17. Public Law 159. Ch. 360, 69 Stat. 322 (1955).

18. Earl W. Edelen and Howard L. Clark, "Odor Control in Los Angeles County," *Air Repair* 1 (1952): 1, 1–2.

19. Pendray & Co., "Opinion Survey on Odors & Fumes as Air Pollution Problems," March 29, 1955. *Cited in* John von Bergen, "Industrial Odor Control," *J. of the Air Pollution Control Association* 8 (1958): 101.

20. National Research Council (NRC), *Odors from Stationary and Mobile Sources*, (Washington, D.C.: National Academy of Sciences, 1979), 15–23, 61–64.

21. Ibid., 15.

22. Robert D. Bullard, *Dumping in Dixie: Race, Class, and Environmental Quality* (Boulder: Westview, 1990), 35.

23. William R. Chalker, "Extent to Which Controls Have Been Utilized by Industry (1)—Chemicals," in *Proceedings: National Conference on Air Pollution* (Washington, D.C.: U.S. Government Printing Office, 1958), 338.

24. Arthur C. Stern, "Summary of the Conference on Odor Control," *J. of the Air Pollution Control Association* 7 (1957): 53, 54.

25. Ibid.

26. Advertisement appearing in *J. of the Air Pollution Control Association* 7 (1957): 8.

27. National Research Council (NRC), *Odors from Stationary and Mobile Sources* 39–40.

28. Copley International Corporation, *National Survey of the Odor Problem: Phase I of a Study of the Social and Economic Impact of Odors* (Springfield, Va.: National Air Pollution Control Administration, 1970), 204.

29. California Health and Safety Code CH. 2.5, Article 10, Section 24360. Cited in Copley International Corporation, *National Survey of the Odor Problem: Phase I*, 204.

30. Kennedy and Portor, "Air Pollution: Its Control and Abatement," 864.

31. Norman A. Huey et al., "Objective Odor Pollution Control," *J. of the Air Pollution Control Association* 10 (1960): 441.

32. Ibid.

33. Copley International Corporation, *National Survey of the Odor Problem: Phase I*, 121. In response to these problems, there developed an alternative, laboratory-based method of odor measurement under which samples of odorous air were collected in special containers and subjected to dilution away from the field. In these tests, primary technical difficulties pertained to the need to ensure that the sample was adequately preserved and not prematurely diluted in the process. See National Research Council (NRC), *Odors from Stationary and Mobile Sources*, 89.

34. J. S. Byrd, "Demonstration—Syringe Odor Measurement Technique," *J. of the Air Pollution Control Association* 7 (1957): 58.

35. Copley International Corporation, *National Survey of the Odor Problem: Phase I*, 92.

36. U.S. Environmental Protection Agency, *Regulatory Options for the Control of Odors* (Research Triangle Park, N.C.: Office of Air Quality Planning and Standards, 1980), 27–28.

37. Jean J. Schueneman, "A Roll Call of the Communities—Where Do We Stand in Local or Regional Air Pollution Control?" in *Proceedings: The Third National Conference on Air Pollution* (Washington, D.C.: U.S. Department of Health, Education, and Welfare; Public Health Service, 1966), 386.

38. Ibid., 390.

39. Bryce Nelson, "Air Pollution: The 'Feds' Move to Abate Idaho Pulp Mill Stench," *Science* 157 (1967): 1020.

40. Ibid., 1018.

41. Scott Hamilton Dewey, *Don't Breathe the Air: Air Pollution and U.S. Environmental Politics, 1945–1970*, 1st ed. (College Station: Texas A&M University Press, 2000), 233.

42. *See* Copley International Corporation, *National Survey of the Odor Problem: Phase I*. See also *Phase II* (1971) and *Phase III* (1973).

43. Ibid., *Phase I*, 4.

44. Ibid., 205.

45. Ibid., 4.

46. Ibid., 182.

47. Ibid., 7. Around the same time of the CIC studies, the reasons behind the paucity of antipollution mobilization in some industrial locales were examined by Mathew Crenson in *The Un-Politics of Pollution*. Crenson investigated variations in air quality policies within similarly polluted locales and—challenging then reigning pluralist theories on the distribution of power in American cities—attributed some of the differences he observed to the impact of industrial influence on the suppression of pollution abatement demands. See Matthew A. Crenson, *The Un-Politics of Air Pollution: A Study of Non-Decisionmaking in the Cities* (Baltimore: Johns Hopkins University Press, 1971).

48. In addition to odors, the Congressional report mentioned fluorides, nitrogen oxides, polynuclear organic matter, and lead. Both nitrogen oxides and lead were subsequently listed as criteria pollutants, the latter under court order. See U.S. Environmental Protection Agency, *Regulatory Options for the Control of Odors*.

49. As the 1980 EPA report on odors explained, "A 'designated' pollutant is one which is subject to an NSPS but which has not been listed as 'hazardous' under Section 112 of the Act or which is not listed as a Criteria Pollutant under Section 108. . . . Any standards applicable to odors under the NSPS program would qualify as 'designated pollutant standards,' thereby triggering existing source controls under Section 111 (d)" (18–19).

50. Clean Air Act of 1970 § 403(b) (1977 amendment).

51. The committee's report ambiguously concluded that "the establishment of federal ambient-air quality or emission standards for odors would confront various conceptual and technical difficulties" and called for more scientific investigation of various related issues (8).

52. U.S. Environmental Protection Agency, *Regulatory Options for the Control of Odors*, 59.

53. Ibid., 14.

54. Ibid.

55. Ibid.

56. Sources subject to Pennsylvania's incineration requirement included asphalt roofing manufacture, core ovens, rendering cookers, varnish cookers, plastic-curing ovens, and all sources of hydrogen sulfide, mercaptans among others. See Ibid., 33.

57. Ibid., 34.

58. Ibid., 53.

59. Ibid., 4.

60. Id., 71–72.

61. William H. Prokop, "Developing Odor Control Regulations: Guidelines and Considerations," *J. of the Air Pollution Control Association* 28 (1978): 9.

62. Stradling, *Smokestacks and Progressives*, 186–87.

63. U.S. Environmental Protection Agency, *Regulatory Options for the Control of Odors*, 44–46.

64. Ibid., 44–45.

65. Ibid., 12.

66. Ibid., 70.

67. National Research Council (NRC), *Odors from Stationary and Mobile Sources*, 64.

68. Prokop, "Developing Odor Control Regulations," 11.

69. Ibid., 14.

70. Howard E. Hesketh and Frank L. Cross, Jr., *Odor Control: Including Hazardous / Toxic Odors* (Lancaster, Penn.: Technomic, 1989), 56–57.

71. U.S. Environmental Protection Agency, *Reference Guide to Odor Thresholds for Hazardous Air Pollutants Listed in the Clean Air Act Amendments of 1990* (Research Triangle Park, N.C.: Office of Research and Development, Environmental Criteria and Assessment Office, Air Risk Information Support Center, 1992), 1–16.

CHAPTER EIGHT
REGULATING "ODORS": THE CASE OF FOUNDRIES

1. About thirteen million tons of castings are produced every year in the United States mostly for the production of automobiles, other types of transportation, and military equipment. See U.S. Environmental Protection Agency, *Notebook Project: Profile of the Metal Casting Industry* (Washington, D.C.: Office of Compliance, 1998), 4.

2. In 1992, when the last industry-wide survey was completed, American foundries employed close to 160,000 workers, with a payroll total of $5.7 billion and a value of shipments totaled at $18.8 billion. Ibid., 7.

3. U.S. National Air Pollution Control Administration, *Economic Impact of Air Pollution Controls on Gray Iron Foundry Industry* (Raleigh, N.C.: US-NAPCA, 1970), 1. Cupolas, or forced air furnaces, which often rained smoke, dust, and ash on their surroundings, served as the main melting apparatus for the industry until the 1970s, and the vast majority of foundries lacked pollution control devices of any kind. For instance, only 15 percent of 1,376 existing gray iron foundries operated any kind of pollution control device in 1967. See American Foundrymen's Society, *Foundry Air Pollution Manual* (Des Plaines, Ill.: AFS, 1967).

4. Morton Sterling, "Current Status and Future Prospects—Foundry Air Pollution Control," in *Proceedings: The Third National Conference on Air Pollution* (Washington, D.C.: Public Health Service, 1966), 255.

5. The exact composition of foundry fumes varies with the particular material and process used by specific foundries. Of the 188 (originally 189) Hazardous Air Pollutants (HAPs) listed in the 1990 Clean Air Act (CAA), according to a 1993

study, at least sixteen are present in some foundries' emissions at levels sufficiently high to cause concern. See Daniel L. Twarog, *Waste Management Study of Foundries Major Waste Streams: Phase I* (Champaign: Illinois Hazardous Waste Research Information Center, 1993); McKinley et al., *Waste Management Study of Foundries Major Waste Streams: Phase II.*

6. With respect to pollution from foundry cupolas, the paper, in fact, goes as far as to describe cupolas as "probably the least controlled stationary major pollution source in the country today" (Sterling, "Current Status and Future Prospects—Foundry Air Pollution Control," 255).

7. Ibid., 257–58.

8. J. F. Elwood, "Monitoring and Analyzing Airborne Emissions in the Casting Facility," in *AFS Transactions: Ninety-Seventh Annual Meeting of the American Foundrymen's Society* (Des Plaines, Ill.: AFS, 1993); McKinley et al., "Waste Management Study of Foundries' Major Waste Streams: Phase II." Because foundries vary in the type of molding materials and technology they employ, so, too, does the composition of their emissions. The foundry processes most responsible for HAPs emissions are core- and mold-making, the pouring and cooling of the metal inside the molds, and, to a lesser degree, the removal or shakeout, of the metal from the molds. Clay-bonded sand (green sand) binds most molds, but cores typically utilize various chemical bonding agents. The type of binding used varies with the temperature of the molten metal, the size of the casting, the type of sand, and other production factors. Foundries generally rely upon disposable molds and cores that either collapse during the casting process or can be separated from the casting during the "shakeout," the final step in the process. See U.S. Environmental Protection Agency, *Notebook Project: Profile of the Metal Casting Industry*, 16–17. The disposal of foundry sand has emerged as an important environmental concern for the industry. After a number of molding cycles, the sand can no longer be reused and must be removed as waste (13).

9. American Foundrymen's Society, *Foundry Air Pollution Manual*, 3.

10. U.S. Environmental Protection Agency, *Notebook Project: Profile of the Metal Casting Industry*, 40.

11. Jack H. Schaum, "The Expensive Sound of Clean Air," *Modern Casting* 63 (1973): 33.

12. Carbon adsorption relies on the capacity of activated charcoal to adsorb practically any organic compound in order to capture emissions from resin-bonded cores. The system used in the Chrysler foundry employed twelve adsorber compartments, each containing approximately 5000 pounds of charcoal, and was able, at least according to its manufacturer, to yield more than 90 percent odor removal. See Jack Schaum, "Chrysler Initiates Odor Control at Huber Avenue Foundry," *Modern Casting* 63 (1973): 35.

13. Schaum, "The Expensive Sound of Clean Air," 33.

14. National Research Council (NRC), *Odors from Stationary and Mobile Sources*, 317.

15. Data documenting the effects of occupational exposure to foundry fumes provide important information regarding the toxicity of foundry emissions. Studies indicate elevated rates of both bladder and lung cancer—in addition to noncancerous respiratory tract damage, including pneumoconiosis, chronic bronchitis,

and occupational asthma—among foundry molders. The International Agency for Research on Cancer deems work in foundries carcinogenic to humans. See David Sherson, Ole Svane, and Elsebeth Lynge, "Cancer Incidence Among Foundry Workers in Denmark," *Environmental Health* 46 (1991): 75; U.K. Health and Safety Executive (HSE), *Criteria Document to Review the Effects on Health of Airborne Substances in the Ferrous Foundry Environment*" (HSE Contract Research Report, 1994). In an effort to lower *indoor* concentrations of hazardous chemicals, vents and fans typically exhaust gases from the mold line from the building. While such diffusion may well reduce the risk to workers, it makes the capture and treatment of HAPs emitted in the molding process more difficult because it results in a much larger volume of air containing low concentrations of HAPs outside the facility. See McKinley et al., "Waste Management Study of Foundries' Major Waste Streams: Phase II."

16. *Organic Emissions from Ferrous Metallurgical Industries: Compilation of Emission Factors and Control Technologies* (Research Triangle Park, N.C.: Research Triangle Institute, 1984), 5–32.

17. Clean Air Act, 42 USC § 7412(d)(3)(A) (1990).

18. *Federal Register* 62 (June 3, 1997): 30322–23.

19. U.S. Environmental Protection Agency, Office of Air Quality Planning and Standards, "MACT Standards Development Survey Data Regarding Iron and Steel Foundries," 1998 (Unpublished database provided by Research Triangle Institute, Research Triangle, North Carolina).

20. Ibid. In addition, twenty (4.3 percent) of the foundries reported use of acid scrubbers, a specialized wet scrubber designed to recover amines that are used as a catalyst in certain cold-box binders. This technology is not directed at general control of HAPs from the molding process. Marvin Branscome (Research Triangle Institute) in email to author, June 30, 1999.

21. Carbon adsorption is among the more effective and costly, methods available for controlling organic emissions. The 1973 *Modern Casting* issue on odor control devoted attention to this method. See Schaum, "Chrysler Odor Control," 4–5. The effectiveness of the method depends on careful management of the spent carbon (through replacement or regeneration via recovery of the captured organics). Adding to the initial cost of installing the system is the need to hood the molding process in order to capture and direct the emissions to the adsorbtion unit (Branscome, email to author).

22. All four foundries would be considered mid-sized if judged by the annual tonnage melted and the number of employees, though they differ among themselves in this regard. The following information is from the EPA "MACT Survey Data." Of the four, the largest at the time in terms of the number of workers employed was PSC (632), followed by Castwell Products, Inc. (429), New Haven Foundry (429), and ME-West (140). The largest in terms of tons of metal melted annually was New Haven Foundry (57,6000), followed by Castwell Products, Inc. (55,051), PSC (27,600), and ME-West (26,130). Castwell was previously named Wells Manufacturing, under which name it appears in the case study. ME-West was previoulsy known as Capital Castings, and is referred to mostly under that name. The case studies focus on the period between the passage of the 1970

CAA and the EPA's inclusion, in 1992, of foundries under the industrial categories whose HAPs were to be subject to MACT standards.

23. John Emmert, "Sewers, Wellwater, Air Pollution Stifle New Haven's Growth," *The Macomb Daily*, October 30, 1969, p. 1D.

24. Ibid.

25. Letter from Bertha Lendzion to William G. Milliken, Governor of Michigan, August 2, 1969. Unless otherwise noted, correspondence and government documents related to the New Haven Foundry are on file with the Michigan Department of Environmental Quality, formerly the Michigan Department of Natural Resources.

26. Clyde Jones, a long-time village resident and New Haven Foundry employee offered, in 1974, the following recollections from that era: "He (Lamkins) set off a division in town for the colored people on property that he purchased. . . . Everybody he hired had to live in that locality. . . . He didn't approve of colored people being scattered all over town." According to Jones, Lamkin paid local officials to help enforce his segregation policies and set up "a special protection agency to keep the colored people where they belonged." Under this system, "if a black was caught by the police in the white section, he would be fined for loitering and brought before the justice of the peace. . . . A representative of the company would attend the trial with a checkbook and pay the fine. It was then deducted from the men's wages" (Charles Thomas, "Sumner Lamkins was a Stern Taskmaster," *The Macomb Daily*, October 8, 1974, p. 2A).

27. See Emmert, "Sewers, Wellwater, Air Pollution Stifle New Haven's Growth." In 1970 out of a total village population of 1855, 1,061 were white, 770 black, and 24 categorized as other. Among heads of households who responded to a 1972 survey, 33 percent did not have any education beyond grade school, and 66 percent reported an annual income of less than $6000. See Parkins, Rogers, and Associates (Planning and Urban Renewal Consultants), "Family Questionnaire for New Haven," 1972 (Files of New Haven Public Library).

28. Out of 772 households counted in the village in 1990, 217 had an income of less than $15,000. U.S. Census Bureau, "Census, Population Data" (1990), 1A Summary Tape File 1. The total population of the village at that time numbered 2, 331 of whom 670 were black. See "Census, Population Data" 3A Summary Tape File 80.

29. Robert Selwa, "New Haven Hopes for Developers with Faith," *The Macomb Daily*, March 20, 1994, p. 8A.

30. Laura Falk, *New Haven: Reflections of a Unique Village* (Romeo, Mich.: Anderson Printing, 1980), 321.

31. Letter from Mary A. Dodd, Center Manager for Neighborhood Aide, to Austin Harrold, Air Pollution Control Section, Bureau of Environmenatl Health, August 27, 1970.

32. Letter from Concerned Citizen of New Haven to William G. Milliken, Governor of Michigan, June 4, 1971.

33. Memorandum from Bob M., Michigan Department of Public Health, to Phil Scozzafave, Division of Air Pollution Control, Michigan Department of Public Health, November 9, 1973.

34. Letter from local resident to Phillip Scozzafave, Division of Air Pollution Control, Michigan Department of Public Health, January 14, 1974.

35. Complaint #107–76-P, AP-35233m to Macomb County Health Department, August 4, 1976.

36. *James Moore et al. v. New Haven Foundry*, Case No. X72 4148, Macomb County Ct. (1975). Plaintiff's First Amended Complaint.

37. Ibid., 4.

38. Ibid., Plaintiff's Pre-Trial Statement.

39. In a 1976 interim opinion, the judge rejected notice by publication as inadequate for this case and ordered that "notice by registered mail must be sent to all current residents of the affected area, *infra*, all those who have lived in the affected area since the establishment of defendant's concern, and all living persons who are or whoever were employed by the defendant, so far as is possible." In addition, the court required that notice be published daily for six weeks in sixteen local and regional publications and be posted in fourteen locations. The opinion noted that "[t]his Court is not oblivious to the fact that the above requirements for notice will require much work and considerable expenditure of money." *James Moore et al. v. New Haven Foundry*. The court cited the Supreme Court's decision in *Eisen* (1974) regarding the proposition, "There is nothing . . . to suggest that the notice requirements can be tailored to fit the pocketbooks of particular plaintiffs." *Eisen v. Carlisle & Jacquelin et al.*, 417 U.S. 156, 158 (1974).

40. *James Moore v. New Haven Foundry*.

41. Bill Wilson, "New Haven Citizens Sue in Bid to Close Foundry," *The Macomb Daily*, November 11, 1980, 1.

42. Letter from Bernard D. Bloomfield, Division of Occupational Health, to S. D. Lamkins, President, New Haven Foundry, May 27, 1968.

43. Letter from James P. Barwick, Plant Engineer, to Lee Jagger, Director, Air Pollution Control Section, Michigan Department of Public Health, April 7, 1972.

44. Rick Jones, Michigan Department of Natural Resources, telephone interview by author, September 21, 1994.

45. Activity Report No. 974, November 29, 1973, Division of Air Pollution Control, Bureau of Industrial Health and Air Pollution Control, Michigan Department of Public Health.

46. Letter from Phillip Scozzafave, Division of Air Pollution Control, to Tim Kaltenback, Administrative Assistant, Village of New Haven, December 3, 1973.

47. Activity Report No. 971, August 31, 1976, Division of Air Pollution Control, Michigan Department of Public Health.

48. Activity Report No. 565–87, November 13, 1987, Air Quality Division, Department of Natural Resources.

49. Activity Report No. 448–91, October 2, 1991, Air Quality Division, Department of Natural Resources.

50. Letter from David Kee, Director, U.S. EPA Region 5, Air and Radiation Division, to William Hopton, New Haven Foundry, December 23, 1993.

51. "Upon arrival to New Haven I observed the area downwind of the plant and confirmed the evidence of a foggy condition and a slight odor. During a conversation with plant officials, we learnt that they have experienced some difficulties in getting the additional air pollution control equipment installed on their

operations. . . . Follow-up investigations with this plant are planned to assure proper compliance" (Scozzafave to Kaltenback, December 3, 1973). Likewise the installation of dust collectors that OSHA required of the foundry was cited in a 1974 DNR letter as a promising solution to complaints against both particulates and odors. See letter from Engineer Dennis M. Drake, Air Pollution Control Division, to President S. D. Lamkins, New Haven Foundry, and Plant Engineer James P. Barwick, June 27, 1974.

52. Petition submitted by Leonard E. Hool, Village Administrator, to Fred Reith, Department of Natural Resources, February 25, 1985.

53. "Notes of meeting held between Foundry Officials and Village Officials." Submitted to Village Council by Linda Addis, January 12, 1985.

54. Letter from Valdas V. Adamkus to New Haven citizen, June 13, 1994.

55. U.S. Environmental Protection Agency, *Regulatory Options for the Control of Odors*, 59.

56. In explaining why there existed no need for the Berkeley Board of Adjustments to require pollution control as part of its own permitting process, the board's secretary wrote, "Heavy industry of this type is pretty closely regulated by agencies such as BAAPCD, and the need for conditional approval, if that should be the decision by the Board, may simply rely on other agency review." The BAAQMD was previously named Bay Area Air Pollution Control District (BAAPCD). Letter from Robert B. Humphrey to members of the Board of Adjustments, July 5, 1974 (on file with the City of Berkeley).

57. Pacific Steel Casting Company, Plant Expansion permit request, November 8, 1979 (on file with the City of Berkeley).

58. Memorandum from Robert B. Humphrey to the Berkeley Board of Adjustments, November 14, 1979 (on file with the City of Berkeley).

59. The BAAQMD's website offers the following statement regarding the district's investigation of air pollution complaints: "The Bay Area Air Quality Management District receives approximately 3,000 air pollution complaints against stationary sources every year from members of the public. Nearly 1,700 of these complaints are related to odor. Satisfactory resolution of these complaints is one of the most important and difficult responsibilities of District staff. Indeed, other than a violation in progress, responding to complaints from the public takes precedence over all other duties assigned to inspectors" (Bay Area Air Quality Management District "Air Pollution Complaints" http://www.baaqmd.gov/enf/inspect/complain.htm; last visited 12/14/2002 11:46 a.m.

60. California Health & Safety Code § 41700 (1999).

61. Laurence G. Chaset, "Enforcement Mechanism for Resolving Community Odor Problems: A Legal Viewpoint," paper presented at the Eightieth Annual Meeting of the Air Pollution Control Association, June 21–26, 1987.

62. Thus the BAAQMD failed to take any action against PSC between November 1987 and November 1988, despite the confirmation, during that period, of fifty out of the 200 complaints that were filed against the company's odors. This was because on no single day were five complaints confirmed. In testimony before the BAAQMD's hearing board in February 1989, the BAAQMD's Senior Assistant District Council offered the following interpretation of the state of the dispute: "Now we are in a gray area. We don't have a public nuisance, but we are

very close to a public nuisance situation. If the community is effectively mobilized, as they were in the past, we know we will have a public nuisance next year." Transcript of BAAQMD Hearing regarding PSC, February 2, 1989. Unless otherwise noted, correspondence and government documents related to PSC are on file with the BAAQMD.

63. Martha Ture, "The Pollution Game," *Express*, June 24, 1983, p. 10.

64. Ibid.

65. BAAQMD Case Summary, Pacific Steel Casting Company, February 25, 1982.

66. Under California law, all air pollution districts are composed of a governing board of directors, which appoints both an Air Pollution Control Officer (APCO) to whom the rest of the staff reports, and a quasi-adjudicative hearing board. Three of the five members of each hearing board must be licensed practitioners in law, engineering, and medicine, respectively. Appointments are for renewable three-year terms, and hearing board members cannot be otherwise employed by the air districts.

67. Public hearing before the BAAQMD Hearing Board, May 27, 1982.

68. Application for Intervention and Request for Hearing Board to Make Motion for Order of Abatement, filed by Michael Freund, attorney at law, May 20, 1982.

69. Respondent's Final Brief, *Air Pollution Control Officer of the Bay Area Air Quality Management District v. Pacific Steel Casting Co.* (1983).

70. Letter from Helen B. Rudee, Chairperson, Board of Directors, to Peter J. Holloway, Neighbors for Clean Air, January 14, 1983.

71. Air Pollution Control Officer, Petition for New Hearing, May 12, 1983.

72. Miranda Ewell, "Industry in Trouble in West Berkeley," *Montclarion*, April 6, 1983.

73. *Air Pollution Control Officer v. Pacific Steel Casting Co.*, 41 (No. 832) (1984), revised and consolidated order for abatement.

74. Unconditional Order of Abatement, *Air Pollution Control Officer v. Pacific Steel Casting Co.* (1984).

75. Transcript, BAAQMD Hearing Board, February 2, 1989.

76. Memorandum from the BAAQMD Inspections Manager to the Director of Enforcement.

77. *Bay Area Air Quality Management District v. Pacific Steel Casting Company*, Complaint for Civil Penalties, November 30, 1989.

78. Christina S. Chan, "Pacific Steel Casting Becomes Better Neighbor: Solution to Plant Odor Emission Problem," *Foundry Management and Technology* 120 (1992): 126.

79. Pacific Steel Casting website, http://www.pacificsteel.com/envirosafety.html (last visited 3/4/2001).

80. In 1992 an internal BAAQMD memo offered the following assessment: "The most recent abatement equipment modifications have gone far in reducing the potential for odor episodes, however, odors still exist. One can safely project that the odors leading to the 42 Violative Episodes in 1989–1990 have been mitigated to the point where, unless demographics of the immediate neighborhood of

PSC change, a consistent long-term reduction of odors and related complaints is expected." Memorandum from BAAQMD Inspections Manager to Director of Enforcment, "District Enforcement Actions to Reduce and/or Minimize Odors from PSC," February 1992.

81. See Judith Scherr. "Neighbors Raise Stink over Odors: Air Quality Officials Downplay Dispute over Pacific Steel Casting," Berkeley. *Daily Planet*. June 13, 1999. Judith Scherr. "Odorous Order: Air Quality Board Places New Conditions on Foundry" *Berkeley Daily Planet*. January 10, 2000.

82. Steve Yoziwak, "Nasty Odor Keeps Area Homes Shut: Tempe Residents Blame Foundry," *The Arizona Republic*, March 30, 1993, B1.

83. Ariz. Rev. Stat. § 49–471 (1993).

84. Letter from citizen to Senator Dennis DeConcini, April 20, 1989.

85. Letter from Senator DeConcini to Daniel W. McGovern, September 28, 1989.

86. VOCs are a precursor of ozone, which is a criteria pollutant subject to National Ambient Air Quality Standards under the CAA. The MCAPCD restrictions on VOCs were consequently aimed at compliance with the pertinent ambient standards. The rule that Capitol Castings was suspected of violating in 1989 restricted VOCs emissions from core ovens to 4.86 tons per year.

87. Letter from John C. Wise, Acting Regional Administrator, Region 9, to Virginia Turner, Special Assistant, Office of Senator DeConcini, June 28, 1993; letter from Mark Mayer, Air Quality Engineer, MCAPCD, to Jill Schlesiger, Office of Senator John McCain, Jan. 25, 1994. Unless otherwise noted, all correspondence and government documents related to Capitol Castings/ME-West are on file with Maricopa County Air Pollution Control District (MCAPCD).

88. The principal repeated this claim in a formal letter to the MCAPCD Hearing Board in June 1993: "Since becoming principal at Aguilar School nine years ago, I have experienced noticeable heavy fumes in the air on our school campus during school hours. . . . Since twenty-five per cent of our student population suffers from asthma and allergies, it is my concern (as well as that of our school nurse) as to how these fumes are affecting our students." Letter from Loretta B. Pacheco, Agular School Principal, to Maricopa County Air Pollution Control Office, June 3, 1993.

89. Yoziwak, "Nasty Odor Keeps Area Homes Shut: Tempe Residents Blame Foundry," B1.

90. David Hoye, "Air of Discontent: Residents Say Odors Fouling Air Near Foundry," *The Phoenix Gazette*, March 31, 1993, B1.

91. Letter from Mark Mayer to Jill Schlesiger, office of John McCain, U.S. Senator from Arizona, January 25, 1994.

92. Citizen Statement / Comment submitted to the MCAPCD Hearing Board, June 10, 1993.

93. Letter from Capitol Castings employee to MCAPCD Hearing Board, June 10, 1993.

94. Letter from Capitol Castings sales administration supervisor to MCAPCD Hearing Board, June 2, 1993.

95. Transcript, MCAPCD Hearing Board, June 2, 1993, pp. 8–9.

96. Ibid., 41–42.

97. Ibid.

98. Transcript, MCAPCD Hearing-Capital Castings, March 10, 1994, 58, 60.

99. Letter from local activist to author, April 28, 1994.

100. Bob Petrie, "Foundry Plans to Stifle the Odors," *The Arizona Republic*, March 15, 1995.

101. A growing number of foundries implemented during the 1960s a similar shift away from outdated, dirty, and difficult-to-control coke-powered cupolas to the cleaner and more efficient electric furnaces. See U.S. National Air Pollution Control Administration, "Economic Impact of Air Pollution Controls on Gray Iron Foundry Industry."

102. Letter from citizen to *Chicago Tribune*, "Action Express," October 27, 1969.

103. Letter from Mario G. Tonelli, Chief Air Pollution Supervisor, to Richard Phillips, "Action Express," Mobile City Desk, November 17, 1969.

104. A Cook County Air Pollution Control Bureau inspection report from March 1971 indicates that the agency was well familiar by that time with the type and source of the fumes of which complainants spoke. That report described the problem as one of "phenol type odor and foundry type fumes and odors," and described the odor as very strong. See Cook County Air Pollution Control Bureau, Complaint No. 71–3/3, March 29, 1973.

105. Letter from Peter Loquercio, Environmental Control Bureau of Cook County, to Marshall K. Wells, Wells Manufacturing Company, May 13, 1971. Unless otherwise noted, all correspondence and government documents relating to Wells Manufacturing are on file with the Illinois Environmental Protection Agency.

106. Ill. H.B. 3788, 76th Gen. Assem., Sec. 1033(b) (o), 1035 (1970).

107. *Moody v. Flinkote Co.*, 2 Op. Ill. P.C.B. 341, 350 (1971), cited in *Mystik Tape v. The Pollution Control Bd.*, 60 Ill. 2d 330, 337 (1975).

108. Thus, in 1974 the Illinois Supreme Court ruled that in determining whether an alleged air pollution interference was unreasonable under section 9 (b) of the act, the Pollution Control Board "must take into consideration the factors referred to in section 33 (c) and must indicate that it has done so in its written opinion by stating the facts and reasons leading to its decision" (*Incinerator, Inc. v. The Pollution Control Bd.*, 59 Ill. 2d 290, 296 [1974]). The court concluded that the control board substantially complied with the act though it "was not as specific as it might have been in making written findings as to each of the Section 33 (c) criteria" when it imposed a $25,000 fine and a requirement to install odor abatement technology on a solid waste incinerator. The court upheld both the fine and the order but added that it expected the control board in the future to be more specific in its treatment of the four criteria to which section 33 (c) referred. The following year the Illinois Supreme Court remanded another odor-related decision of the Pollution Control Board under the argument that "(t)he opinion of Board does not indicate that it took into consideration the various factors, bearing upon 'reasonableness,' as set forth in Section 33 (c)" (*Mystik Tape v. The Pollution Control Bd.*, 60 Ill. 2d 330, 337 [1975]). In *Processing & Books, Inc.*, a decision it issued in 1976, the same

court reinstated an odor abatement order that had been overturned on appeal and explained that "(t)he appellate court apparently concluded that this court's opinion in the *Incinerator* case had placed upon the Agency the burden of proving, by evidence which it offered, the unreasonableness of the respondents' conduct in terms of each of the four criteria mentioned in section 33 (c). No such result was intended by our decision in *Incinerator*" (*Processing & Books, Inc v. The Pollution Control Bd.*, 64 Ill. 2d 68, 76 [1976]).

109. Resolution, Board of Trustees of the Village of Morton Grove, Cook County, January 28, 1974.

110. *Wells Mfg. Co. v. Pollution Control Bd.*, 48 Ill. App. 3d 337 (1977).

111. Ibid., 339–40.

112. Ibid., 340.

113. *Wells Mfg. Co. v. Pollution Control Bd.*, 73 Ill. 2d 226 (1978), citing *Processing & Books, Inc. v. Pollution Control Bd.* (1976).

114. Letter from S.T.O.P. to IEPA, September 16, 1985.

115. Ibid.

116. Permit Denial 217/782–2113 from Bharat Mathur, IEPA, to Marhall K. Wells, Wells Manufacturing, February 28, 1985.

117. Brief of respondent, *Wells Mfg. Co. v. Illinois Environmental Protection Agency*, PCB 86–49, p. 5 (1986).

118. Transcripts, *Wells Manufacturing Company v. Illinois Environmental Protection Agency*, P.C.B. 86–48, p. 23, 47 (1986).

119. *Wells Mfg. Co. v. Illinois Environmental Protection Agency*, Ill. P.C.B. 86–49, (1987).

120. *Wells Mfg. Co. v. Illinois Environmental Protection Agency*, Op. Ill. P.C.B. 86–49, p. 12 (1987).

121. *Wells Mfg. Co. v. Illinois Environmental Protection Agency*, 195 Ill. App. 3d 593 (1990).

122. Letter from Wells Manufacturing to Division Manager, Division of Air Pollution Control, IEPA, March 24, 1990.

123. BAAQMD, "Report Regarding District Complaint Confirmation," June 14, 1989.

124. *Bay Area Air Quality Management District v. Pacific Steel Casting Co. Inc.*, No. BCV0067442 (1991). On file at the Berkeley-Albany Municipal Court.

125. Minutes, BAAQMD Advisor Council-Public Health Committee, December 3, 1991.

126. Comments of BAAQMD Hearing Board Chairman Kenneth Manaster at hearing regarding *APCO v. Becton-Dickinson* (no. 2087), July 6, 1989.

127. Thomas A. Cobett, "A New Look at Nonhazardous Binders," *Foundry Management and Technology* 117 (1989): 30.

128. A 1994 report on the development of a new resin, based on lignin, a natural by-product of the paper pulping process, noted that the availability of this technology "is well-timed for U.S. foundries. Environmental Protection Agency regulations for best achievable and maximum achievable control technologies are being formulated for introduction by 1997 for iron and steel foundries" ("New Resin Developed for Foundries," *American Metal Market* 102 [1994] 8).

CHAPTER NINE
CONCLUSION

1. See e.g. Theda Skocpol and John Ikenberry, "The Political Formation of the American Welfare State in Historical and Comparative Perspective," *Comparative Social Research* 6 (1983); Ann Shola Orloff, "The Political Origins of America's Belated Welfare State," in *The Politics of Social Policy in the United States*, ed. Margaret Weir, Ann Shola Orloff, and Theda Skocpol (Princeton: Princeton University Press, 1988).

2. Sonja Bohemer-Christiansen and Jim Skea, *Acid Politics: Environmental and Energy Policies in Britain and Germany* (London: Belhaven, 1991), 185–230. Albert Weale, Geoffrey Pridham, Michelle Cini, Dimitrios Konstadakopulos, Martin Porter, and Brendan Flynn, *Environmental Governance in Europe: An Ever Closer Ecological Union?* (Oxford: Oxford University Press, 2000), 385, 392–94.

3. Weale et al., *Environmental Governance in Europe*, 157, 177.

4. Richard A. Harris and Sidney M. Milkis, *The Politics of Regulatory Change: A Tale of Two Agencies*, 2nd ed. (New York: Oxford University Press, 1996), 56.

5. Ibid., 242–43.

6. Kathleen Thelen and Sven Steinmo, "Historical Institutionalism in Comparative Perspective," in *Structuring Politics: Historical Institutionalism in Comparative Analysis*, ed. Sven Steinmo, Kathleen Thelen, and Frank Longstreth (Cambridge: Cambridge University Press, 1992), 3.

7. Common exceptions to the uniformity of technology standards are exemptions for existing or nonmajor sources. But the distinctions between new and old, or major and nonmajor, sources that are prominent in the United States are not inherent in the regime but are concessions to political opponents of across-the-board controls. Feasibility-based technology standards can consider difficulties of compliance on a case-by-case basis without offering blanket exemptions. See Wagner, "Innovations in Environmental Policy: The Triumph of Technology-Based Standards."

8. See Bullard, *Dumping in Dixie*.

9. *See* Vicki Been, "Locally Undesirable Land Uses in Minority Neighborhoods: Disproportionate Siting or Market Dynamics," *Yale L. J.* 103 (1994): 138.

10. Drury et al., "Pollution Trading and Environmental Injustice," 283–85.

11. Dwyer, "The Pathology of Symbolic Legislation," 234.

12. Brickman, Jasanoff, and Ilgen, *Controlling Chemicals;* Badaracco, *Loading the Dice;* Kagan, *Adversarial Legalism;* Stark, "Germany: Rule by Virtue of Knowledge.";* Vogel, *National Styles of Regulation;* Keith Hawkins, *Environment and Enforcement: Regulation and the Social Definition of Pollution* (Oxford: Clarendon, 1984).

13. Badaracco, *Loading the Dice*, 153–54.

14. Kagan, *Adversarial Legalism*, 3–4.

15. Mirjan R. Damaška, *The Faces of Justice and State Authority: A Comparative Approach to the Legal Process* (New Haven: Yale University Press, 1986), 73, 80.

16. Brickman, Jasanoff, and Ilgen, *Controlling Chemicals.*

17. For an extensive critique of the German air pollution regime, based largely on its insularity from both public participation and judicial review, see Susan Rose-Ackerman, *Controlling Environmental Policy: The Limits of Public Law in Germany and the United States* (New Haven: Yale University Press, 1995). For a similar argument by a German author, see Carsten Stark's contention that "corporatism is certainly feasible. This feasibility, however, can exist only by giving up the liberal participating democratic idea and an orientation toward the ideal of enlightened democracy. In the end, this form of democracy is not based on participation and the pursuit of interests but rather on a few experts' search for truth and the enlightenment of the public. . . . My conviction is that a 'rule by virtue of knowledge' or, to be precise, a 'rule by virtue of engineering knowledge' is the basis of legitimation for an institutionalized exclusion of the public in the political process, which, in terms of democratic theory, can be designated as 'democracy by enlightenment' " (Stark, "Germany: Rule by Virtue of Knowledge," 103).

18. *See* Rose-Ackerman, *Controlling Environmental Policy,* 209, n. 62; Molly Elizabeth Hall, "Pollution Havens? A Look at Environmental Permitting in the United States and Germany," *Wis. Envtl. L. J.* 7 (2000): 1.

19. Wagner, "The Science Charade in Toxic Risk Regulation."

20. William D. Ruckelshaus, "Stopping the Pendulum," *The Environmental Forum* 12 (1995): 25, 27.

21. Ibid., 29.

22. David Schoenbrod, "Protecting the Environment in the Spirit of the Common Law," in *The Common Law and the Environment,* ed. Roger E. Meiners and Andrew P. Morriss (Lanham, Md.: Rowman and Littlefield, 2000), 6.

Index

Cases Cited

Natural Resources Defense Council v. EPA, 824 F. 2d 1146 (1987).

Northwestern Laundry v. City of Des Moines, 239 U.S. 486 (1916).

Panama Refining Co. v. Ryan, 293 U.S. 388 (1935).

Processing & Books, Inc. v. The Pollution Control Bd., 64 Ill. 2d 68, 76 (1976).

Richards's Appeal, 57 Pa. 105 (1868).

Schechter Poultry Corp. v. United States, 295 U.S. 495 (1935).

Slaughter-House Cases, 83 U.S. 36 (1872).

St. Helen's Smelting Co. v. Tipping, 11 Eng. Rep. 1483 (1865).

Sullivan v. Jones & Laughlin Steel Co., 208 Pa. 540 (1904).

Sullivan v. Jones & Laughlin Steel Co., 222 Pa. 72 (1908).

U.S. v. Carolene Products, 304 U.S. 144 (1938).

Versailles Borough v. McKeesport Coal & Coke Co., 83 Pa. 379 (1935).

Waschak v. Moffat, 379 Pa. 441 (1954).

Wells Mfg. Co. v. Illinois Environmental Protection Agency, 195 Ill. App. 3d 593 (1990).

Wells Mfg. Co. v. Pollution Control Bd., 48 Ill. App. 3d 337 (1977).

Wells Mfg. Co. v. Pollution Control Bd., 73 Ill. 2d 226 (1978).

Whalen v. Union Bag & Paper Co., 208 N.Y. 1 (1913).

Whitman v. American Trucking Associations, 531 U.S. 457 (2001).

Selected Bibliography

Ackerman, Bruce A. *The Uncertain Search for Environmental Quality.* New York: Free Press, 1974.

Ackerman, Bruce A., and William T. Hassler. *Clean Coal / Dirty Air or How the Clean Air Act Became a Multibillion-Dollar Bail-Out for High-Sulfur Coal Producers and What Should Be Done about It.* New Haven: Yale University Press, 1981.

Ackerman, Bruce A., and Richard B. Stewart. "Reforming Environmental Law," *Stan. L. Rev.* 37 (1985): 1333.

American Foundrymen's Society. *Foundry Air Pollution Manual.* Des Plaines, Ill.: AFS, 1967.

American Metal Market. "New Resin Developed for Foundries," *American Metal Market* 102 (1994): 8.

Ashby, Eric, and Mary Anderson. *The Politics of Clean Air.* Oxford: Clarendon, 1981.

Ashford, Nicholas A. "An Innovation-Based Strategy for the Environment." In *Worst Things First? The Debate over Risk-Based National Environmental Priorities,* edited by Adam M. Finke and Dominic Golding. Washington, D.C.: Resources for the Future, 1994.

Ashford, Nicholas, Christine Ayers, and Robert F. Stone. "Using Regulation to Change the Market for Innovation," *Harv. Envtl. L. Rev.* 9 (1985): 419.

Badaracco, Joseph L. *Loading the Dice: A Five-Country Study of Vinyl Chloride Regulation.* Boston: Harvard Business School Press, 1985.

Baker, J. H. *An Introduction to English Legal History.* 3rd ed. London: Butterworth, 1990.

Baker, J. H., and S.F.C. Milsom. *Sources of English Legal History: Private Law to 1750.* London: Butterworth, 1986.

Bardach, Eugene, and Robert A. Kagan. *Going By the Book: The Problem of Regulatory Unreasonableness.* Philadelphia, Pa.: Temple University Press, 1982.

Barker, T. C., and J. R. Harris. *A Merseyside Town in the Industrial Revolution: St. Helen's 1750–1900.* London: Frank Cass, 1959.

Been, Vicki. "Locally Undesirable Land Uses in Minority Neighborhoods: Disproportionate Siting or Market Dynamics," *Yale L. J.* 103 (1994): 138.

Berman, Harold. "The Origins of Western Legal Science," *Harv. L. Rev.* 90 (1977): 894.

Bingham, Eula. "The New Look at OSHA: Vital Changes," *Labor L. J.* 29 (1978): 487.

Black, Henry Campbell, and Joseph R. Nolan. *Black's Law Dictionary: Definitions of the Terms and Phrases of American and English Jurisprudence, Ancient and Modern.* 6th ed. St. Paul, Minn.: West, 1990.

Blackstone, William. *Commentaries on the Laws of England*. Chicago: University of Chicago Press, 1979.

Boehmer-Christiansen, Sonja. "The Precautionary Principle in Germany-Enabling Government." In *Interpreting the Precautionary Principle*, edited by Timothy O'Riordan and James Cameron. London: Cameron and May, 1994.

Boehmer-Christiansen, Sonja, and Jim Skea. *Acid Politics: Environmental and Energy Policies in Britain and Germany*. London: Belhaven, 1991.

Bone, Robert. "Normative Theory and Legal Doctrine in American Nuisance Law: 1850 to 1920," *S. Cal. L. Rev.* 59 (1986): 1101.

Brazil, W. D. "Authority to Refer Discovery Tasks to Special Masters: Limitations on Existing Sources and the Need for a New Federal rule." In *Managing Complex Litigation: A Practical Guide to the Use of Special Masters*, edited by Wayne D. Brazil, Geoffrey C. Hazard, Jr., and Paul R. Rice. Chicago: American Bar Foundation, 1983.

Brennan, Troyen A. "Environmental Torts," *Vand. L. Rev.* 46 (1993): 1.

Brenner, Joel Franklin. "Nuisance Law and the Industrial Revolution," *J. Legal Stud.* 3 (1974): 403.

Breyer, Stephen. "Analyzing Regulatory Failure: Mismatches, Less Restrictive Alternatives, and Reform," *Harv. L. Rev.* 92 (1979): 547.

———. *Regulation and Its Reform*. Cambridge: Harvard University Press, 1982.

———. *Breaking the Vicious Circle: Toward Effective Risk Regulation*. Cambridge: Harvard University Press, 1993.

Brickman, Ronald, Sheila Jasanoff, and Thomas Ilgen. *Controlling Chemicals: The Politics of Regulation in Europe and the United States*. Ithaca: Cornell University Press, 1985.

Briggs, L. Vernon. *Smoke Abatement: What Has Been Done and Is Being Done Today to Abate this Nuisance*. Boston: Old Corner Bookstore, 1941.

Brimblecombe, Peter. *The Big Smoke: A History of Air Pollution in London Since Medieval Times*. London: Methuen, 1987.

Bryner, Gary C. *Blue Skies, Green Politics: The Clean Air Act of 1990 and Its Implementation*. 2nd ed. Washington, D.C.: CQ Press, 1995.

Bullard, Robert D. *Dumping in Dixie: Race, Class, and Environmental Quality*. Boulder: Westview, 1990.

Buzbee, William W., and Robert A. Schapiro. "Legislative Record Review," *Stan. L. Rev.* 54 (2001): 87.

Byrd, J. S. "Demonstration—Syringe Odor Measurement Technique," *J. of the Air Pollution Control Association* 7 (1957): 58.

Calabresi, Guido, and Philip Bobbitt. *Tragic Choices*. 1st ed. New York: W. W. Norton, 1978.

Caplan, Christina C. "The Failure of Current Legal and Regulatory Mechanisms to Control Interstate Ozone Transport: The Need for New National Legislation," *Ecology L.Q.* 28 (2001): 169.

Cappelletti, M., John Henry Merryman, and Joseph M. Perillo. *The Italian Legal System*. Stanford: Stanford University Press, 1967.

Chadwick, Edwin. *Report on the Sanitary Condition of the Labouring Population of Great Britain*. Edited by Michael W. Flinn. Edinburgh: University Press, 1965.

Chalker, William R. "Extent to Which Controls Have Been Utilized by Industry (1)—Chemicals." In *Proceedings: National Conference on Air Pollution*. Washington, D.C.: U.S. Government Printing Office, 1958.

Chan, Christina S. "Pacific Steel Casting Becomes Better Neighbor: Solution to Plant Odor Emission Problem," *Foundry Management and Technology* 120 (1992): 26.

Chaset, Laurence G. "Enforcement Mechanism for Resolving Community Odor Problems: A Legal Viewpoint," Paper presented at the Eightieth Annual Meeting of the Air Pollution Control Association, June 21–26, 1987.

Chass, Robert L. "Extent to Which Available Control Techniques Have Been Utilized by Communities (1)—Los Angeles County." In *Proceedings: National Conference on Air Pollution*. Washington, D.C.: U.S. Government Printing Office, 1958.

Chicago Association of Commerce. *Report on Smoke Abatement and Electrification of Railway Terminals in Chicago*. Chicago: Chicago Association of Commerce, 1915.

Cobett, Thomas A. "A New Look at Nonhazardous Binders," *Foundry Management and Technology* 117 (1989): 30.

Cole, Daniel H., and Peter Z. Grossman. "When is Command-and-Control Efficient? Institutions, Technology, and the Comparative Efficiency of Alternative Regulatory Regimes for Environmental Protection," *Wis. L. Rev.* 1999 (1999) 887.

Cook, Charles M. *The American Codification Movement: A Study of Antebellum Legal Reform*. Westport, Conn.: Greenwood, 1981.

Cooley, Thomas. "State Regulation of Corporate Profits," *N. Am. Rev.* 137 (1883): 205.

———. *Treatise on Constitutional Limitations*. 6th ed. Boston: 1890.

Copley International Corporation. *National Survey of the Odor Problem: Phase I of a Study of the Social and Economic Impact of Odors*. Springfield, Va.: National Air Pollution Control Administration, 1970.

Coquillette, Daniel R. "Mosses from an Old Manse: Another Look at Some Historic Property Cases about the Environment," *Cornell L. Rev.* 64 (1979): 761.

Corwin, Edward S. "The Basic Doctrine of American Constitutional Law." In *Selected Essays on Constitutional Law*. Chicago: Foundation Press, 1938.

Cranor, Carl F. *Regulating Toxic Substances: A Philosophy of Science and the Law*. New York: Oxford University Press, 1993.

Crenson, Matthew A. *The Un-Politics of Air Pollution: A Study of Non-Decisionmaking in the Cities*. Baltimore: Johns Hopkins University Press, 1971.

Cross, Frank B. "Section 111 (d) of the Clean Air Act: A New Approach to the Control of Airborne Carcinogens," *B. C. Envtl. Aff. L. Rev.* 13 (1986): 215.

———. *Environmentally Induced Cancer and the Law: Risks, Regulation, and Victim Compensation*. New York: Quorum, 1989.

Currie, David P. "Air Pollution Control in West Germany," *U. Chi. L. Rev.* 49 (1982): 355.

Damaška, Mirjan R. *The Faces of Justice and State Authority: A Comparative Approach to the Legal Process*. New Haven: Yale University Press, 1986.

Damon, W. A. "Legal Aspects of Atmospheric Pollution and Methods of Control Used in Great Britain." In *Air Pollution: Proceedings of the U.S. Technical Conference on Air Pollution*, edited by Louis C. McCabe. New York: McGraw-Hill, 1952.

Dewey, Scott Hamilton. *Don't Breathe the Air: Air Pollution and U.S. Environmental Politics, 1945–1970*. 1st ed. College Station: Texas A&M University Press, 2000.

Dicey, A. V. *Introduction to the Study of the Law of the Constitution*. 8th ed. London: Macmillan, 1915. The first edition appeared in 1885.

Dickinson, John. *Administrative Justice and the Supremacy of Law in the United States*. Cambridge: Harvard University Press, 1927.

Driesen, David M. "Is Emissions Trading an Economic Incentive Program? Replacing the Command and Control / Economic Incentive Dichotomy," *Washington & Lee L. Rev.* 55 (1998): 289.

Drury, Richard Toshiyuki, Michael E. Belliveau, J. Scott Kuhn, and Shipra Bansal. "Pollution Trading and Environmental Injustice: Los Angeles' Failed Experiment in Air Quality Policy," *Duke Envt'l L. & Pol'y F.* 9 (1999): 231.

Dwyer, John P. "The Pathology of Symbolic Legislation," *Ecology L. Q.* 17 (1990): 233.

Dyson, Kenneth H. F. *The State Tradition in Western Europe: A Study of an Idea and Institution*. Oxford: Oxford University Press, 1980.

Edelen, Earl W., and Howard L. Clark. "Odor Control in Los Angeles County," *Air Repair* 1 (1952): 1.

Eghigian, Greg. *Making Security Social: Disability, Insurance, and the Birth of the Social Entitlement State in Germany*. Ann Arbor: University of Michigan Press, 2000.

Elwood, J. F. "Monitoring and Analyzing Airborne Emissions in the Casting Facility." In *AFS Transactions: Ninety-Seventh Annual Meeting of the American Foundrymen's Society*. Des Plaines, Ill.: AFS (1993).

Falk, Laura. *New Haven: Reflections of a Unique Village*. Anderson Printing Co.: Romeo, MI., 1980.

Faure, Michael, and Marieke Ruegg. "Environmental Standard Setting through General Principles of Environmental Law." In *Environmental Standards in the European Union in an Interdisciplinary Framework*, edited by Michael Faure, John Vervaele, and Albert Weale. Antwerpen: Maklu, 1994.

Feller, Joseph M. "Non-Threshold Pollutants and Air Quality Standards," *Envtl. L.* 24 (1994): 821.

Fine, Sidney. *Laissez Faire and the General-Welfare State: A Study of Conflict in American Thought, 1865–1901*. Ann Arbor: University of Michigan Press, 1956.

Forbath, William E. *Law and the Shaping of the American Labor Movement*. Cambridge: Harvard University Press, 1991.

Freeman, A. Myrick, III. "Air and Water Pollution Policy." In *Current Issues in U.S. Environmental Policy*, edited by Paul R. Portney. Baltimore: Johns Hopkins University Press, 1978.

Freund, Ernst. *The Police Power, Public Policy and Constitutional Rights*. Chicago: Callaghan, 1904.

Friedman, Barry. "The History of the Countermajoritarian Difficulty, Part Three: The Lesson of *Lochner*," *N.Y.U. L. Rev.* 76 (2001): 1383.

Friedman, Lawrence Meir. *A History of American Law.* New York: Simon and Schuster, 1973.

Garrett, Theodore L. "Judicial Review After Chevron: The Courts Reassert Their Role," *Nat. Resources & Env't.* 10 (1995): 59.

German, Ralph H. "Regulations of Smoke and Air Pollution in Pennsylvania," *U. Pitt. L. Rev.* 10 (1948): 494.

Gildea, Robert. *Barricades and Borders: Europe 1800–1914.* 2nd ed. Oxford: Oxford University Press, 1996.

Gillman, Howard. *The Constitution Besieged: The Rise and Demise of Lochner Era Police Powers Jurisprudence.* Durham: Duke University Press, 1993.

Goklany, Indur M. *The Precautionary Principle: A Critical Appraisal of Environmental Risk Assessment.* Washington, D.C.: Cato Institute, 2001.

Goldner, Lester. "Air Pollution Control in the Metropolitan Boston Area: A Case Study in Public-Policy Formation." In *The Economics of Air Pollution*, edited by Harold Wolozin. New York: W. W. Norton, 1966.

Graham, John D. "The Failure of Agency-Forcing: The Regulation of Airborne Carcinogens under Section 112 of the Clean Air Act," *Duke L. J.* 1985 (1985): 100.

Graham, John D., Laura C. Green, and Marc J. Roberts. *In Search of Safety: Chemicals and Cancer Risk.* Cambridge: Harvard University Press, 1988.

Green, H. Marlow. "Common Law, Property Rights and the Environment: A Comparative Analysis of Historical Developments in the United States and England and a Model for the Future," *Cornell Int'l L.J.* 30 (1997): 541.

Grinder, R. Dale. "The Battle for Clean Air: The Smoke Problem in Post–Civil War America." In *Pollution and Reform in American Cities, 1870–1930*, edited by Martin V. Melosi. Austin: University of Texas Press, 1980.

Haber, L. F. *The Chemical Industry During the Nineteenth Century: A Study of the Economic Aspect of Applied Chemistry in Europe and North America.* Oxford: Clarendon, 1958.

Hall, Molly Elizabeth. "Pollution Havens? A Look at Environmental Permitting in the United States and Germany," *Wis. Envtl. L. J.* 7 (2000): 1.

Halper, Louise A. "Nuisance, Courts and Markets in the New York Court of Appeals, 1850–1915," *Alb. L. Rev.* 54 (1990): 301.

Hamilton, Alexander. "Federalist No. 78." In *The Origins of the American Constitution: A Documentary History*, edited by Michael Kammen. New York: Penguin, 1986.

Hamilton, Walton H. "The Path of Due Process of Law," *Ethics* 47 (1938): 269.

Harris, Richard A., and Sidney M. Milkis. *The Politics of Regulatory Change: A Tale of Two Agencies.* 2nd ed. New York: Oxford University Press, 1996.

Hawkins, Keith. *Environment and Enforcement: Regulation and the Social Definition of Pollution.* Oxford: Clarendon, 1984.

Heinzerling, Lisa. "Selling Pollution, Forcing Democracy," *Stan. Envtl. L. J.* 14 (1995): 300.

Hesketh, Howard E., and Frank L. Cross, Jr. *Odor Control: Including Hazardous / Toxic Odors.* Lancaster: Technomic, 1989.

Hodas, David R. "Private Actions for Public Nuisance: Common Law Citizen Suits for Relief from Environmental Harm," *Ecology L. Q.* 16 (1989): 883.

Horwitz, Morton J. *The Transformation of American Law, 1780–1860.* Cambridge: Harvard University Press, 1977.

———. *The Transformation of American Law, 1870–1960: The Crisis of Legal Orthodoxy.* New York: Oxford University Press, 1992.

Houck, Oliver A. "BAT Birds and B-A-T: The Convergent Evolution of Environmental Law," *Miss. L. J.* 63 (1994): 403.

Huey, Norman A., Louis C. Broering, George A. Jutze, and Charles W. Gruber. "Objective Odor Pollution Control," *J. of the Air Pollution Control Association* 10 (1960): 441.

Humbach, John A. "Evolving Thresholds of Nuisance and the Takings Clause," *Colum. J. Envtl. L.* 18 (1993): 1.

Jones, Charles O. *Clean Air: The Policies and Politics of Pollution Control.* Pittsburgh: University of Pittsburgh Press, 1975.

Kagan, Robert A. *Adversarial Legalism: The American Way of Law.* Cambridge: Harvard University Press, 2001.

Kagan, Robert A., and Lee Axelrad. *Regulatory Encounters: Multinational Corporations and American Adversarial Legalism.* Berkeley: University of California Press, 2000.

Kaufman, Herbert. "The Federal Administration Procedure Act," *B. U. L. Rev.* 25 (1946): 479.

Kelman, Steven. *Regulating America, Regulating Sweden: A Comparative Study of Occupational Safety and Health Policy.* Cambridge: MIT Press, 1981.

Kennedy, Harold W. "The Legal Aspects of Air Pollution Control with Particular Reference to the County of Los Angeles," *S. Cal. L. Rev.* 27 (1954): 373.

Kennedy, Harold W., and Andrew O. Portor. "Air Pollution: Its Control and Abatement," *Vand. L. Rev.* 8 (1955): 854.

Kens, Paul. "*Lochner v. New York*: Rehabilitated and Revised, but Still Reviled," *J. Sup. Ct. His.* 1995 (1995): 31.

Kneese, Allen V., and Charles L. Schultze. *Pollution, Prices, and Public Policy.* Washington, D.C: Brookings Institution, 1975.

Knermeyer, Franz-Ludwig. "*Polizei*," *Economy and Society* 9 (May 1980): 174.

Krier, James E., and Edmund Ursin. *Pollution and Policy: A Case Essay on California and Federal Experience with Motor Vehicle Air Pollution, 1940–1975.* Berkeley: University of California Press, 1977.

Kurtz, Paul M. "Nineteenth Century Anti-Entrepreneurial Nuisance Injunctions—Avoiding the Chancellor," *Wm. & Mary L. Rev.* 17 (1976): 621.

La Pierre, D. Bruce. "Technology-Forcing and Federal Environmental Protection Statutes," *Iowa L. Rev.* 62 (1976–77): 771.

Laitos, Jan G. "Legal Institutions and Pollution: Some Intersections Between Law and History," *Nat. Resources J.* 15 (1975): 423.

Latin, Howard. "Ideal Versus Real Regulatory Efficiency: Implementation of Uniform Standards and 'Fine-Tuning' Regulatory Reforms," *Stan. L. Rev.* 37 (1985): 1267.

———. "Regulatory Failure, Administrative Incentives, and the New Clean Air Act," *Envtl. L.* 21 (1991): 1647.

Lazarus, Richard. "Pursuing 'Environmental Justice': The Distributional Effects of Environmental Protection," *Nw. U. L. Rev.* 87 (1992): 787.

Letwin, William. "Economic Due Process in the American Constitution and the Rule of Law." In *Liberty and the Rule of Law*, edited by Robert L. Cunningham. College Station: Texas A&M University Press, 1979.

Levy, Leonard Williams. *The Law of the Commonwealth and Chief Justice Shaw.* Cambridge: Harvard University Press, 1957.

Lewin, Jeff L. "*Boomer* and the American Law of Nuisance: Past, Present, and Future," *Alb. L. Rev.* 54 (1990): 189.

Lieberman, David. *The Province of Legislation Determined: Legal Theory in Eighteenth-Century Britain.* Cambridge: Cambridge University Press, 1989.

Loengard, Janet. "The Assize of Nuisance: Origins of an Action at Common Law," *Cambridge L. J.* 37 (1978): 144.

Lowi, Theodore J. *The End of Liberalism: Ideology, Policy, and the Crisis of Public Authority.* 1st ed. New York: Norton, 1969.

Lübbe-Wolff, Gertrude. "Efficient Environmental Legislation—On Different Philosophies of Pollution Control in Europe," *J. of Envtl. L.* 13 (2001): 79.

Lundqvist, Lennart. *The Hare and the Tortoise: Clean Air Policies in the United States and Sweden.* Ann Arbor: University of Michigan Press, 1980.

MacLeod, Roy M. "The Alkali Acts Administration, 1863–84: The Emergence of the Civil Scientist," *Victorian Studies* 9 (1965): 85

McBride, Michael S. "Critical Legal History and Private Actions Against Public Nuisances, 1800–1865," *Colum. J. L. & Soc. Probs.* 22 (1989): 307.

McCabe, Louis C., ed. *Air Pollution: Proceedings of the U.S. Technical Conference on Air Pollution.* New York: McGraw-Hill, 1952.

McCurdy, Charles W. "The 'Liberty of Contract' Regime in American Law." In *The State and Freedom of Contract*, edited by Harry N. Scheiber. Stanford: Stanford University Press, 1998.

McKinley, Marvin D., Irvin A. Jefcoat, William J. Herz, and Christopher L. Frederick. *Waste Management Study of Foundries Major Waste Streams: Phase II.* HWRIC TR-016. Champaign: Illinois Hazardous Waste Research Information Center, 1994.

McLaren, John P. S. "Nuisance Law and the Industrial Revolution—Some Lessons from Social History," *Oxford J. of Legal Studies* 3 (1983): 155.

Mcquillin, Eugene. "Abatement of Smoke Nuisance in Large Cities by Legislative Declaration that Discharge of Dense Smoke is a Nuisance Per Se," *Cent. L. J.* 60 (1905): 343.

McRae, William A. "The Development of Nuisance in the Early Common Law," *U. Fla. L. Rev.* 1 (1948): 27.

Melnick, R. Shep. *Regulation and the Courts: The Case of the Clean Air Act.* Washington, D.C.: Brookings Institution, 1983.

Melosi, Martin V. "Environmental Crisis in the City: The Relationships Between Industrialization and Urban Pollution." In *Pollution and Reform in American Cities, 1870–1930*, edited by Martin V. Melosi. Austin: University of Texas Press, 1980.

Merryman, John Henry. *The Civil Law Tradition: An Introduction to the Legal Systems of Western Europe and Latin America.* 2nd ed. Stanford: Stanford University Press, 1985.

Nader, Ralph, and John C. Esposito. *Vanishing Air: The Ralph Nader Study Group Report on Air Pollution.* New York: Grossman, 1970.

Nash, Jonathan Remy, and Richard L. Revesz. "Markets and Geography: Designing Marketable Permit Schemes to Control Local and Regional Pollutants," *Ecology L. Q.* 28 (2001): 569.

National Research Council (NRC). *Odors from Stationary and Mobile Sources.* Washington, D.C.: National Academy of Sciences, 1979.

Nelson, Bryce. "Air Pollution: The 'Feds' Move to Abate Idaho Pulp Mill Stench," *Science* 157 (1967): 1018.

Newell, Edmund. "Atmospheric Pollution and the British Copper Industry," *Technology & Culture* 38 (1997): 655.

Noble, Charles. *Liberalism at Work: The Rise and Fall of OSHA.* Philadelphia: Temple University Press, 1986.

Novak, William J. *The People's Welfare: Law and Regulation in Nineteenth-Century America.* Chapel Hill: University of North Carolina Press, 1996.

Obermeyer, Henry. *Stop That Smoke!* New York: Harper, 1933.

O'Brien, David M. *What Process is Due? Courts and Science-Policy Disputes.* New York: Russell Sage Foundation, 1987.

Organisation for Economic Co-Operation and Development. "Hazardous Air Pollutants." Paper presented at the London Workshop, 1995.

Orloff, Ann Shola. "The Political Origins of America's Belated Welfare State." In *The Politics of Social Policy in the United States*, edited by Margaret Weir, Ann Shola Orloff and Theda Skocpol. Princeton: Princeton University Press, 1988.

Pehle, Heinrich. "Germany: Domestic Obstacles to an International Forerunner." In *European Environmental Policy: The Pioneers*, edited by Mikael Skou Andersen and Duncan Liefferink. New York: St. Martin's, 1997.

Pildes, Richard H., and Cass R. Sunstein. "Reinventing the Regulatory State," *U. Chi. L. Rev.* 62 (1995): 1.

Pocock, J.G.A. *The Ancient Constitution and the Feudal Law: A Study of English Historical Thought in the Seventeenth Century.* 2nd ed. Cambridge: Cambridge University Press, 1987.

Post, Robert C. "Defending the Lifeworld: Substantive Due Process in the Taft Court Era," *B. U. L. Rev.* 78 (1998): 1489.

Pound, Roscoe. "Common Law and Legislation," *Harvard L. Rev.* 21 (1908): 383.

Prokop, William H. "Developing Odor Control Regulations: Guidelines and Considerations," *J. of the Air Pollution Control Association* 28 (1978): 9.

Prosser, William L. *Handbook on the Law of Torts.* 4th ed. St. Paul, Minn.: West, 1971.

Reed, Peter. "Robert Angus Smith and the Alkali Inspectorate." In *The Chemical Industry in Europe, 1850–1914: Industrial Growth, Pollution, and Professionalization*, edited by Ernst Homburg, Anthony S. Travis, and Harm G. Schröter. Dordrect: Kluwer, 1998.

Rees, Ronald. "The Great Copper Trials," *History Today* 43 (1993): 38.

Reitze, Arnold W., Jr. "Overview and Critique: A Century of Air Pollution Control Law: What's Worked; What's Failed; What Might Work," *Envtl. L.* 21 (1991): 1549.

———. *Air Pollution Control Law: Compliance and Enforcement.* Washington, D.C.: The Environmental Law Institute, 2001.

Reitze, Arnold W., and Randy Lowell. "Control of Hazardous Air Pollution," *B. C. Envtl. Aff. L. Rev.* 28 (2001): 229.

Research Triangle Park. *Organic Emissions from Ferrous Metallurgical Industries: Compilation of Emission Factors and Control Technologies.* PB84–141548. Research Triangle Park, N.C.: Research Triangle Institute, 1984.

Ritter, Gerhard Albert. *Social Welfare in Germany and Britain: Origins and Development.* Leamington Spa: Berg, 1986.

Rodgers, Daniel T. *Atlantic Crossings: Social Politics in a Progressive Age.* Cambridge: Belknap, 1998.

Rodgers, William H. *Environmental Law.* St. Paul: West, 1994.

———. "A Hard Look at Vermont Yankee: Environmental Law Under Close Scrutiny," *Georgetown L. J.* 67 (1979): 699.

Rose-Ackerman, Susan. *Controlling Environmental Policy: The Limits of Public Law in Germany and the United States.* New Haven: Yale University Press, 1995.

Rosen, Christine. "Differing Perceptions of the Value of Pollution Abatement Across Time and Place: Balancing Doctrine in Pollution Nuisance Law, 1840–1906," *Law and History Review* 11 (1993): 371.

Rowe, Gary D. "*Lochner* Revisionism Revisited," *L. & Soc. Inquiry* 24 (1999).

Ruckelshaus, William D. "Stopping the Pendulum," *The Environmental Forum* 12 (1995): 25.

Schaum, Jack. "Chrysler Initiates Odor Control at Huber Avenue Foundry," *Modern Casting* 63 (1973): 33.

———. "The Expensive Sound of Clean Air," *Modern Casting* 63 (1973): 35.

Scheiber, Harry N. "Economic Liberty and the Modern State." In *The State and Freedom of Contract*, edited by Scheiber. Stanford: Stanford University Press, 1998.

Schoenbrod, David. "Goals Statutes or Rules Statutes: The Case of the Clean Air Act." *UCLA L. Rev.* 30 (1983): 740.

———. *Power Without Responsibility: How Congress Abuses the People Through Delegation.* New Haven, Conn.: Yale University Press, 1993.

———. "Protecting the Environment in the Spirit of the Common Law." In *The Common Law and the Environment*, edited by Roger E. Meiners and Andrew P. Morriss. Lanham, Md.: Rowman and Littlefield, 2000.

Schuck, Peter H., and E. Donald Elliott, "To the Chevron Station: An Empirical Study of Federal Administrative Law," *Duke L. Rev.* 1990 (1990): 984.

Schueneman, Jean J. "A Roll Call of the Communities—Where Do We Stand in Local or Regional Air Pollution Control?" In *Proceedings: The Third National Conference on Air Pollution.* Washington, D.C.: U.S. Department of Health, Education, and Welfare; Public Health Service, 1966.

Schwartz, Gary T. "Tort Law and the Economy in Nineteenth-Century America: A Reinterpretation," *Yale L. J.* 90 (1981): 1717.

Shapiro, Martin. *Courts, a Comparative and Political Analysis*. Chicago: University of Chicago Press, 1981.

———. "APA: Past, Present, Future," *Va L. Rev.* 72 (1986): 447.

———. "The Supreme Court's 'Return' to Economic Regulation," *Studies in American Political Development* 1 (1986): 139.

Shapiro, Martin M. *Who Guards the Guardians? Judicial Control of Administration*. Athens: University of Georgia Press, 1988.

Shapiro, Sidney A., and Thomas O. McGarity. "Not So Paradoxical: The Rationale for Technology-Based Regulation," *Duke L. J.* 1991 (1991): 729.

Sherson, David, Ole Svane, and Elsebeth Lynge. "Cancer Incidence Among Foundry Workers in Denmark," *Environmental Health* 46 (1991): 75.

Silberman, Linda J. "Masters and Magistrates Part II: The American Analogue," *N.Y.U. L. Rev* 50 (1975): 1297.

Simon, E. D., and Marion Fitzgerald. *The Smokeless City*. London: Longmans Green, 1922.

Simpson, A.W.B. *Leading Cases in the Common Law*. Oxford: Clarendon, 1995.

Skocpol, Theda, and John Ikenberry. "The Political Formation of the American Welfare State in Historical and Comparative Perspective," *Comparative Social Research* 6 (1983).

Skowronek, Stephen. *Building a New American State: The Expansion of National Administrative Capacities, 1877–1920*. Cambridge: Cambridge University Press, 1982.

Spence, David B., and Lekha Gopalakrishnan. "Bargaining Theory and Regulatory Reform," *Vand. L. Rev.* 53 (2000): 599.

Stark, Carsten. "Germany: Rule by Virtue of Knowledge." In *Democracy at Work: A Comparative Sociology of Environmental Regulation in the United Kingdom, France, Germany, and the United States*, edited by Richard Münch, Christian Lahusen, Markus Kurth, Cornelia Borgards, Carsten Stark, and Claudia Jaufs. Westport: Praeger, 2001.

Stein, Peter. *Civil Law in Post-Revolutionary America: The Character and Influence of the Roman Civil Law*. London: Hambledon, 1988.

Steinzor, Rena I. "Reinventing Environmental Regulation: The Dangerous Journey from Command to Self-Control," *Harv. Envtl. L. Rev.* 22 (1998): 103.

Sterling, Morton. "Current Status and Future Prospects—Foundry Air Pollution Control." In *Proceedings: The Third National Conference on Air Pollution*. Washington, D.C.: Public Health Service, 1966.

Stern, Arthur C. "Summary of the Conference on Odor Control," *J. of the Air Pollution Control Association* 7 (1957): 53.

Stewart, Richard B. "Controlling Environmental Risks Through Economic Incentives," *Colum. J. of Envtl. L.* 13 (1988): 153.

———. "Madison's Nightmare," *U. Chi. L. Rev.* 57 (1990): 335.

———. "Models for Environmental Regulation: Central Planning versus Market-Based Approaches," *B. C. Envtl. Aff. L. Rev.* 19 (1992): 547.

———. "Antidotes for the 'American Disease,' " *Ecology L. Q.* 20 (1993): 85.

Stone, Alec. *The Birth of Judicial Politics in France: The Constitutional Council in Comparative Perspective*. New York: Oxford University Press, 1992.

Stone, Judith F. *The Search for Social Peace: Reform Legislation in France, 1890–1914.* Albany: State University of New York Press, 1985.

Stradling, David. *Smokestacks and Progressives: Environmentalists, Engineers and Air Quality in America, 1881–1951.* Baltimore: Johns Hopkins University Press, 1999.

Sunstein, Cass R. "*Lochner*'s Legacy," *Colum. L. Rev.* 87 (1987): 873.

———. *After the Rights Revolution: Reconceiving the Regulatory State.* Cambridge: Harvard University Press, 1990.

———. "Administrative Substance," *Duke L. J.* 1991 (1991): 607.

———. "Neutrality in Constitutional Law (With Special Reference to Pornography, Abortion, and Surrogacy)," *Colum. L. Rev.* 92 (1992): 1.

———. "Is the Clean Air Act Unconstitutional?," *Mich. L. Rev.* 98 (1999): 303.

———. *Risk and Reason: Safety, Law, and the Environment.* Cambridge: Cambridge University Press, 2002.

Tampke, J. "Bismark's Social Legislation: A Genuine Breakthrough?" In *The Emergence of the Welfare State in Britain and Germany,* edited by W. J. Mommsen. London: Croon Helm, 1981.

Technical Coordinating Committee T-4. "Coal Report," *J. of the Air Pollution Control Association* 6 (1956): 105.

Thelen, Kathleen, and Sven Steinmo. "Historical Institutionalism in Comparative Perspective." In *Structuring Politics: Historical Institutionalism in Comparative Analysis,* edited by Sven Steinmo, Kathleen Thelen and Frank Longstreth. Cambridge: Cambridge University Press, 1992.

Thomas, Charles. "Sumner Lamkins was a Stern Taskmaster." *The Macomb Daily,* Oct. 8, 1974, 2A.

Thorne, Samuel Edmund. *Sir Edward Coke, 1552–1952.* London: Bernard Quaritch, 1957.

Tiedeman, Christopher G. *A Treatise on the Limitations of the Police Power in the United States Considered from Both a Civil and Criminal Standpoint.* St. Louis, Mo.: F. H. Thomas Law Book Co., 1886.

Tomlins, Christopher L. *Law, Labor, and Ideology in the Early American Republic.* Cambridge: Cambridge University Press, 1993.

Tucker, Raymond C. "The St. Louis Code and Its Operation." In *Air Pollution: Proceedings of the U.S. Technical Conference on Air Pollution,* edited by Louis C. McCabe. New York: McGraw-Hill, 1952.

Ture, Martha. "The Pollution Game." *Express,* June 24, 1983, 10.

Twarog, Daniel L. *Waste Management Study of Foundries Major Waste Streams: Phase I.* HWRIC TR-011. Champaign: Illinois Hazardous Waste Research Information Center, 1993.

U.S. Environmental Protection Agency. *Regulatory Options for the Control of Odors.* EPA-450/5-80-003. Research Triangle Park, N.C.: Office of Air Quality Planning and Standards, 1980.

———. *Environmental Investments, The Cost of a Clean Environment: Report of the Administrator of the Environmental Protection Agency to the Congress of the United States.* EPA-230-11-90-083. Washington, D.C.: U.S. EPA, Policy, Planning, and Evaluation, 1990.

————. *Reference Guide to Odor Thresholds for Hazardous Air Pollutants Listed in the Clean Air Act Amendments of 1990*. EPA-425/K-00–002. Research Triangle Park, N.C.: Office of Research and Development, Environmental Criteria and Assessment Office, Air Risk Information Support Center, 1992.

————. *Notebook Project: Profile of the Metal Casting Industry*. EPA/310-R-97–004. Washington, D.C.: Office of Compliance, 1998.

————. *Taking Toxics Out of the Air: Progress in Setting "Maximum Achievable Control Technology" Standards Under the Clean Air Act*. EPA-425/K-00–002. Research Triangle Park, N.C.: Office of Air Quality Planning and Standards, 2000.

————. *Latest Findings on National Air Quality: 2000 Status and Trends*. EPA 454/K-01–002. Research Triangle Park, N.C.: U.S. EPA, Office of Air Quality Planning and Standards, 2001.

U.S. National Air Pollution Control Administration. *Economic Impact of Air Pollution Controls on Gray Iron Foundry Industry*. Raleigh, N.C.: 1970.

Uekoetter, Frank. "Divergent Responses to Identical Problems: Businessmen and the Smoke Nuisance in Germany and the United States, 1880–1917," *Business History Review* 73 (1999): 641.

Vogel, David. *National Styles of Regulation: Environmental Policy in Great Britain and the United States*. Ithaca: Cornell University Press, 1986.

von Bergen, John. "Industrial Odor Control," *J. of the Air Pollution Control Association* 8 (1958): 101.

von Moltke, K. *"The Vorsorgeprinzip" in West German Environmental Policy*. London: Royal Commission on Environmental Pollution, HMSO, 1988.

Wagner, Wendy E. "Innovations in Environmental Policy: The Triumph of Technology-Based Standards," *Univ. of Ill. L. Rev.* 2000 (2000): 83.

————. "The Science Charade in Toxic Risk Regulation," *Colum. L. Rev.* 95 (1995): 1613.

Weale, Albert. *"Vorsprung durch Technik*? The Politics of German Environmental Regulation." In *The Politics of German Environmental Regulation*, edited by Kenneth Dyson. Aldershot: Dartmouth, 1992.

Weale, Albert, Geoffrey Pridham, Michelle Cini, Dimitrios Konstadakopulos, Martin Porter, and Brendan Flynn, *Environmental Governance in Europe: An Ever Closer Ecological Union?* Oxford: Oxford University Press, 2000.

Weber, Edward P. *Pluralism by the Rules: Conflict and Cooperation in Environmental Regulation*. Washington, D.C.: Georgetown University Press, 1998.

White, Leonard Dupee. *Introduction to the Study of Public Administration*. 4th ed. New York: Macmillan, 1955.

Wilmot, Sarah. "Pollution and Public Concern: The Response of the Chemical Industry in Britain to Emerging Environmental Issues, 1860–1901." In *The Chemical Industry in Europe, 1850–1914*, edited by Ernst Homburg, Anthony S. Travis, and Harm G. Schröter. Dordrect: Kluwer, 1998.

Wilson, Bill. "New Haven Citizens Sue in Bid to Close Foundry." *The Macomb Daily*, November 11, 1980, 1.

Wilson, Woodrow. "The Study of Administration," *Pol. Sci. Q.* 2 (1887): 197.

Wohl, Anthony S. *Endangered Lives: Public Health in Victorian Britain*. London: J. M. Dent, 1983.

Wood, H. G. *A Practical Treatise on the Law of Nuisances in their Various Forms: Remedies Therefore at Law and in Equity*. Albany, N.Y.: John D. Parsons, Jr., 1875.

Yale Law Journal. "Note: A Remedy for the Victims of Pollution Permit Markets," *Yale L. J.* 92 (1983): 1022.

GPSR Authorized Representative: Easy Access System Europe - Mustamäe tee
50, 10621 Tallinn, Estonia, gpsr.requests@easproject.com

www.ingramcontent.com/pod-product-compliance
Lightning Source LLC
Chambersburg PA
CBHW031352290326
41932CB00044B/987